To Christine, Charlotte and Patrick

Preface

Because this book is something of a hybrid in that it deals with both psychological and philosophical topics, my problem in deciding how to pitch the presentation was particularly acute. If I had started with Piaget's theory then proceeded by way of Baldwin to philosophical questions about the nature of knowledge and thence to consider genetic epistemology the material might have proved more immediately accessible to those without a philosophical background but would have resulted in a less satisfactory whole: the logical and historical order would have been quite wrong. Therefore, my advice to a reader whose only perspective on these issues has been provided by a slight acquaintance with Piaget's developmental psychology and who does not feel ready to tackle the generalities is to read Part 2 and 3 first and then go on to Part 1 and 4. Also the psychological readership might feel some impatience with what they may regard as an over-detailed historical introduction in Section 1.1. I believe, however, that anything much briefer would have had to be so general or so elliptical as to be almost meaningless.

J. M. Baldwin's work is unfamiliar to the great majority of those with either a psychological or a philosophical interest in the acquisition of knowledge; and many of those who do know of it may feel that it is best left to languish in the murky prehistory of psychology. But I have given myself the task of introducing this work because I am certain that not only is it impossible to give a serious treatment of genetic epistemology without a full consideration of Baldwin but also that the theory is interesting and important in itself. The past 70 years of psychology have, if anything, increased rather than diminished its importance. As I say in Part 4 the aim is to give the theory a 'run for its money' not to advocate a wholesale adoption of his proposals. We cannot return to a cosier era of pre-behaviourism as some may like to think, but neither is psychology yet as cumulative a discipline as many more may like to believe!

I am very grateful to Professor D. W. Hamlyn, Professor L. S. Hearnshaw and Professor Wolfe Mays for reading and commenting on portions of an earlier draft of the book. These comments did in some cases influence the scope and emphasis of the text, though not the substance.

viii PREFACE

Thanks are also due to Mrs Myfanwy Thompson for preparing the final typescript so swiftly and well.

Chester, 1978   J.R.

Contents

Introduction

What can we know of human knowledge or understand about human understanding? The very reflexiveness of the questions can make us chase our own tails for a starting point. As this book is concerned with the *acquisition* of knowledge, the knowledge that things are the case, there seem to be at least two main starting points, one psychological and the other philosophical. Psychologists interested in the genetic psychology of cognition study the processes of coming to know in the human child, at the most general level the way in which biological and experiential factors interact to produce and maintain this development. Philosophers who study the theory of knowledge, or epistemology, wish to determine the status, extent and character of knowledge in the individual and/or the scientific community.

The main purpose of this book is to confront the proposition that these two starting points are really one, that although psychological and philosophical questions can and must be treated in different ways, the central questions about knowledge concern its acquisition, and they must be answered by coordinating philosophical theses and developmental theory and data. Such an approach exists within what has come to be known as *genetic epistemology*.

It is a popular error to take the phrase 'genetic epistemology' to be the invention and property of the Swiss psychologist Jean Piaget, and the area of enquiry which it encompasses to be centred at Geneva. In fact, the phrase was coined by the American James Mark Baldwin in 1906. Bernard Kaplan (1971) has claimed that Wundt, Sigwart, Enriques, Bosanquet, Hobhouse and Cassirer all produced genetic epistemological theories apart from Baldwin himself. Indeed, taking an evolutionary perspective on knowledge became almost fashionable under the influence of Darwin's evolutionary theory. As we shall see the 'evolutionary epistemology' of Karl Popper is not a million miles from such an approach. The philosopher D. W. Hamlyn has interpreted Aristotle as producing a kind of, what he would claim to be, genetic epistemology and has himself recently attempted to tackle genetic epistemological questions within the same framework. Thus it is evident that Piaget is one, though a major one, among many.

If we attempted to extract a common denominator from among the questions which these theorists were asking we would probably end up with something of a bland generality which would hardly distinguish genetic epistemology as a definite sphere of interest, if indeed we found any such common questions. Perhaps the best way of characterising genetic epistemology is to present some of the theories; at least this is what I will be doing here. Principally we will be studying the theories of Baldwin and Piaget because although their interests were very similar they represent two of the major *alternatives* within genetic epistemology; and also because their theories have the greatest relevance to cognitive development.

But what of this starting point? I have set out a figure including some of the major kinds of question which are encountered in the study of knowledge and its acquisition in order to give genetic epistemology a location relative to these. The two columns represent the ontogeny (development in the individual) and the phylogeny (in the species) of knowledge, and each of the three sets of questions represents in turn a progression towards more genetic concerns. The descending arrows indicate not only the direction of genetic interests

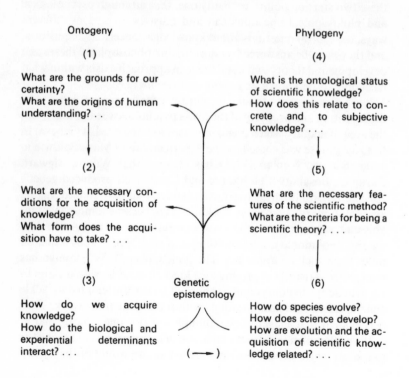

Ontogeny

(1)

What are the grounds for our certainty?
What are the origins of human understanding? . .

(2)

What are the necessary conditions for the acquisition of knowledge?
What form does the acquisition have to take? . . .

(3)

How do we acquire knowledge?
How do the biological and experiential determinants interact? . . .

Genetic epistemology

(⟶)

Phylogeny

(4)

What is the ontological status of scientific knowledge?
How does this relate to concrete and to subjective knowledge? . . .

(5)

What are the necessary features of the scientific method?
What are the criteria for being a scientific theory? . . .

(6)

How do species evolve?
How does science develop?
How are evolution and the acquisition of scientific knowledge related? . . .

but also that answers to the higher questions can influence the framing of the lower ones. It is, of course, inevitably artificial to compartmentalise sets of issues in this way—more properly there should be a continuous series of questions, and many would find the absolute distinction between the ontogenetic and the phylogenetic objectionable—but whatever disadvantages a caricature has over a painting it does possess the advantage of clarity! As will be seen, the points at which the columns begin also represent different traditions and different interpretations of the word 'epistemology'.

At (1) are located the classic questions in what philosophers working within the Anglo-Saxon tradition call epistemology. There is here a quest for certainty in our everyday claims to know that things are the case . . . What are the grounds for our certainty that three-dimensional, solid, perduring objects exist in an 'external world'; that we can predict concrete events such as that the sun will rise tomorrow morning 'only' on the basis of past experience? What is the nature of and grounds for our certainty that an effect of a certain kind will follow a cause of a certain kind, or indeed that cause will precede effect and not vice versa? What is the nature of our certainty regarding the seemingly timeless truth of the principles of logical inference, mathematics and geometry, and how does this certainty differ from that which we have of truths about the concrete world? With what element of certainty do perception and memory provide the experiential raw materials and props to our knowledge? Is there an *a priori* form of knowledge that is not acquired from experience; might this be identical or similar to the structural principles of logic and mathematics? What kind of certainty can we possess of the mental states of other people; and how does it relate to our immediate awareness of our own mental life and to our knowledge of concrete matters? What prior understanding of concepts, ideas and meanings supports what kinds of knowledge? What is the significance and extent of the intimate relation between knowledge and belief, and between knowledge and truth?

Considered *in vacuo* by the unphilosophical mind such questions might appear somewhat idle: although they present some nice intellectual teasers they are merely making us reflect on and formalise that which we already know—a puny advantage compared with that from science which actually increases our stock of knowledge. Yet the arguments of philosophers take on their proper relevance and urgency when thrown into relief by the skepticism which they were forged to combat. Indeed this species of epistemology can be seen as a bulwark against skepticism and only when considered in this light are its issues fully intelligible. Traditionally the skeptic's claim has been that knowledge is impossible (the Greek Skeptics), or that knowledge is nothing beyond convention or subjective judgment (The Greek Sophists). To take one example of a traditional answer, Descartes, as we shall later see in more detail, took skepticism to its limits in order to show that although perceptual knowledge could be reasonably doubted the facts of mental activity could not. We will also discuss how the British Empiricists took the opposite tactic in combating the skeptic by emphasising the certainty that *perceptual* data give us and suggesting that only in judgment and in the 'imagination' was error to be found.

Traditional epistemology thus seeks to provide *justifications* for the plain man's confidence in his own knowledge. Indeed if such justifications could not be provided and skepticism were to insinuate into ethics, matters of practical conduct and judgment, all human affairs would surely become coloured by it. Moreover, one reason why we now have the luxury of treating the skeptic's objections as 'academic' is that we live in a scientific age: the more we know, the less subjective, arbitrary, ambiguous and relative to immediate context our everyday world reveals itself to be—the very qualities of knowledge which the skeptic was able to exploit. Indeed the establishment of science and its methodology would not have been possible had not a sound epistemological groundwork been provided by philosophers. This is certainly not meant to imply though that the issues outlined above are now only of historical interest or of relevance only to the academic philosopher. By way of illustration here are just two examples of epistemological issues in cognitive development we shall be considering in Part 3: the role we give to truth and justification in the ascription of knowledge to children determines our view of mental development; this in turn determines the importance we place on memory as a process in the acquisition of knowledge.

It should be made clear what is being intended in saying that such epistemology is not genetic, indeed agenetic. This may seem especially strange in view of the fact that the traditional epistemological polarities of empiricism and rationalism can be construed as answering a question about the *origin* of our understanding—for all the world, it would appear, some kind of genetic question. As we shall see in Section 1.1 the European Rationalist philosophers of the seventeenth century held knowledge to originate in the innate predispositions of the mind, even in congenital states of knowledge, and that the British Empiricist philosophers of the seventeenth and eighteenth centuries proposed that knowledge was derived from experience. Surely, it may be objected, there is more than a developmental flavour to such epistemologies, and surely the heirs of such theories are easily located within psychology? Notwithstanding this, the theories are fundamentally agenetic, for although they can serve as influences towards developmental theories in a way we shall be discussing in Section 4.3 the view of knowledge which they expressed was that of a static, stable possession, whose status was not greatly different to that of a medulla or opposable thumbs. There is no suggestion in the traditional epistemologies that knowledge is a process, and that it is the product of a dialectic between the individual and the world of things and persons. After all, indicating the origins of a mineral in the earth is to tell us nothing about the principles by which it came to be formed and about the continuous geological processes still taking place within the earth's crust. To put it crudely, classical empiricism involved a kind of pointing to the perceptible world and classical rationalism to the mind; and pointing is a finite act not a process. Stopping the process of doubting within the mind or perceptual experience served, rightly or wrongly, to provide justifications for certainty.

By broadening our investigation towards such questions as: What are the limits of knowledge? How is any knowledge possible? What kinds of knowledge can we acquire? What are the necessary features of knowledge acquisition? We are moving towards more genetic interests and what are labelled as type (2) questions in the figure. The more ambitious we become in asking about any *possible* knowledge that there could be the more definitely do our answers take on a genetic flavour. Instead of saying that our certainty is grounded in perception or mental faculties the answers to this group of questions concern sets of conditions which are logically prior to knowledge of an objective, spatio-temporal world. Here the philosopher will be careful to distinguish between those aspects of acquisition which are contingent, such as its timing or how labile are its stages, and those aspects without which knowledge could never result, such as self-consciousness or a notion of causality. As we shall see, there are in Aristotle elements of such an epistemology which reaches its fullest expression in Kant. Perhaps the reader will also appreciate that interests of this kind in turn involve questions—given that we have to know in a certain way—about what can we possibly know, what are the limits of any kind of understanding, not just human, and what is the nature of the necessity which supports any possible understanding. These are Kantian questions.

It is indeed a far cry from this to the study of cognitive development and we have to draw a line between the philosopher who plots out the logical framework within which the necessary features of knowledge acquisition are located and the psychologist who observes, questions and experiments with children: the difference between asking how has knowledge to develop and how does it develop in fact. It should be emphasised that this does not encompass merely the bloodless research findings which only exist as products of the abstracting services, but the *theories* of cognitive development and the more modest sets of hypotheses which gave rise to the data.

In the second column in the figure we have again a series of three parcels of questions, moving from less to more genetic but concerned this time with the phylogeny of knowledge. Generally this means scientific knowledge—but not exclusively. For example there can be said to be an evolution in artistic knowledge whereby, as E. H. Gombrich has argued, certain 'schemas' or 'vocabularies' for representing reality become incorporated into a transmissable culture. The case is also strong for an evolution of musical and of literary knowledge. Nevertheless to the extent that it is 'knowledge *that* something is the case' rather than 'knowledge of *how* to do something' with which we are concerned, science is the exemplar. As a means of providing a focus for these still more heterogeneous bunches of questions, I will organise the discussion around the work of Karl Popper, certainly the most influential and possibly the greatest philosopher of science this century has produced, because it represents answers to the three kinds of question.

In each of the phylogenetic categories I intend there to be some kind of parallel with the ontogenetic category across from it, so that our agenetic set of questions is that regarding the ontological status of scientific knowledge—the way in which it exists as an entity relative to other kinds of knowledge such as that of the concrete world of immediate experience or knowledge of our own states of mind. Popper characterises this kind of knowledge as 'objective knowledge' and as existing in what he calls world 3; with world 1 being that of physical objects and world 2 that of 'subjective' experiences such as thought processes (Popper, 1972). He does not intend this third world to be constituted only out of scientific facts such as that the heart pumps blood around the body or that falling objects accelerate at 32 feet per second per second, for there are also problems, critical arguments and theories. Indeed he even includes the objective element in thinking (what the logician Frege called the 'content' of the thought), an idea which, though subjective in mode of apprehension, can be objectivised as a statement with a greater or lesser degree of truth and coherence: it can exist apart from any particular cognising agent. Unlike the knowledge considered under ontogeny this is what Popper calls 'epistemology without a knowing subject'. Objective knowledge has been thought in the past and, as it were, 'stays thought' in an objective world. One example he gives is that of log tables, to which we have access in their printed form but which cannot and do not have to be known by one person at any particular time. Likewise, as regards an idea example such as the idea of a solution to a mathematical problem, there is something about an idea that is not private, which can, in principle, be thought by anyone and communicated to anyone; if it can only be private property then it cannot be an idea—and here there is an intimate connection with the linguistic form in which knowledge has to be expressed. From such considerations Popper claims that the classic epistemological problems considered above are inherently uninteresting and tangential to the true study of epistemology as they deal with what he regards as the subjective, belief side of knowing. Popper, rightly or wrongly, construes type (1) questions really to be of the form: What are the grounds for *my belief* that the external world exists? . . . that effect will follow cause? and so on.

Popper's conception of objective knowledge was not constructed as a bulwark against skepticism. To the extent that it has any kind of bulwark status it is as against this species of subjectivism just mentioned. He distrusts the whole enterprise of answering the skeptic with empiricist or rationalist arguments and of looking for one kind of source or grounding of knowledge; many different kinds of thing, he argues, can be sources of knowledge. The classic epistemologies are subjective because they take as their starting point the individual's *so-called* 'direct' or 'immediate' observational experience: in reality these are themselves the result of a process of theory-testing and thus have no kind of status as absolute truths, as pegs on which to hang epistemological theories. The objectivity with which he is concerned does not belong to the subject but has its character precisely because it exists apart from him. Similarly, he sets himself against trends in science which rely on a form of individual belief for coherence: 'epistemic logic' which has premises such as 'a knows p'; the subjectivist interpretation of the probability calculus by Bayesians; subjectivist theories of entropy in physics.

However, this is not to say that subjectivity cannot be taken so far as to become a form of skepticism. Although Popper has not, to my knowledge, commented on such trends, there has been a movement in recent years—though with clear historical antecedents—within the philosophising flank of sociology towards the adoption of a radically subjectivist view of reality, regarding it as a social construct. (*Towards Deep Subjectivity* is the title of one work in the area; papers in the collection edited by M. F. D. Young, *Knowledge and Control*, provide a fair cross section of views.) Such theorists go far beyond studying the social determinants of the individual's world view or of the ideological aspects of knowledge to argue that knowledge, even in some cases up to and including mathematical and natural scientific knowledge, is determined by social conditions and that there is no essential difference between the sense in which a legal system is a social construction and in which the axioms of Euclidean geometry, for example, are social constructions.

Because the reader might come to equate this kind of notion with genetic epistemological suggestions to be discussed later regarding the necessarily social, intersubjective nature of knowledge it is worth emphasising that the former but not the latter has to be treated as a species of skepticism which it is the business of philosophy to counter. Although the classic epistemologies of Platonism, Aristotelianism, Empiricism, Rationalism and Kantianism are capable of combating such a thesis, its mode of expression and concern with knowledge in the culture makes it a more suitable nut for Popperians to crack. Stated as a bold fact it is trivially true that knowledge, broadly, is necessarily dependent on interpersonal conventions and it remains trivial unless it is used as a basis for, or a lead in to, the solution of epistemological problems or an explanation of knowledge acquisation, or both: the significance of this obvious fact has to be exploited. Clearly it cannot be exploited merely by using it to take away from knowledge the very thing that makes it knowledge—its objectivity. Although it is fairly easy to appreciate that this kind of

skepticism is a similar species of nonsense to that of the thoroughgoing skeptic who claims that we can never really know if anything
exists or that mathematics has no real certainty because we can make
errors of calculation, the production of justifications for regarding it
as such, as we saw in connection with type (1) questions, is an
important function of philosophy. Moreover, the constitution of a
field which calls itself the 'sociology of knowledge' presupposes
skepticism: opinion and belief have a sociology but not knowledge.
Similarly, there can be a sociology of science *qua* the scientific
endeavour, but not a sociology of scientific knowledge.

The parallel of type (5) questions with type (2) resides in the fact
that they both deal with necessary conditions for knowledge
acquisition, so we are asking here about the essential features of the
scientific method. Just as in (2) where we indicated a boundary
between these and cognitive developmental issues, the present set
have to be distinguished from the study of how scientists actually
conduct their investigations. The traditional view, proposed by
Francis Bacon, was that the scientist has to begin by collecting data,
perhaps by controlled experimental procedures, until a general
pattern emerges on the basis of which he can formulate testable
hypotheses. If these hypotheses are supported by the evidence then a
scientific 'law' has resulted and the stock of knowledge been
increased. This is known as the inductive method, about which
Hume, as we shall see, raised doubts of a skeptical nature.

Popper's extremely influential alternative account focuses on the
falsification rather than the verification of hypotheses as a means of
plotting the boundary between the scientific and the pseudo-
scientific. It is in the nature of scientific theories that they can never be
proved by collecting supportive empirical data because this means
that the testing of each hypothesis would have to be continued to
infinity. However, although hypotheses *qua* empirical generalisations
are not verifiable, they are falsifiable. Thus, scientific laws are such
because they can be subjected to systematic attempts to refute them.
Furthermore, the starting point of the scientific investigation could
never be pure observation or experimentation because this, given
human nature, is impossible; rather there is always a prior problem,
conjecture, or expectation of regularity which comes not from the
world but from the creative intelligence of the scientist. So instead of
the Baconian sequence of 'data → emerging regularity → prediction →
supportive evidence → fact' we have a sequence which Popper (1972)

represents as:

$$P_1 \rightarrow TT \rightarrow EE \rightarrow P_2$$

The initial problem gives rise to a tentative theory, followed by a process of error elimination by empirical testing and some conceptual refinement which produces not a finite result which can be stored away with all the other scientific facts but a new problem on a higher level, so that the process can begin again.

So, although Popper sets his face against any hint of subjectivism (and presumably social relativism) in science his theory results in something very far from an absolutist, static view of knowledge. Indeed he says himself: 'I regard world 3 as being essentially the product of the human mind' (Popper, 1976) and his theory of scientific method is that of a series of closer and closer approximations to the truth about nature, a truth which we can never know whether we have attained and which therefore can have no real epistemic status. He has been misunderstood on this score, but emphatically this does not mean there is no such thing as truth, that it is an illusion or merely a shifting symptom of rational coherence, which would be a meaningless proposal; but that The Truth as the absolute end-point of knowledge acquisition cannot be regarded as the holy grail of science.

The parallel between questions (3) and (6) derives from their common concern with the actual process of knowledge acquisition, theories of its nature and the management of relevant empirical data. First of all, evolutionary theories such as that of Darwin are, in one aspect, theories of the acquisition of knowledge by organic life: the human 'knows' more than the chimpanzee, the chimpanzee more than the dog, the dog more than the rat and so on. Natural selection is like a theory of learning but the learning of species rather than of individual organisms. Within the same very broad category there are also theories of the growth of scientific knowledge which seek to extract the processes fundamental to scientific investigation. These are historical processes, the evidence for which has been gleaned from what has taken place in the past, not necessary processes which must constitute individual acts of scientific discovery.

However, one must be particular not to gloss over the huge difference between theories of scientific advancement and of theories of species evolution. Clearly, Darwin's theory of evolution is science in the important sense in which T. S. Kuhn's (1962) much discussed account of the nature of scientific change is not. The latter, which proposes that the challenges which scientific theories receive within a certain framework of accepted principles or 'paradigms' (Newtonian physics for example) are different in kind to those which are thrown up when the paradigm itself is challenged (the theory of relativity), is a closer kin to the philosophy, history or sociology of scientific progress than to science itself. Nevertheless theories of evolution and theories of scientific development do share one important feature: they are both answerable to evidence concerning what actually took place in a way that philosophy is not. For example, it has been objected that only in caricature did the change from Newtonian to Einsteinian physics actually involve a fundamental theoretical discontinuity (Toulmin, 1972).

Of particular interest is the possibility of a systematic relationship existing between the two kinds of phylogenetic process; and here we return to Popper. Popper's theory of knowledge and criterion of demarcation shades into a theory of evolution via the problem-solving activity. Problem solving, far from being the exclusive function of the scientist or even of the plain man, is the primal activity. The environment sets problems for the organism which are solved on the level of the species. Moreover, the initial conjectures or expectations by means of which scientific investigation gets off the ground are founded in the inborn 'reactions or responses' of the (especially neonatal) animal. The corollary of such a view is that animals possess a form of objective knowledge—from spiders' webs to social hierarchies. However Popper does not accept a strict parallelism between natural selection in evolution and in science; not because he is against parallelism as such but because he takes mutationism to be neglecting the *active* principle which adaptation must involve. Because organisms select and organise their behaviour and preferences on the basis of environmental contingencies, because there is a certain variability programmed into their behavioural repertoire, they are able to select the selective pressures, which will thereby influence the course evolution will take.

As we shall see in Section 1.2 the genetic epistemologist J. M. Baldwin produced a similar kind of account around the turn of the century and indeed Popper makes reference to Baldwin's work and to that of H. S. Jennings (1906), usually known as 'organic selection' or 'the Baldwin effect'. Overall, there is little difficulty in regarding Popper's (1972, chapter 7) suggestions about evolution as speculative science rather than philosophy: he conjectures that there should be two fundamentally different kinds of gene (what he calls a 'genetic dualism'), 'a-genes' for anatomy and 'b-genes' for behaviour within which there are 'p-genes' controlling aims and 's-genes' controlling skills, which influence adaptation and organic selection in different ways. Regarding our scientist/organism parallel therefore, P_1 can be regarded as a problem set by the environment to the organism, TT as the 'theory' which it adopts, such as some new way of behaving or selecting a new ecological niche, EE is the way in which the environment limits this reaction and P_2 is another survival problem on a higher level.

Another recent attempt to draw a parallel of a similar kind is made in Stephen Toulmin's book *Human Understanding*, to which we shall return in Section 4.5. Yet Toulmin rejects Popper's demarcation principle as arbitrary and reliant on formal, *a priori* logical principles, to press a more relativistic view whereby the rationality of each age determines the formal demarcation between science and pseudo-science. He does not follow such an argument towards skepticism however.

Having plotted out the 'ecological niche' of genetic epistemology how are we to characterise it? As I said at the outset it is difficult to extract from all kinds of genetic epistemology one common denominator apart from 'a theory of knowledge given from a genetic point of view'; and on this broad definition Popper is surely doing genetic epistemology. Let us, however, limit ourselves to the sphere within which the originator of the phrase and its main current practitioner are located. What Baldwin and Piaget share is an interest in *reversing* the arrow of genetic progression as indicated in the figure. This kind of genetic epistemology involves accepting not only that there is a progression from agenetic to genetic explanations of knowledge but that answers to type (3) or type (6) questions—often as the result of empirical research—can influence the way the other kinds of question are treated and answered. The basic credo is that developmental theories can, and *must*, contribute to the explanation of human knowledge in its broadest sense: if we want to know about knowledge we must see how it develops. The extent to which a theorist will hold that there is a cross-over of the arrow of influence from one side of the figure to the other ((3) to (4) for example or (6) to (2)) will largely be determined by the degree to which he accepts that ontogeny recapitulates phylogeny in the acquisition of knowledge.

Such a theorist, Piaget for example, might also take the view that the growth of knowledge in the child must be at least partly isomorphic to that in the natural sciences; but such a proposal need not be regarded as part of genetic epistemology's essential baggage and so the bottom horizontal arrow is in parenthesis. I wish to leave this highly schematic characterisation as it is in the hope that the remainder of the book will flesh it out and in the fear that anything much less schematic would pre-empt the remainder.

Regarding the rather artificial distinction made here between ontogeny and phylogeny, this is also roughly isomorphic to one between two different meanings of the word epistemology which in turn reflects two divergent academic traditions. Within the Anglo-Saxon tradition epistemology commonly means type (1) and (2) questions and thus genetic epistemology as interpreted by a philosopher such as D. W. Hamlyn means (quite properly) something at the most genetic extreme of (2) and (less properly) something around the interface of type (2) and (3) questions. However, within the European, especially French, tradition epistemology means something much closer to the rational structure of specifically scientific knowledge—as in 'the epistemology of mathematics' for example—and so the constitution of such a field as genetic epistemology with its empirical, scientific content is achievable without too much stretching of existing conceptual frameworks.

It is the former kind of epistemology that this book is principally about: it is deliberately one-sided. My concern is with everyday knowledge (within civilised societies), with the cognitive development of the child and with the genetic epistemology which a coordination of these interests can produce. The phylogenetic, scientific face is not and cannot be ignored entirely but, for good or ill, the perspective here is cognitive developmental.

Part 1 is mainly historical, dealing with traditional approaches to the issues lumped in the figure under (1) and (2). Baldwin's theory, which is presented in this section is 'historical' in that it belongs to the distant past of psychology, but is not, I hope to show, of only historical relevance. Piaget's theory, presented in Part 2 is not dressed up as anything much more than a theory of cognitive development because, whatever importance Piaget has as a practitioner of genetic epistemology, his broader proposals cannot be made fully intelligible apart from his cognitive theory. The main novelty in the presentation is that we shall follow the order in which Piaget developed the main features of the theory, taking some of his important books as located within the development of Piaget's thought rather than that of the child.

The experimental material presented in Part 3 may appear to be somewhat incongruous set against the generalities of some of the preceding discussions. But if genetic epistemology has any viability such that experiments with and observations of children can influence our conception of knowledge, these experiments must reveal phenomena sufficiently robust to support the weight of such generalities. Therefore, some pains have to be taken to determine whether the relevant experiments do, in fact, show what their authors intend them to; and thus what may look to the outsider like minutiae have to be gone over. This section should generally show the dependence of empirical research on conceptual frameworks which can be derived from the experimenters' (usually implicit) answers to type (1) and (2) questions.

In Part 4 we will stand back from the patchwork of philosophical and psychological issues which will have been raised to see if some coherent pattern can be made out within which the fruitful and the less fruitful aspects of genetic epistemology are plainly marked. Baldwin's and Piaget's theories will be compared, some general issues discussed and one particular construal of genetic epistemology championed.

Part 1

Philosophical Origins and Baldwin's Theory

1.1 THE PROBLEM OF KNOWLEDGE

Philosophers do not take Plato (428–347) merely to have been Socrates' Boswell. Although many of the dialogues take the form of disputes between Socrates and another in which the master demonstrates some truth or principle by the dialectical method, this is generally agreed to be more Platonic philosophy than reportage. We find in Plato (or Socrates–Plato) the distinguishing feature of the philosophical enterprise: the tireless worrying away at a problem by argument and counter argument—in contrast to the Pre-Socratic philosophers who generally presented world views *ex cathedra*. Plato has had more influence than any other single philosopher, with the bromide being that 'all philosophy is footnotes to Plato'.

Plato regarded the prevailing epistemologies of his time as all unsatisfactory. The Sophist view that reality is nothing beyond what we judge it to be, the Heraclitean view that reality is a state of constant flux, the Eleatic view that reality is one and unchanging all failed to do justice to the certainty of our knowledge as being something beyond the data of sense experience. In one of the dialogues the Sophist Protagoras contends that there can be no question of objectivity, truth or falsity in our judgments of reality because everything is what it seems to be to the person making the judgment. Plato refutes this by showing how we regard some people as more expert at judging reality than others, that we do not behave as if one judgment is as good as another; a point which also relates to his insistence that knowledge has to be distinguished clearly from opinion and belief. Moreover, by the very nature of Protagoras's thesis no truth can be claimed for it. In the same spirit he refutes the doctrine of Heraclitean flux by pointing out that if reality were constantly changing we would never be able to say anything about it because the truth value of our statements would change from one time to another; in fact we are well able to make true and coherent judgments about reality. The Eleatic view seems to be rather the opposite side of the same bad coin: saying that reality is one and unchanging does not resolve the paradox that our sense perceptions are often of change, progression, transformation and decay whilst our judgments and knowledge necessarily involve reference to properties which are perduring and entities which are independent of our perception of change.

We wish to claim certain knowledge and we find ourselves forced to accept the independent existence of the world, yet the medium whereby this knowledge is apprehended—our sense organs—provides us with manifestly relative, often indistinct, ambiguous and fleeting data. Plato's theory of Forms can be seen as an attempt to resolve this paradox by positing a separate, ideal world of standard exemplars of all the things we confront in sense experience. Thus, the things that we see and touch are merely instances of these paradigms. For example, one particular table which we see is not a thing of which we have direct knowledge but one instance of the ideal standard of the 'Table'. In this way our notion of 'knowledge' is maintained because we do at least have *access* to this separate absolute world but our *possession* of knowledge is just as uncertain as our senses make it appear.

The difficulty with such a theory is that it works much more easily for awareness of concrete facts than for rational knowledge like the rules of logic, mathematics and grammar, or ideas like that of God. Plato was aware of this problem and initially attempted to solve it by employing the Socratic doctrine of 'anamnesis' or the theory of recollection, which held that individuals have an unconscious store of knowledge carried over from a previous existence. He reports that Socrates was able to elicit from a small boy the solution to a complex geometrical problem without instruction by bringing into his awareness the latent knowledge with questioning. But Plato later rejected this on the grounds that even geometrical knowledge is basically sensible (derived from the senses) and therefore uncertain in the same way as knowledge of material things. For the opponent of skepticism one of the major problems in the quest for certainty is accounting for the fundamental difference he takes there to be between true belief and knowledge. Plato later considered whether an accompanying *justification* of the claim to know is what sets genuine knowledge apart. Giving the *logos*, the justification/reason/ground for a true belief, might establish the resultant judgment as different in kind from merely perceiving objects, relations or events and from the belief itself. It is unclear how Plato meant these *logoi* to be regarded. He presented three possible characteristics of them—(1) manifestations of judgments in speech; (2) the recounting of the elements of a known object; (3) the identification of objects by a distinguishing characteristic—and rejected them all as inadequate (or rather had Socrates reject them to Theaetetus).

But though Plato was not able to characterise the *logos* satisfactorily, the suggestion of an intimate relation between justification and knowledge was of immense importance. We shall see in Part 3 how inescapable is the criterion of justification when we are studying the nature of the child's concrete knowledge—another 'footnote' to Plato! In general, although the Platonic theory of an absolute reality beyond sensation is as agenetic a view as it is possible to express, Plato's *problem*—the status of certainty within sense data—has to be confronted by everyone engaged in the study of knowledge.

Aristotle's (384–322) conception of the problem of knowledge was much less influential than that of Plato and divergent from it in at least two important respects. First, his account was not developed in response to skeptical arguments so his aim was not to justify claims to know. Second, the type of knowledge with which Aristotle was mainly concerned was scientific knowledge; an interest which may well have been determined by the fact that he was a practising scientist, having carried out zoological, and other, researches. The act of knowing, according to Aristotle, essentially involved that of subsuming something under a larger category and then this in turn as a subclass of a still larger category and so on; entailing that the higher the state of knowledge the wider its generality. We can only be said to possess full-blown scientific knowledge (*espisteme*) when we are able to provide an account of how the phenomenon in question came about, its cause or reason; so *episteme* is closely linked to an understanding which can be demonstrated.

Of special interest is that when Aristotle came to attempt an explanation of *episteme* the account he gave was genetic in character; indeed D. W. Hamlyn (1976) has characterised it as a piece of genetic epistemology. Aristotle's problem was to explain how we can have immediate knowledge of the 'raw material' for a full epistemic judgment prior to *episteme*, knowledge of the first principles or premises which the knower should be able to provide in the demonstrative argument for his scientific judgment. These first principles, he argued, were grasped by an act of intuition and the process of gaining such an intuition he called *epagoge*, normally translated as 'induction'. Although he rejected the Platonic notion of inherited knowledge, Aristotle did propose that the mind, or soul, contains universals which determine how particulars from the flux of sensory experience come to be sorted out; which might be conceived psychologically as a proposal of an innate tendency to make certain kinds of discrimination. And thus the process of the hierarchical subsuming under broader and broader categories gets off the ground. Aristotle's famous metaphor for this is of an army which has been thrown into chaos by an attack, gradually reforming for defence as one man after another stands firm; just as the cumulative sorting out of particulars from diffuse sensations produces perceptions with the status of judgments. As to why certain particulars 'stand firm' rather than others, Aristotle says that this is due to their repetition in the stream of experience: they recur and make themselves noticed, with those that recur coming to be lodged in memory.

Whatever the shortcomings of this account—not the least of which are the characterisation of knowledge acquisition as the progressive *generality* of judgments and the fact that the *epagoge* process seems to provide little more than an account of discrimination between items rather than the emergence of unities out of an amorphous whole—its genetic rationale makes it relevant to our interests. It can reasonably be classified under type (2) questions (see Introduction) because *epagoge* provides us with a necessary feature of the process of knowledge acquisition. An individual cannot be said to have acquired knowledge of a general truth unless he can appreciate how individual instances together constitute this truth. Knowing that 'Strawberries are red' *necessarily* involves the ability to understand how this, and this, and this red strawberry are instances of the statement. (We are not very far here from the Platonic notion of giving the *logos*: the *logos* of an epistemic judgment is seeing its instances *as* instances.) Also, on the basis of this necessity we can determine when knowledge should be attributed to individuals: knowing a fact is more than using it to make generalisations. Aristotle also held that the ultimate dependence of *epagoge* on sense perception and the repetition of instances were necessary features of knowledge acquisition.

The founder of Neoplatonism, Plotinus (205–270), elaborated the theory of Forms and investigated the nature of conciousness and the essential self-consciousness of human beings. St Augustine (354–430), who represents a bridge between classical and mediaeval thought, took up the challenge of skepticism in a Platonic spirit; both thinkers pursuing the *dualism* inherent in Plato—that between reason and the sensible world and that isomorphic to it between mind and body. This was the inherited conceptual framework within which Descartes (1596–1650) undertook his investigations.

We pass two thousand years so swiftly because the later Greek philosophers either did not make their major contributions in epistemology or their theories are mainly of historical interest. In the Middle Ages philosophical controversies raged fiercely; so fiercely indeed that blood was spilt between the proponents of 'Nominalism', 'Realism' and 'Conceptualism'. Yet more energy was expended on controversy than on the preparation of theses; there was much entrenched opinion but little presentation of arguments for a point of view because the main concern was with characterising knowledge (as being of universals or particulars for example) not in unearthing the bedrock of certainty on which our everyday judgments are based.

The quest for certainty is the chief characteristic of Descartes' method. As a mathematician he was greatly impressed by the different kinds of certainty which mathematical and sense judgments possess, but unlike Plato he did not postulate a separate world of ideal Forms to characterise the certainty of the latter. Also his method was not that of dialogue between intellectual opponents but rather the meditations of one mind on its own functioning: introspection in contrast to dialectic. It would, though, be wrong to regard this as an experimental technique—although Descartes did himself spend much time meditating, preferably in a 'hot-cupboard'*—for it was in essence a means of logically establishing the limits of skepticism. He held that all knowledge can be rationally doubted. We have hallucinations, are susceptible to illusions, our perceptual experiences are relative to context, indeed the existence of dreams furnishes us with strong evidence that we often think we are experiencing what we are not. All these facts mitigate against the certainty of sensible experience, argued Descartes. (The individual truth of the arguments need not detain us, save only to mention that J. L. Austin was able to argue that as regards the *absence* of criteria for distinguishing sleeping from waking states which Descartes proposed, there were at least 50 such criteria!) Yet even if our senses were trustworthy there was always the possibility that we were being tricked into believing in a substantial world by some malevolent demon.

Even mathematics is not immune from Cartesian doubt simply

---

* Many of Descartes' personal predilections as well as his philosophy are reflected in the work of Samuel Beckett. In this instance there is a parallel with Murphy's fondness for thinking his time away in an over-heated garret.

because our reasoning can be led into error, so that Descartes was eventually driven back to the one species of certainty of which not even an omnipotent deceiver could rob him: that of his own existence. The three words *cogito ergo sum* encapsulate the notion that the objects of consciousness may be uncertain but that we have experience of such objects is not. Philosophers have since expended many more words debating the status of this credo (whether it is an intuition or an inference for example) but for our purposes the *cogito* can be said to be important in a simple and almost non-controversial sense: it asserts that the consideration of consciousness is inescapable in epistemology. (How this 'consideration' is going to enter the explanation is, of course, another matter, for we can admit that talk of consciousness may have to enter the explanation without believing that it is either logically (Hegel, see below) or temporally (Freud) primary.) Descartes then went on from the *cogito* to argue for the existence of God from this foundation and thereby for the existence of the external world because no perfect, divine being would dupe us into believing something which was not true. Of course this strategy reflects the fact that Descartes was writing in an age of faith; but more important it reflects his faith in rational procedures, of which the formal proof is the paradigm, by which knowledge could be justified and which gave the rationalists their name.

The groundwork of Descartes' arguments for the certainty of our knowledge is the proposal that many of our ideas are innate. Much of Cartesian doubt can only be defended by assuming the innateness of some ideas (Kenny, 1968), and one of Descartes' 'proofs' of the existence of God relies upon the innateness of the idea of God. Descartes held that thought itself was innate and indeed the truth of the *cogito* relies on the 'unlearned' nature of thinking. He shared this belief with other seventeenth century rationalists such as Spinoza (1637–1677) and Leibniz (1648–1716) who held the doctrine in a more mystical and, in a sense, more extreme form. Leibniz was able to argue that none of the ideas are literally produced in us by the external world affecting our sense organs, whereas Descartes only believed that some of them were strictly innate. He wrote in 1641 that the infant in the womb 'has in itself the ideas of God, itself, and all truths which are said to be self-evident; it has these ideas no less than adults have when they are not paying attention to them, and it does not acquire them afterwards when it grows up' (Adam and Tannery, III, p. 424).

It should be stressed that Descartes was not proposing that the child is born thinking of God or the isosceles triangle, as he more often in his writings presented the doctrine in such a way as to suggest that the child had an innate predisposition to develop certain kinds of knowledge. Thus, ideas are innate ' . . . in the sense of the word that we say generosity is innate in certain families; or again that in others certain diseases, e.g. gout and the stone are innate: not that infants of these families suffer from these diseases in the mother's womb, but because they are born with a certain disposition or liability to contract them' (op. cit., VIII p. 357). Of course there was some ambiguity in Descartes usage, but suffice it to say that he was certainly aware of this more plausible interpretation of the doctrine.

A reaction against the very notion of the innateness of knowledge was represented by three British philosophers, John Locke (1632–1704), George Berkeley (1685–1753) and David Hume (1711–1776) who are collectively known as the British Empiricists. They were not empiricists in the modern sense of performing experiments but in that they held, in varying degrees and for different reasons, that knowledge is derived from experience. Instead of trusting reflective consciousness and the rational faculties, the British Empiricists held that certainty lay in direct perception.

Locke, in Book I of the *Essay Concerning Human Understanding* directed a polemic against the doctrine of innate ideas, although it is not always clear which proponents or versions of the account he was attacking (see Aaron, 1965). But it is clear that Locke did not take issue with the notion of innate dispositions; the main thrust of the argument was against those passages in Descartes (and the teaching of certain other philosophical movements) in which he writes as if the infant does possess full-blown, potentially conscious knowledge. This is a fairly easy target—a straw figure some would have it. The major denial on Locke's part is that knowledge, in the full sense of the term employed in ordinary language, is ever acquired other than by intuition and demonstration (which might perhaps trade on innate dispositions). A Cartesian would hold in opposition to this that knowledge is innate in that it is present in a primitive, pre-dispositional form at birth and develops by a process of maturation: the relationship of the bud to the branch. The reader will perhaps appreciate that this innate—learned debate is inescapable in psychology. No matter how sophisticated we try to be with talk of interactions between heredity and environment—often without

bothering to say how the interaction is supposed to take place—
maturation and learning are polarities which have to be represented
in every developmental theory. It is as easy for the theorist to
maintain a neutral stance as for an iron filing to remain stationary
when placed between the prongs of a horseshoe magnet!

Locke is regarded by many as the father of English psychology.
Although a generation earlier Hobbes had produced a mechanistic,
hedonistic psychology, it was Locke who provided the conceptual
framework within which an experimental psychology could develop.
Moreover Hobbes is better regarded as a rationalist, especially in *De
Corpore* (1665). Thus, Anglo-Saxon psychology is Lockian in character. However, when he stated that his aim was to explore the origins of
knowledge and that he would adopt the 'historical plain' method this
did not mean that he was embarking on anything that we would
regard today as developmental psychology; it was primarily a
philosophical examination of the groundwork of knowledge.

Although Locke did allow that there were aspects of nature which
we cannot discern, we find in his writings a firm statement of the view
that knowledge is derived from experience, and a 'building block'
account of its formation. There are two sources of our ideas: ideas
from sense experience and ideas of reflection formed by the operation
of the mind on the ideas. There are two kinds of idea, simple and
complex; the former are passively acquired from sense experience and
the latter are actively acquired by combination. Locke wrote of the
mind in the *Essay* as being like a 'great mirror' on which ideas are
reflected (Section 2.1), and although he allowed some activity to the
mind, its passivity was what he emphasised. To continue the
metaphor, the mirror may bias the reflection by being slightly convex
or concave in places (innate dispositions) and might split up and
recombine images because of variegated surfaces (active combination
of ideas), but its function is primarily to reflect.

This process furnishes us with three kinds of knowledge. Firstly
there is knowledge derived from things which he called 'modes'; and
there is knowledge of relations which is established by comparing
ideas. For the third category, knowledge of substance, we see an
attempt at a solution to the original Platonic problem of how we
know the certain existence of an independent material world if we
only have our senses to rely on for the collection of data. His answer
was that because we cannot imagine how the clusters of 'qualities' or
ideas which we possess when perceiving objects could subsist by

themselves, we 'accustom ourselves to suppose some substratum' which we call substance and which, for man, is a supposition of 'he knows not what'. Philosophically this raises more questions than it answers and psychologically it simply states a doubtful generalisation.

Unlike Plato, Locke did not feel the need to have a different kind of explanation for rule-bound knowledge such as geometry, but argued that space, time and number were modes—derived from things. Rationalists such as Leibniz strongly criticised Locke for failing to do justice to the difference between knowledge of objects and rational knowledge, putting his mistake down to ignorance of mathematics.

It should be pointed out at this juncture that the difference between rationalism and empiricism must not only be seen in terms of the question of innate knowledge. The rationalist emphasises the *relational* nature of our understanding, like a logical or formal framework within which sense can be made of individual objects and events; which for him, rightly or wrongly, implies that the formal structure is not derived from experience. The empiricist, on the other hand, regards the *absolute*, either—or knowledge of things or their qualities as fundamental and believes that the rational aspects of understanding are built up by an additive process: that they result from this building rather than presuppose it. Therefore it is easy to see that knowledge such as that of mathematics certainly favours the rationalist case. Imagine how difficult it is to argue that we learn the rules of addition or subtraction from our experience of things alone without the mind being actively structuring.

At bottom the empiricist's difficulty is in explaining our relational knowledge, and we see this difficulty reflected in the contention in psychology between the American, neo-behaviourist, S—R theorists and those who regard relational knowledge as primitive (broadly but not necessarily, Gestaltists). The behaviourists had to postulate covert chains of verbally mediated S—R links in the brain in order to account for the fact that we are capable of certain kinds of relational learning (Kuenne, 1946) and can 'abstract' dimensions like shape and colour (Kendler and Kendler, 1962). However, the fact that rats, who are not verbal creatures, can be trained to perform these relational (Riley, 1958) and abstracting (Shepp and Eimas, 1964) tasks considerably weakens the behaviourists' case. Here is our first example of a conceptual issue contended between philosophers being fought out again by psychologists with experimental rather than logical weapons.

In fact, regarding the question of abstraction it is instructive to contrast Locke with Aristotle. How abstraction is possible was precisely Aristotle's genetic problem, but for Locke positing a process of abstraction was the explanation itself—general concepts are formed by abstracting common features from disparate instances. This faith in abstraction as a sufficient explanation was a consequence of his agenetic view point. As we shall see later, the genetic epistemologists Baldwin and Cassirer both rejected abstraction as the foundation of concept formation because it is a mere circular characterisation: *how* we are able to abstract is the fundamental problem.

Finally, one of the best known features of Locke's epistemology was his rather unclearly drawn distinction between 'primary' and 'secondary' qualities, which originated with Robert Boyle. Knowledge of primary qualities such as solidity, extension, figure, motion and rest and number are derived directly from the object, generally because no object can lack them. On the other hand, secondary qualities such as colour, sound and smell are a function of the way the individual perceives the object, his sensory capacities and the perceptual context. But the fact that Locke argued that these secondary qualities were produced by 'powers' inherent in the object may be seen to be partly a consequence of his pure empiricist conception of how objectivity is constituted in knowledge. On this model, objectivity cannot be conceived as being anything other than a property of the concrete datum, and the more objective then the more indissociable from the object itself, the less mediated by ideas and hence the more 'primary'. Even perceptual experiences like those of sound and smell derive an objectivity from properties of the object which produced them. Nevertheless, the notion that there are different degrees and kinds of perceptual immediacy in our concepts is of great significance as we shall see in Section 3.3.

The second of the British Empiricists, Berkeley, is a paradoxical figure for although his presentation of the empiricist standpoint was the most extreme of the three, there is at the same time a mystical strain in his philosophy. His main work was the *Principles of Human Knowledge*. Although one of his aims was to purify the Lockian doctrine so that only the data of sense perception—not even intuition and demonstration—could furnish us with knowledge, his solution to the Lockian problem of the 'he-knows-not-what' existence of substance was piously mediaeval rather than empiricist. Indeed an explanation of our belief in the independent existence of the concrete world was all the more pressing for Berkeley precisely because he would only admit of sense perception in knowledge. His account was that the existence of objects is constituted only in their being perceived (*esse est percipi*). But what of their independent, enduring existence when they are not being perceived? They exist in the mind of God who is the source of all knowledge and who is manifest to us through our ideas of the material world. Therefore the problem of the status of substances was removed by removing substances themselves.

Although Berkeley's solution was mystical, the problems which he raised were not, for he demonstrated the consequences and paradoxes of a thoroughgoing empiricism. Also he produced arguments for his position which were of more than historical interest: his criticisms of Locke's theory of abstract ideas and the meaning of words, the theory of optics which he developed from empiricist principles in *Towards a New Theory of Vision*.

The aims of Hume were quite different. Like Berkeley though, his initial position was more purely empiricist than Locke's, as he assumed the derivation of *all* our ideas from experience. He held that for every idea in the mind there is a corresponding impression or perception of sense. Inevitably this presented him with many difficulties in explaining our knowledge of space and time. His answer was that ideas of space and time originate from the order in which the impressions arrive in the mind. Nevertheless Hume is the most interesting of the three to the psychologist because he employed arguments which are essentially psychological to explain our knowledge of the external world and causality. Again, this is a form of solution to the original Platonic problem of why we are certain about the existence of a concrete world when this belief is not logical (it cannot be demonstrated by rational argument) and when the senses can only furnish us with 'impressions' of things. Hume's approach was to attack the nature of the *belief* in these things—and belief is a psychological state. In this connection Popper's strictures against Anglo-Saxon epistemology are recalled: he regarded it as subjectivistic in that it is concerned with states of belief rather than with objective knowledge.

Why do we believe in the existence of objects when we have no *reason* to do so? Hume's answer was in terms of the quality of our experience: we receive the impressions of the external world as being coherent and constant although gappy. We are able to predict that, and how, things will be perceived given certain conditions and that processes will go on in things whether or not we observe them. (He gives the example of lighting a fire in his study, then returning some hours later to find it burned out.) The synthesis of sense-data is carried out by the imagination, working on the basis of custom and habit. Price (1940) has argued that the emphasis on the synthesising activity of the mind foreshadowed Kant and to the extent that the habit of completing gappy sequences of sense-data is a rule-like process comparable to the 'grammar' of material object words and phrases Hume anticipated logical positivism.

Hume's famous account of causality makes a similar kind of reference to psychological states. *Habit* and *custom* determine our belief in causality. We witness the constant conjunction between C and E so often that an association of ideas is set up in the imagination whereby the impression, then idea, of C makes us automatically pass to the idea of E: the belief that cause will inevitably produce an effect. We believe in the necessity of C → E because when we reflect on our inference we see ourselves being determined to move from C to E. This however is a psychological impression of necessity, not true logical necessity.

Whatever the shortcomings of this account, it has been immensely influential at least in part because it suggests a skeptical construal of scientific knowledge though *within* an epistemology; indeed taken in an extreme form it can be interpreted to mean that science has no rational basis. Hume himself is often characterised as a skeptic of sorts. One of the most cogent criticisms of Hume's theory is that he made the error of believing that the only kind of necessity there can be is logical and that anything else is subjective: a consequence of his pure empiricism. It should also be added that although Hume makes reference to psychological processes it is not, in the present-day sense, a psychological theory; for he was not presenting an *hypothesis* about the psychological processes which underly the causal inference. Rather he was examining the grounds for this knowledge and saying (1) that it was basically psychological and (2) what the only possible psychological inference *could* be, excluding other explanations through *conceptual*, not empirical, considerations.

The empiricism of Locke and Berkeley could be taken as characterising their general view of the developmental process as well as their epistemology. Locke was also interested in what would be called today developmental or educational psychology. Shortly after writing the *Essay* he produced a tract, rather behaviourist in flavour, entitled *Some Thoughts Concerning Education* (1693). In addition Berkeley's writings on optics can be regarded as embryo psychophysics. Hypotheses were to be expected from such an empiricist writing on perception: Berkeley stated at one point that a man born blind who acquired his sight in adulthood would have to *learn* to see by tactual manipulation; a prediction which has been supported (Von Senden, 1932).

To some degree European rationalism and British empiricism were resolved in Germany by Immanuel Kant (1724–1804). Kant was the first to have faced these divergent currents in order to produce a system which did justice to the fact that there are rational elements in experience and experiential elements in reasoning. There are many ways of construing the task which Kant set himself in the *Critique of Pure Reason*. Some have stressed the demarcation between metaphysical and scientific questions, some the plotting of the limits within which language can be meaningful or the limits to what we can conceive of or make intelligible to ourselves. But for our present purpose we must emphasise the way in which Kant rejected the notion of knowledge being *either* innate *or* experiential and attempted to determine how structures and sense experience contributed and interacted, thereby developing a system in which the mind is seen as constructing reality through experience from certain general principles. Kant emphasises throughout that we require both general concepts in order to make sense of experience and the raw material of sensation if these concepts are themselves to have a foothold in knowledge; in Kant's own words 'thoughts without content are empty, intuitions without concepts are blind.' This is the essence of Kant's *interactional* view of knowledge.

Kant began by demarcating different kinds of judgment. A judgment can be 'analytic' or 'synthetic'—either true by definition as in 'My black cat has dark fur' or giving us new information as in 'My black cat is fierce'. Also, it can be either logically independent of and prior to experience, *a priori*, or logically dependent on it, *a posteriori*. For example $2 + 2 = 4$ could not conceivably be false as its truth is in a way independent of what we know about the concrete world. In contrast to this our knowledge that swans are white is dependent on experience. (It will be appreciated that for each distinction the first is more amenable to a rationalist explanation and the second to an empiricist.) The most distinctive element in Kant's system was his assertion that there is a kind of judgment which is synthetic *a priori*, that is, not derived from experience yet neither self-evident. These judgments, he argued, are found in mathematics and geometry, but, more importantly, they form the presuppositions on which objective experience and scientific knowledge are based. In attempting to show how synthetic *a priori* judgments are possible Kant was stating the conditions without which objective knowledge could not obtain—the necessary conditions for objective experience.

All knowledge begins with 'intuition' (sensation) which comes to us in a necessarily spatio-temporal form. This sense experience is empirically real but itself cannot provide us with certain knowledge that objects have an independent existence. We can never know the thing as it exists in itself in the world of 'noumena' (compare Locke's problem with 'substance'). We have only knowledge of a world of 'phenomena' which is nevertheless objective. How does this objectivity arise? Kant's answer was that we organise sensory data in accordance with certain formal, general principles of the understanding which are themselves objective in that they are true for all mankind. Kant did not wish to have to argue that because we cannot know the 'thing in itself' within the world of noumena then therefore our concrete experience is subjective: the objectivity of the sensible world resides in the very fact that physical and temporal characteristics are valid for all men. Hamlyn (1967) calls this a 'criterion of intersubjectivity'*. In Kantian terminology this intersubjectivity was characterised by saying that physical and temporal reality was empirically real but transcendentally ideal. Here we see the empiricism—rationalism resolution at work in Kant's account of the physical world. He did not adopt the empiricism of Locke which was content to locate objectivity in the immediate perception of primary qualities, nor the Cartesian faith in objectivity as arising out of logical

---

*Kant did not say that judgments gain objectivity by being shared among human beings via contingently common rules of thought, but rather that truth for all men is a necessary characteristic of objectivity. Indeed Bennett (1966, pp. 129–130) has argued (rightly or wrongly) that although Kant tends to slide between the first person singular and plural in his account he really stresses the first person, the *individual* consciousness, and that he is right to do so. We shall be much concerned later with the relation between contingently shared judgments and the Kantian kind of necessary intersubjectivity.

deduction; rather objectivity was seen as the *application* of logical categories to the primary data of experience in certain necessary ways.

These general principles of the understanding Kant called the categories, and believed that he did not have to look far beyond the Aristotelian system of logic to find them. His establishment of the table of categories is now held to be misguided for a number of reasons. Also, he tended to argue that the necessity of the categories is a *consequence* of man's, presumably innate, cognitive constitution. This is philosophically unsatisfactory and P. F. Strawson (1966) has argued that Kant's nativist construal of the categories was mainly responsible for the unpalatably metaphysical notion of a world of unknowable entities of which we can never gain an understanding by reason of our fixed cognitive capacities. More interesting and important than the categories themselves is Kant's argument for their existence in the Transcendental Deduction section. In this section Kant showed how the understanding controls the process of 'synthesising' the manifold of sensation into objective knowledge by deploying the faculties of imagination and memory. For our purposes it would be valuable to discuss one major theme which Kant treats under the 'transcendental unity of apperception' and which he discusses in the Analogies section which comes later. This is concerned with the necessary features of the relation between thinking and perceiving, objective knowledge and the possibility of being conscious of the self.

Kant held that although our perceptions have a rulebound connectedness which is necessary for our ever coming to make objective judgments, this quality alone is not sufficient. What is also required is that the subject should be able to conceive of this rulebound sequence of sense-data as being independent of the order and arrangement of his awareness of it. This reflexive self-awareness, my being able to separately cognise that there *is* a pen in my hand and that *I think* that there is a pen in my hand, is necessary for my ever coming to know that something is objectively the case. Kant expressed it by saying that there must be the *possibility* of 'I think' accompanying any objective judgment, and he employed the term 'apperception' to refer to the conscious, objective kind of perceiving as distinct from 'perception' which is simply the reception of sensory information in space and time. Furthermore, the unity of sense-data that we receive from objects (for example we see a thing where we touch it, where we hear it, where we smell it) is necessary for us to be able to judge them to be existent. Some sense data, such as hallucinations, dreams and tickles do not possess this unity. Or in Kantian terminology: only objects have the synthetic unity necessary for the application of the categories. The three strands of the argument—the application of the categories, objective knowledge, self-consciousness—entail each other so that they do not represent steps towards a conclusion but a unity. This means that for an individual to have genuine knowledge, he must be in principle capable of ascribing this to himself, that this capacity comes about through applying certain general, formal principles which make intersubjective validity possible, and that these processes interdepend.

Kant's next task was to give an account of how we come to apply the categories to concrete instances. This is the question of how we identify a given thing as coming under a given concept: how we classify, describe and recognise. He said that for each category there is a corresponding 'schema' which can be thought of as a kind of rule which must be followed in the application of concepts (see Bennett, 1966, p. 141). The Analogies section is of particular relevance as it concerns, in part, an examination of the rulebound procedure for ordering percepts such that they are taken to be of a substantial, causal world. As concrete experience is time-bound, the general problem is how the intellect orders perceptual events in *time* to attain objectivity.

The First Analogy asserts the importance of a conservation principle: that there can be no concept of time without a corresponding notion of a substance perduring through time; knowledge of permanence and identity are necessary for any objective experience. In the Second Analogy Kant presents one of the most interesting (for the psychologist) arguments in the *Critique*. This concerns knowledge of cause and effect which Kant saw as the result of the application of the logical category of 'ground and consequent' in temporal experience via a schema. In contrast to Hume he argues that knowledge of causality is not consequent on knowledge of objects but that the principle of causality is necessary for any objective experience (hence derived from a category). Knowing that the sequence of portions of an object and of events is independent of the order in which we observe them is necessary for our being able to distinguish objective existence from subjective experience. He gives the example of standing in front of a house and viewing it from top to bottom where the sequence of the percepts can be followed in the other direction by then looking from bottom to top. Any sequence which is thus 'reversible' (Körner, 1955, p. 85) can be judged to be of an independent object. On the other hand there are irreversible sequences where, to take Kant's example again, we see a ship sailing downstream; we must necessarily see it upstream before we see it downstream. Similarly, in viewing causal sequences between objects we necessarily see the cause before the effect. All perception which is not thus determined is subjective and self-produced. The perceptible world is refractory and therefore independent; but, argues Kant, we need to apply the categories by schemata if we are to extract these necessary features of reversibility and irreversibility. Distinguishing between the cases in which we are active and cases in which the action takes place outside us is necessary for experience, that is, synthetic *a priori*.

Although only a sketchy account has been presented, the reader may be able to extract some idea of Kant's general aim. Though this is made especially difficult by the fundamental ambiguity in the *Critique* between Kant's desire to give a philosophical account of the necessary, general features of our experience, and his tendency to declare when these are found that they lie in our cognitive faculties, which is an empirical hypothesis. This is the difference between saying that intersubjectivity is necessary and produced by the application of formal categories and saying that intersubjectivity is possible because of the *common cognitive constitution* of human beings. P. F. Strawson (1966) has called these the 'two faces of the Critique' and has argued that the 'crude, innatist psychology' that was inherent in the latter tendency was responsible for the 'unacceptable face of the Critique' which produced the disastrous model of an unknowable world of noumena, as was mentioned above. But perhaps it is not quite so difficult to appreciate how, given the distinction made in the Introduction between type (2) and type (3) questions, some sliding towards cognitive psychology is almost inevitable in theorising about the necessary features of knowledge acquisition; and especially if, as in Kant's day, there is no science of psychology with which to contrast the philosophical enterprise. On this construal therefore, Kant was tending towards a genetic epistemology of a nativist variety.

G. W. F. Hegel (1770–1831) challenged the absolutism of Kant's system wherein fixed principles are enshrined in the categories, with a thoroughgoing relativism, which was opposed to the whole enterprise of epistemology. Classical epistemology, as we have seen, essentially involves a quest for justification, but Hegel argued that in order to undertake such a quest we must be already in a position to trust our directly acquired cognitions, otherwise we could not undertake anything—a circularity. Hegel did not regard the genesis of knowledge as being at the point at which objective judgment, application of formal principles and self-consciousness interdepend, but rather in consciousness itself. Kant founded knowledge on the 'I think' that accompanies all our perceptions, whereas Hegel asserted that this is in fact the result of consciousness reflecting on itself—one stage in the development of consciousness. Knowledge develops through continuous self-reflection. By means of this proposal Hegel wished to avoid the circularity of epistemology by making the foundation of knowledge the rational activity of the mind. Rather than begin with the question 'How do we know that this table exists?' when we must assume that it does to begin the questioning, he starts with consciousness that has only data. The reason then proceeds to confront each datum with its opposite and to synthesise these opposites, the result of which can be negated again and so on: 'thesis', 'antithesis' and 'synthesis'. The acquisition of knowledge can only take place by this process, which Hegel called the 'dialectic'. Thus, the mind can attain higher and higher stages of knowledge: from consciousness to self-consciousness to the stage of reason (understanding the 'real'), the stage of spirit (religion and art), attaining absolute knowledge when the mind can reflect on its own self-formative process.

Perhaps the main feature of Hegel's system is the way in which every truth, or datum, or piece of knowledge, is treated as a stage in a process, relative to what precedes and succeeds it. Indissociable from this relativism is a subjectivity which views the developmental stages as 'alienations'—creations of the reason, not independent of it.

It is now time to take a broader view of the development of epistemology, for in the nineteenth century it becomes possible to construe the search for the origins of our understanding as moving off in many different directions. I will mention four of these directions which all have relevance to the establishment of genetic epistemology, though some more than others. The first direction was mainly French and German and took either a Kantian or Hegelian flavour. The common element in this thought was a concern with consciousness, a concern which characterised the phenomenologists, the most influential of whom was Edmund Husserl (1859–1938). Husserl believed that epistemology should investigate the different modes of consciousness and by a method similar to Cartesian doubt ('*epoche*') arrive at pure consciousness, free of all presuppositions, which would be the foundation of our understanding. The French philosopher Merleau-Ponty is heavily influenced by phenomenology.

There are two other tributaries which are more obviously Hegelian: Marxism and (mostly as a negative influence) existentialism. Marx began his system with a critique of Hegel and takes over some of Hegel's concepts, notably the dialectic and the notion of alienation. Marxist historians reflect the determinism in the system whereby no human agent can divert the sure march of the dialectic. The relativism and subjectivity is also found in much present-day sociological theorising such as that considered in the Introduction. Although the existentialism of Kierkegaard represented a reaction against the hyper-rationalism and determinism of Hegel, many existentialist writers, especially Heidegger and Sartre, almost outdo Hegel with their abstruse, multi-hyphenated style, producing a system just as reason-bound.

The second direction was mainly British and German. Although there had been an almost unbroken train of empiricist thought in Britain running from Locke and reaching its fullest nineteenth-century expression in J. S. Mill, an Hegelian Idealism as presented by F. H. Bradley was the prevailing orthodoxy in the early years of this century. As young men Bertrand Russell (1872–1970) and G. E. Moore reacted against this; Moore from a distrust of the cloudy, autistic verbiage of Hegel and a desire to establish a philosophy founded on common-sense Realism, and Russell from a wish to plot the logical structure of knowledge—having been influenced by Leibniz and the German logician Gottlieb Frege.

In 1912 Ludwig Wittgenstein (1889–1951) became a pupil of Russell. His early work the *Tractatus Logico Philosophicus* greatly influenced Russell's thinking with its atomic theory of meaning, whereby the ultimate constituents of knowledge were taken to be atomic particulars and the relations between these particulars the universal structure of knowledge, which could be represented in the symbolism of formal logic. The *Tractatus* also influenced a group of philosophers, mainly interested in the philosophy of science, who became known as the Vienna Circle and their doctrine as logical positivism. The main tenet of logical positivism was the verification principle, which stated that either propositions were analytic (mathematics, logic) or empirically *verifiable* (as in science) or meaningless— a stringent empiricism imported into Britain by A. J. Ayer. Karl Popper was originally located on the fringes of the Vienna Circle. His development of the *falsifiability* principle was mainly responsible for logical positivism falling out of favour as a philosophy of science (see p. 9).

Wittgenstein's later philosophy, which became profoundly influential, can be seen as a reaction against his early theory of meaning and significance. His notion that meaning grows out of our conduct in the everyday world, the'forms of life' of the human community, and that language is made up of a complex network of procedures with their own implicit rule-systems ('language games') is of manifest relevance to the social sciences. Wittgenstein believed that philosophical problems were really conceptual confusions generated by an ignorance of the different functions of language. We earlier characterised philosophy as the tireless worrying away at a problem; but what if the problem is of our own making? Is the philosopher, as Voltaire put it, like the man who looks in a darkened room for a black cat which is not there? Or, as Wittgenstein wrote: 'What is your aim in philosophy? To show the fly the way out of the fly bottle'—or indeed the bee out of the bonnet.

No less radical in intent though more conservative in style was the philosophy of J. L. Austin who likewise believed in appealing to ordinary linguistic usage to extricate philosophers from their metaphysical entanglements. Austin's method was the painstaking analysis of the different usages of words and expressions and his goal the construction of a kind of 'super-grammar' by means of which the net of philosophical problems could be unravelled. Both these philosophers will be re-encountered later.

Another philosopher who has had some influence on psychological thinking is Gilbert Ryle, who, in *The Concept of Mind* (1949) adopted a philosophical behaviourism in order to purge theories about human behaviour and thinking of mentalism: intentions could be translated as dispositions to act for example. In opposition to this Beloff (1962) has argued that Ryle's 'ghost in the machine' analogy of the mind— body relationship in so-called 'mentalistic' psychology was really a gibe against a position which nobody in psychology or philosophy seriously held.

The third direction is biological and developmental and leads more directly towards genetic epistemology. This train of influence really continues into the next section, but one thinker who should be included here, not only because of his (partly negative) influence on Piaget's thought, is Henri Bergson (1859–1941). He represents something of the genetic epistemological approach in a primitive form insofar as he did not see the necessity for treating philosophical and biological–developmental questions separately. Bergson held that the intellect has practical roots in action and tool use, being later elaborated in language. Man has a need to predict and control nature and develops effective action patterns to this end; intellectual endeavours such as science represent a further development of this capacity rather than a separate speculative faculty. Also, the intellect does not create new structures in the course of its development but rather rearranges more primitive procedures from a lower level. One of the main achievements of the developing intellect is to 'break up' the continuous flux of time into discrete units by the application of formal methods in order to construct stability in the ever-changing environment (compare Kant).

However, Bergson's reading of *The Origin of Species* (published in the year of his birth) had a fundamental influence on his thinking. His major work *Creative Evolution* sets out a rejection of Darwin's account of evolution insofar as it was proposed in materialistic, mechanistic terms of random mutations being selected for their adaptive value. In contrast Bergson stressed that an animal or an organ is a whole whose parts coordinate to produce efficient functioning. If one of these parts comes to vary independently from the rest the functioning breaks down. How then can random variation account for the fact that all the integrated elements of the system *co*-adapt as a totality? Darwin's emphasis on the random production of more adaptive characteristics, argued Bergson, ignored the necessity for some kind of biological organising agency in maintaining the continuity of the organism throughout successive changes in form. The other aspect of evolution which Bergson believed Darwin could not account for was that the process moves from lesser to greater complexity. Bergson's conception of the agency which could account for these features of evolution was metaphysical, indeed religious. He postulated a vital impulse (*élan vital*) which 'insinuated itself' into early physicochemical systems and which was the coordinating force, a 'current of consciousness' passed on from generation to generation. This found its highest expression in human intelligence; ending with the thesis that the 'appearance of man is the *raison d'être* of life on earth'. By and large, Bergson's questions have been more influential than his answers.

The fourth and final direction was mainly American, with its European progenitor being Kant. American Pragmatism was originated by Charles Peirce (1839–1914) in the 1870s, though its most famous protagonist was the philosopher–psychologist William James; other notable pragmatists being John Dewey and the English philosopher F. C. S. Schiller. Pragmatism is difficult to define as a whole because James's conception of it was really quite divergent from that of Peirce, in whom the Kantian influence was predominant—indeed Peirce reports that he devoted two hours a day to the study of the *Critique* until he almost knew it by heart (Buchler 1940, p. 2). He took the term pragmatic from Kant's use of the word *pragmatisch* as referring to rules of thought which have their application in experience, or empirically. Thus Peirce's theory of meaning is produced: meanings are determined by schemata or rules of application that prescribe results or anticipatable consequences in the world of experience and action. That is, a concept has meaning only in so far as we can conceive of its application in a practical context.

There is another direct line of influence from Kant to modern pragmatism which produced Hans Vaihinger's *Philosophy of the As-If.* Kant had proposed that there are certain 'Ideas', *a priori* notions, to which nothing in experience can correspond but which can have a kind of application by being treated *as if* they did, as indicating the upper limit of our understanding. As regards knowledge of the mind, for example, we can 'connect all appearances, actions and the receptivity of our mind . . . *as if* it were a simple substance, which endowed with personal identity (at least during life) permanently exists'. In this way concepts can be justified by their heuristic value.

But it was *American* pragmatism which contributed to the development of genetic epistemology. Peirce's main philosophical concern was with language or 'signs'; and he was many years ahead of his time in this respect. Signs are of such crucial importance in human thought because it is by virtue of their socially conventionalised nature that we can communicate and thus share meanings and knowledge. On this basis, his conception of pragmatism was of a technique for promoting the clarification of concepts by showing their practical application, and expediting communication by encouraging linguistic clarity. The pragmatist has to apply the acid test of what are the practical consequences of adopting this or that intellectual construct or linguistic form. On this model therefore, the classical philosophical problems are discounted as meaning*less*. So Peirce was here anticipating the verification principle of logical positivism and, more interestingly, the linguistic philosophy of Wittgenstein encompassed in the slogan that meaning is use. Regarding any direct filiation from pragmatism to Wittgenstein it is difficult to judge, although we know that Wittgenstein did work through James' *Principles of Psychology* in his Cambridge lectures. As to James himself, his pragmatism was in many ways more extreme, more concerned with moral questions and much closer to the ordinary language meaning of 'pragmatic'. His notion of truth was very like that of expediency and value; indeed he characterised the truth of our ideas in a famous phrase as their 'cash value'.

The guiding principle of pragmatism was functionalist: beliefs, truths, concepts have a significance only in so far as they can be understood to have a function in human life. When carried over to psychology this meant that the stuff of mental life was to be understood as the product of the continuous interrelationship between organism and environment rather than a set of mental structures or faculties. Clearly functionalism, in that it stresses process against state, must tend towards a genetic view of knowledge; but when it is untempered by the Kantian principles that human knowledge is necessarily structured in definite ways and that certain forms of individual–environment interaction are necessary for any knowledge and thus transcend mere practical expediency, functionalism can slip into subjectivism and behaviourism. Both tendencies are *derivable* from the work of the pragmatist G. H. Mead (1863–1931) who studied under James and came to produce an influential social psychology. Mead developed a form of 'social behaviourism' in which he saw no need for any principles beyond the mutual determination of organism and environment in the growth of mind. Although he was not an opponent of introspection (unless when used as the prime experimental tool as by the 'structuralist' Titchener) his view of mental phenomena was not unlike the dispositional account of Ryle, in which the idea was treated merely as an inner, prior stage of the total act of which the overt behaviour was the final stage. As regards subjectivism we have Mead's emphasis on the socially constituted nature of reality, on the individual's incorporation of *his conception* of the group (the 'generalised other'), as his personal reality and the view that the self is constructed out of reactions to 'significant others'—notions that have greatly influenced current theoretical sociology. His functionalism carried over into a philosophy of science takes on a Bergsonian flavour, with science being originated in the desire to control nature rather than understand it: abstract physical concepts like space, time and mass being regarded as having developed out of manipulatory experience. There is also a flavour of subjectivism: physical reality is the intersection of the perspectives of individuals and thus there is a 'subjectivity' in every scientific judgment which has not been totally assimilated to the experiences of others (see Strauss, 1956, pp. 43–60). This is in exact contrast to Popper who regards even a trial solution by a lone thinker as within the world of objective knowledge.

1.2　JAMES MARK BALDWIN AND GENETIC EPISTEMOLOGY

It is no exaggeration to say that before Darwin there was nothing that would be recognisable today as developmental psychology. Major landmarks had been Locke's writings on education and J. J. Rousseau's *Emile* (1762). Childhood was more often the exercising-ground for hobby horses rather than the domain of the scientist until the appearance of *The Origin of Species* (1859).

Adopting an evolutionary perspective to view man *qua* species, led many of Darwin's contemporaries to regard childhood as the mirror of racial history: ontogeny (development of the individual) re-capitulating phylogeny (evolution of the species). This had the effect of legitimising the child as a source of scientific information and the baby biography as a scientific exercise (Kessen, 1965). Darwin himself published an account of the development of his own infant son William Erasmus (or 'Doddy')in the journal *Mind* in 1877, in which sophistication and accuracy of reporting was allied to unmistakably Darwinian interpretation, especially regarding the infant's aggressive behaviour.

Yet Darwin's was not the first evolutionary theory. Many years before Jean Lamarck (1744–1829) had proposed an evolutionary principle whereby organisms inherited characters acquired by their parent during the parent's lifetime, and although there is no empirical support for the direct heritability of acquired characters Lamarckism has by no means been confined to the dustbin of history. As a theoretical construct it retains some usefulness because there are phenomena which mimic a Lamarckian mode of inheritance, and because a thoroughgoing mutationism is not satisfactory—as we shall be discussing later (see also p. 44).

Moreover, nine years before the publication of the *Origins* the English philosopher Herbert Spencer (1820–1903) had attempted in his first book *Social Statics* an evolutionary theory strongly Darwinian in flavour though with Lamarckian overtones. Having thoroughly assimilated Darwin's theory Spencer then set about producing an all-inclusive system of thought which he called a *synthetic philosophy* wherein the unity of the various sciences would be achieved by relating them to fundamental evolutionary processes.

For our interests, Spencer's mediation of Darwinian principles into psychological and social areas was more important than the evolutionary and psychological theories which he himself proposed. But though these were often vague and devoid of empirical content, they did provide useful conceptual frameworks for later workers. For example, he proposed that complementary processes of *integration* and *differentiation* were at work in any progressive change: the parts of things—organic and inorganic—become increasingly differentiated but at the same time better integrated and organised into superordinate and subordinate levels. Likewise in mental development, in evolution and in society there is a gradual movement towards complexity and higher levels of organisation. He also employed a principle of *equilibrium*, to show how natural selection cannot be regarded as working only through the mutation of single organs but that 'all other organs become equilibrated in the change. The Functions performed by them have to constitute a moving equilibrium.' As Popper (1972) indicates, Spencer's concepts and terminology anticipate present-day systems theory: he referred to the organism as an 'open system in fluent equilibrium', for example. During the middle period of an organism's or a society's life, after its development and before its decay, it was regarded as being in a state of equilibrium. Also, Spencer's characterisation of intelligence as basically *adaptive*—as a set of tendencies and behaviour patterns which enabled the organism to interact effectively with a harsh environment—became very influential.

Spencer cannot, however, be regarded as a genetic epistemologist for although he did a great deal of work in epistemology he never attacked epistemological questions from a developmental perspective. He expressed at first an empiricism not unlike that of J. S. Mill and although he later adopted a more Kantian approach Kant's influence was realised in his proposal of the Unknowable (the 'noumenon' in Kant) which was manifested to us through phenomena; he did not adopt the Kantian quest for the necessary forms which man's relation to his environment has to take—which might have led him towards a genetic epistemology.

Another evolutionary thinker of this period worth mentioning is the English comparative psychologist George Romanes (1848–1918), not merely because he was typical, but because his account of mental evolution and development contained some proposals about the special evolutionary status of human knowledge which are similar to arguments to be presented in Part 4. Romanes is also notable for his insistence that the evidence against Lamarckism did not warrant its total rejection and for his championing of cultural factors, such as writing, in human evolution. It is in his *Mental Evolution in Man* (1888) that some of his most interesting suggestions appear.

Like many others he contended that the possession of language clearly delineates human from animal intelligence but did not believe that this was due to the syntactic or semantic structure of language moulding human intelligence and thus determining the categories and transformations which it can apply to reality; rather because it is only through a sign system that *propositions* can be made about *truths*. 'In any case', he wrote, 'the psychological distinction between a brute and a man consists in the latter being able to *mean a proposition*; and the kind of mental act which this involves is technically termed a "judgment"' (p. 399). Animals can make *re*ceptual (associative connections between repeated concrete instances) inferences and may even use signs to denote them but although 'there would then be the outward semblance of a proposition, we should not be strictly right in calling it a proposition. It would, indeed, be the *statement of a truth perceived*; but not the statement of a truth perceived *as true*' (p. 405). Young children have a higher form of receptual intelligence which Romanes called *pre-conceptual* because they have yet to attain the ability to state truths 'perceived as true' through their language. 'Of course' he wrote 'the condition required for the raising of this lower kind of judgment and this lower kind of predication . . . into the higher or only true kind of judgment and predication, is the advent of self-consciousness. Or, in other words, the place where a mere statement of truth first passes into a real predication of truth, is determined by the place at which there first supervenes the faculty of introspective reflection' (p. 405). Thus we have Kant's *I think* which must be capable of accompanying all our judgments.

In the USA meanwhile two philosophers were making their transition to psychology via Darwin: Granville S. Hall and James Mark Baldwin (1861–1934). In almost every respect they were quite different kinds of psychologist. Hall, regarded by many as the founder of American psychology, having embraced psychology, decried the relevance of philosophy; metaphysics and epistemology were denounced as two of the three greatest enemies of psychology (the third being mathematics). The child for Hall was a cornucopia of data to be gathered by observation. He had a clear aversion to theorising (although his own speculations were often lavish), and held broadly to the theory of recapitulation, resulting in a maturationist viewpoint later represented in the work of Arnold Gesell.

Baldwin's aim was nothing less than to explain human knowledge developmentally, with reference to both phylogeny and ontogeny though with the emphasis on the latter; that is, to construct a *genetic* epistemology. More akin to William James than he was to many of his more experimentally orientated contemporaries, he was, nevertheless, a psychologist, co-founding the *Psychological Review* and having his heir in Jean Piaget. 'The most vicious and Philistine attempt . . . to put science in the strait-jacket of barren observation' was how he described Hall's approach. 'On the contrary,' he went on to say 'give us theories, theories! Let every man who has a theory pronounce his theory! That is just the difference between the good psychologist and the average mother . . . , (Baldwin, 1906a, p. 35).

Already Darwin had provided psychologists with a framework within which to regard development, to stand back from any biological entity and see it as the result of a progression of trial and error and once an evolutionary principle had been established as universal, explaining the mind and its workings could be construed as a genetic task. Indeed we now know from Darwin's recently published notebooks that he was himself greatly concerned with mental as well as physical evolution (Gruber, 1974). As Baldwin said in *Development and Evolution* (1902), 'The occurrence of psychological change in an animal is a fact in the same sense that the animal's process of digestion is' (p. 4). Also, biological and psychological phenomena do not inhabit separate watertight compartments; a point which he illustrates by reference to the fact that in order for male and female members of a species to mate and continue evolution they must recognise each other, which is a psychological process.

As regards the evolution of intelligent behaviour, although Baldwin argued that common principles are operative in ontogeny and phylogeny he did not accept the recapitulation theory. There is a 'parallelism', but of quite a different nature, derived from the fact that both natural selection and the intelligent activity of the individual are selective: natural selection selects the better adapted variations 'after the event' and intelligence selects between actions 'before the event'. Now Baldwin held that the products of natural selection—the phylogenetically evolved repertoire of the organism—could not by themselves be responsible for intelligent behaviour because behavioural adaptation to the environment, at any level, must involve an *active* principle whereby the organism regulates its behaviour in the light of environmental contingencies. The environment does not merely provide a set of triggers for phylogenetically fixed patterns to be elicited from passive organisms. Baldwin called this active principle *accommodation*. Accommodation is *what the organism does* with its innate capacities, acquired through natural selection, in order to make the most of its environmental milieu, so that both the possession of advantageous, congenital, fixed behaviour patterns and the range over which the organism can accommodate, together determine adaptive capacity. Evolution therefore, tends not towards the 'wiring in' of more and more complex behavioural programmes but rather towards an increased plasticity of nervous structure. Baldwin suggests that, in the broadest sense, intelligence can be equated with accommodatory capacity—with lack of specificity in the behavioural repertoire rather than a quantum of advantageous skills. As we move up the phylogenetic scale, therefore, accommodatory capacity increases, implying that the standard dichotomy between congenital and acquired characteristics is not tenable. There is a set of reflexes, of fixed action patterns even, but these are elaborated in a manner dependent on the accommodatory range of the organism and the environmental contingencies. Natural selection is thus a necessary but a negative principle which sets a limit on what kinds of animal will survive. Accommodation, on the other hand, is a positive principle: the putting-to-use of biological raw materials, akin almost to the creative principle which Bergson had envisaged.

There are, therefore, certain basic 'ontogenetic agencies', as Baldwin calls them, which are responsible for accommodatory capacity. The most primitive of these are the functions necessitated by adverse physical influences such as chemical agents, temperature, hindrances to growth and so on, to which the organism has to accommodate within its lifetime in order to survive. These are very close to naturally selected fixed patterns. Next are the agencies which arise from the spontaneous activities of the organism, the capacities for 'rising to the occasion' when faced with a difficulty, such as the animal escaping from a cage. Finally in the highest category Baldwin places the agencies responsible for the accommodations, producing what we normally think of as intelligent behaviour: 'imitation, gregarious habits, parental instruction, the lessons of pleasure and pain and of experience generally, reasoning from means to end' (*op. cit.*, p. 93). (As this list shows, Baldwin regarded these agencies as including both influences from the physical and social environment and things done by the organism, as they each determine the course of accommodation.) Baldwin is saying here that the higher mental functions are not innate within the human species, neither are they a set of skills, or something more general like storage capacity in the brain which has been selected in phylogeny, rather they represent the capacity of the species to accommodate to environmental demands. Human life, for example, presents the child with models, problems, codes, symbols, rules, to which he will accommodate in so far as his brain has the requisite plasticity; heredity provides the raw material. The human brain differs from (say) the chimpanzee brain not in the sophistication or quantity of its programmes but in the range of choice points it gives its owner at the beginning and throughout the course of development.

Natural selection is not alone sufficient to keep the organism alive because the 'storm and stress' of the environment must be met by accommodatory modifications of congenital function. 'By this means *those congenital and phylogenetic variations are kept in existence which lend themselves to intelligent imitative adaptive or mechanical modification during the lifetime of the creatures which have them*' (*op. cit.*, p. 95). Perhaps the clearest example of this process (and most important for Baldwin) is that of imitation. There may be certain kinds of behaviour (catching prey for example) which are necessary for the survival of the species but are not innate action patterns requiring only an environmental trigger; these might be developed by imitation, an ontogenetic process of accommodation. So here, because behaviours developed in one generation can be passed on directly through imitation, we have something that mimics Lamarkian inheritance and disposes of its necessity. 'Tradition' is nothing other than the social development and transmission of behaviours, through such agencies as imitation, to which the young can accommodate.

As we ascend the phylogenetic scale the more we find this accommodatory process determining the course of natural selection rather than just keeping pace with it. For ontogenetic agencies can over-reach the congenitally-fixed potentialities and point the species in a new direction by changing habitat, courtship rituals and so on within a generation, thus making different congenital capacities advantageous and changing phylogeny through ontogeny. Let us consider an example of how this could occur. One suggestion has been that man-like creatures began to evolve from the apes when the apes changed their habitat, moving down from the trees to the plain, thus necessitating the killing of other animals for food when before they had been mainly herbivorous. Thus there would eventually be selection in favour of the necessary congenital capacities which would allow the development of tool use and the concommitant symbolic skills. Baldwin accounts for this kind of process by the 'Orthoplasy' principle: 'It is the theory that individual modifications or accommodations supplement, protect or screen organic characters and keep them alive (certain more advanced apes inventing tools and being imitated for example) 'until useful congential variations arise and survive by natural selection; that this process, combined in many cases with "tradition" give direction to evolution' (*op. cit.*, p. 173).

Baldwin also posited a process—a theory of learning in fact—which is taken to underly all the various ontogenetic agencies. This he called the 'circular reaction': the deliberate repetition (hence 'circular') of an action which produces pleasant stimulation, reproducing the conditions of its previous stimulation. It enables the organism to secure new accommodations precisely because it *overproduces* a wide variety of different movements so that individual movements which it finds advantageous can be selected *by the organism*. In a sense circular reactions are hedonistic but without them behaviour would lack a motive force and the necessary degree of redundancy—a 'pool' of behaviour from which to select the required action 'before the event'. It cannot be overemphasised that circular reactions must not be equated with trial-and-error or S–R learning. The behaviours produced on this latter account are a blind running-through of a repertoire from which the *environment* selects the most advantageous; it is not the production for their own sake of behaviours which are then selected by the organism ('functional selection' is Baldwin's term) for their utility. To put the matter epigramatically, the circular reaction is to orthoplasy as S–R learning is to natural selection.

Baldwin claimed that the orthoplasy principle is able to deal with two often mentioned difficulties with the theory of natural selection: (1) that certain advantageous variations when they first arose were immature and not initially useful (palaeontological evidence), thence how did they come to be selected? and (2) in the cases where there are 'correlations' (later called 'integrations') of structures or functions as, for example, in the elements of the digestive system or complex fixed behaviour patterns. It is difficult to see how the partial correlations through which the species must have passed could have been selected, and difficult to believe that the correlations arose *de novo* from a mutation (see Bergson's criticism above). The orthoplasy principle meets the first objection by stating that the yet-to-be-useful characters would be supplemented by individual accommodations keeping the organism alive until they became fully advantageous through natural selection, and it meets the second in much the same way by saying that the correlations which were not adequate at first would be supplemented by accommodations until the complete correlations became congenital through natural selection.

Relating these arguments to what has gone before in this book, the connection between the philosophical accounts of Section 1.1 and the theoretical biology of this section is not obvious but it is definite. We saw that one fundamental issue in epistemology is the relative contribution of experience and prior structure to knowledge, with empiricism putting the weight on experience, rationalism on innateness and Kantian theory attempting a synthesis of the two approaches. Naturally the innate–learned dichotomy is also psychobiological. What the notion of orthoplasty seeks to achieve is a kind of Kantian resolution between the unfolding of phylogenetically fixed patterns in development—an innatist principle—and the empiricism which sees the environment as selecting certain advantageous behaviours from a passive organism which blindly produces them. We have in the principle of orthoplasy both the active, predisposed organism of rationalism and the determining environment of empiricism. Baldwin had no doubt that the explanation of the acquisition, and indeed the nature of, knowledge was psychological as well as philosophical, that as knowledge is itself a biological phenomenon, epistemological systems cannot exist independently of theoretical biology.

In another book, *Mental Development in the Child and the Race* (1906a), Baldwin extends these principles into the realms of psychology to explain the genesis of memory, logical thought, perception, imagination, volition, attention, internal speech and so on. Although the organisation of the book is somewhat diffuse, there is a definite theme, which is the relation between habit and accommodation in mental development especially as found in imitation— the process fundamental to both the ontogeny and the phylogeny of mind. Although Baldwin holds that common principles are at work in the ontogeny and phylogeny of mental development, and tends to follow each section in the book with a treatment of the relevant phylogenetic considerations, he is careful as before to disclaim any recapitulation. One piece of evidence given for this rejection is that because the brain evolves from specificity to plasticity by accommodation, there is no stage in the development of the human infant that might be called 'instinctive' in the sense in which the fixed action patterns studied by ethologists might be so termed.

Baldwin sees development from birth as the interaction between two opposing but complementary principles—habit and accommodation—one conservative and the other innovatory. Habit is the repetition of the pleasurable and reflects the predispositions of the organism to repeat *vitally beneficial* actions, and is phylogenetically determined. For example, actions which result in nurture (sucking), warmth (clinging), freedom from noxious stimulation (crying) all serve to maintain life. However such a principle is adevelopmental, and could only be effective, argues Baldwin, given a highly uniform environment. The following question must be posed: if habit is the maintenance of advantageous states, how is the infant able to effect the 'right' movements given a complex and changing world? Baldwin says that the infant is able to do this by the accommodatory principle of the circular reaction. This account takes certain habits as phylogenetically fixed by natural selection, because it is of selective value to find pleasure in the repetition of certain actions—such as sucking, grasping, blinking. The circular overproduction and repetition of movements for their own sake then provides a necessary process whereby the infant can elaborate on, and develop away from, purely habitual, automatic *re*action and accommodate to the changing world. An example of this process would be how the infant begins by habitually sucking protruberances which enter its mouth, then sucks its own fingers if they happen to brush past his lips, then intentionally brings the hand to the mouth for sucking, then explores new objects by putting them into the mouth, then sucks different objects (blanket, rattle) in different ways—it accommodates to them. Yet although accommodation arises out of habit it is fundamentally opposed to it; firstly because it produces new movements where habit repeats old ones, and secondly, in that it *selects* new movements, it tends to disintegrate habits.

The bridge between the purely motoric notion of the circular reaction and the course of *mental* development is formed by imitation. The nature of the circular reaction itself is imitative: 'an imitation is an ordinary sensori-motor reaction which finds its differentia in the single fact that it imitates . . . It is what we have called "circular activity" on the bodily side' (*op. cit.*, p. 251). A circular reaction repeats itself, is thus self-imitative and from this other kinds of imitation flow. The imitative component of circular reaction is also the origin of memory. Repetition of an action *recalls* the original action—repeating something implies the presence of some internal record of the initial performance, however primitive. Baldwin sketches the physiological basis of memory in the following way: in order to imitate there must be a 'copy for imitation' so that as accommodation proceeds this action-to-be-imitated becomes an-action-imitated and is thus 'rung up' in the brain. The cortex thus stores a mass of past imitations which 'make up a larger and larger mass of connected centres which vibrate in delicate counterpoise together' (*op. cit.*, p. 266) in the association cortex. In this way one imitation can evoke another by association, or an immediate experience can recall a past imitation.

Thus memory on Baldwin's account is an instance of the principle of association of ideas. The child, for example imitates his parent speaking the name of an object so that speaking-name and seeing-object are 'rung up' together in his memory. Thus, by association, the later sight of the object evokes a past sound and the child says the word. Indeed Baldwin's use of the association principle goes beyond the field of memory and he subsumes the various forms of association under the principle of *assimilation*, a term he borrowed from Wundt. Assimilation is the general process whereby old 'mental elements' impose their character on the new, giving a cognitive context. Also, a new habit can be assimilated to an old one. Thus assimilation, again a conservative principle like habit, serves to place every new action in the light of what has been achieved previously, to establish a context for it in the stream of behaviour. It is also very close to recognition; recognising a knife *as* a knife is a case of assimilation.

Baldwin says later 'Passing on to the sphere of conception and thought, we find an opening for the law of imitation. The principle of Identity which represents the mental demand for consistency of experience, and the mental tendency, already remarked, to the assimilation of new material to old schemes, is seen genetically in the single fact that the repetitions are pleasurable to the infant, and to us all, because of the law of habit in our reactions' (*op. cit.*, p. 306). Baldwin employs the principle of assimilation to explain the formation of concepts: 'His earliest experiences, carried over into memory, become general copies which stand as assimilative nets for every new event or object' (*op. cit.*, p. 309). These 'nets' will begin by being of too coarse a mesh; for example, the child may tend to call all men 'daddy'. These first early concepts are—using Kant's term—*schematic*, and they take past experience as a model for the accommodatory needs of the future, because particular experiences are 'all that the organism is accommodated to and they are the copies to which all experiences are assimilated if possible' (*op. cit.*, p. 310). But of course it is *not* always possible to assimilate new experiences to old schemes and thus new accommodations are necessitated, abstract concepts being produced by the complementary processes of generalisation and erosion of schematic concepts (see also p. 65).

The role of imitation in psychic development was displayed by Baldwin on a broader canvas in his *Social and Ethical Interpretations* (1906b). The notion is extended beyond cognitive development to encompass what would be called today ego development, socialisation and theoretical sociology. Firstly he seeks to explain the development of the child's consciousness of himself as a thinking, feeling being by the 'dialectic of personal growth'—an imitative process. The child's earliest understanding of the person is *projective*, that is, he cognises other people as unpredictable and 'self-propelling' in contrast to things, without having any notion of himself as being likewise. A later *subjectivity* is then brought about by his imitation of others. By imitating actions he finds that certain subjective feelings, of strain and resistance for example, accompany the action, and indeed the fact that this involves an effort of his own towards some end produces the earliest consciousness of volition. Yet this subjective sense cannot exist without a complementary ascription by the child of subjective states to others, an *ejection*—'They are also *me's*; let them be assimilated to my me-copy'—and thus the social self is born. 'My sense of myself grows by imitation of you and my sense of yourself grows in terms of my sense of myself' (*op. cit.*, p. 14).

This same dialectical, 'give-and-take' process is again encountered when Baldwin comes to consider the development of societies—the 'dialectic of social growth'. The first stage of the dialectic is the existence in the mind of one individual or set of individuals of some new 'thought' (such as Christianity or Socialism) which is projective in that it is extra-social. When society assimilates this thought and embodies it in its institutions (Monarch made the head of the Church, public ownership) it becomes subjective; and finally society makes it ejective by imposing these principles on the people by what we might today call indoctrination. It should be mentioned, however, that although this is a dialectical theory, that the initial impetus is seen as coming from the *individual* or set of individuals makes it distant from Hegel and Marx. Imitation—in this context the process of taking from others—is therefore what makes individuals self-aware and social, what integrates individuals into society and what determines the development of societies. Baldwin was not alone among his contemporaries in emphasising imitation within a theory of society: Bagehot, Sighele and especially Tarde did so.

It would be wrong to have the impression that Baldwin's reliance on imitation implies a view of the individual as passive in the developmental process, however dialectical the account may be. He stresses that imitation and invention do not represent opposite poles but rather are indissociable elements in psychic development. Invention comes about, not by any instinct to create novelties, but almost willy-nilly. Imitation takes place in a context of past accommodations and a current assimilatory capacity so that the child who sets out to imitate will end up creating some kind of novelty so long as his assimilatory capacities are relatively immature; he will see and do things in his own way because he *cannot* do them in any other.

Also, in the process of imitation he may, by chance, create new combinations which lead him away from the straight and narrow path to follow his own interests. Here Baldwin gives the example of his daughter starting to build in bricks a copy of a tower in a picture book and finishing up with a model of what she called an animal. This balancing of the production of novelties against imitation leads to a measure of self-regulation.

As regards language use and play Baldwin sees these as representing the aspects of the child's life where the inventive function is uppermost. For example the child learns the words of his language by imitation but expresses his own needs and interests when he speaks, so that the main thrust towards the development of language is the *inventive interpretations* of adult speech which are confirmed or disconfirmed as he puts them to use. 'There is no end, of course, to this give-and-take between the child and me; he takes what I give and gives it back in his own form of assimilation or invention, only to have his construction rejected by me with further direction whereby he can make it conform better to the demands of the developed system of meanings, which I have already acquired by precisely the same process' (*op. cit.*, p. 145). 'Interpretations' is the name Baldwin gives to the child's inventive imitations. He interprets new data, puts his interpretation to the test by appealing to his fellows through usage, and on the basis of the result effects a new synthesis, and so on.

What are the implications of this dialectical account for a theory of knowledge? Firstly our knowledge can only be regarded as private in a very limited and relative sense, and likewise only in a relative sense is knowledge public; the fact is they are identical. 'The social judgment gets its competence from the common absorption of the same imitative copies by all individuals; and the individual's private judgment gets its validity from the conditions of social origin' (*op. cit.*, p. 133). Therefore, in trying to discover the origin of truth and error we must look not to the individual's innate capacities, nor to the nature of the physical world, but to society which *includes* the individual.

With this conclusion we are anticipating the dominant motif of Baldwin's major work *Thought and Things; or Genetic Logic* (Vol. I, 1906; Vol. II, 1908; Vol. III, 1911) in which he set out a genetic theory of all knowledge. Yet, as one child psychologist puts it, '*Thought and Things*, brilliant and one of the few truly original documents in psychology, crowded with invented words and all the apparatus of a philosophical system, caused a slight flurry among philosophers and was steadfastly and monotonously ignored by psychologists' (Kessen, 1965, p. 165). The reasons for this neglect are not hard to appreciate: the Kantian scale, the difficulty of the language (a mixture of heartiness and spiralling abstraction), but mostly its very indefinability—was it philosophy or psychology? Although the arguments have a more or less clear empirical relevance they are presented largely in an empirical vacuum. Many of Baldwin's theoretical proposals 'unfolded as a result of the observational research that he conducted on his own two children, Helen and Elizabeth' (Mueller, 1976), but examples of actual child behaviour are quite rare in the work. Indeed even the most fervent anti-behaviourist, when reading certain passages, might feel how tempting Watson's approach must have seemed to one accustomed to such a rich diet—something clear and hard after Baldwin's often elusive abstractions. Yet the importance of the arguments transcends these difficulties, an importance which lies, as we shall see, not merely in its historical role in the development of Piaget's genetic epistemology, but in the fact that we find expressed a quite different view of the acquisition of knowledge from Piaget's within a complete system of a comparable *scale* to that of Piaget.

'Professor Baldwin likes to make his readers work' wrote Yerkes in a review, and indeed *Thought and Things* is difficult reading: new terms appear, reappear and generate others, abstractions breed abstractions and disappear into the shadows. But, as W. B. Yeats wrote of a work which is almost comparable in this respect (Blake's *Jerusalem*), there is despite it all a 'mumbling wisdom'. Baldwin is saying something important and that is why I have attempted here to distil the essence of his 950 closely-argued pages.

In *Thought and Things* Baldwin begins by defining genetic logic, distinguishing it first from *formal* or exact logic. This is the study of the abstract structure of reasoning which has no necessary connection with the way people actually think, with psychology. *Metaphysical* logic refers to the kind of theorising carried on by Hegel and his followers. We are then left with two kinds of genetic logic, *functional* and *real*. Baldwin intended by functional logic a conceptual inquiry into the nature of how we think, what thinking is for and the end result, what we think about. He stressed that these 'How', 'Why' and 'What' questions require developmental answers. Real logic, on the other hand, is best understood by contrasting it with the traditional philosophical position that takes reality to have a definite logical structure of which we attain knowledge through the vehicle of thought. The genetic logic of the real does not distinguish between thought and reality but rather 'studies the actual movement of thought as instrument to a genetically built up and evolving reality, and interprets all its meanings in their hierarchical relationships and complex settings' (Vol. I, p. 13). This entails standing back from our thought about the world and viewing it as we would the evolution of a species in which study we do not distinguish between the process of phylogeny and some ideal end-state of adaptation. The term *genetic epistemology* he applied to this.

Volumes I and II are both concerned with functional logic. Volume I, is a developmental enquiry into the pre-logical conditions for the later judgments and inferences of logical thought. Volume II seeks to explain the operations of the cognitive faculties in judging and inferring. Baldwin called it 'Experimental' because, as we shall see, he held that logicality can be traced back to the primitively experimental nature of early pre-logical functioning.

1.2.1 *Interest and datum*

In the beginning, consciousness is *adualistic*: the infant has no notion of the distinction between inner and outer, ego and alter. He has two modes of experience, the conative–affective in which he is trying to attain some goal (such as the nipple) and the passive reception of the shifting stuff of consciousness. Baldwin proposed that the concrete world is determined by conative–affective striving, which would be insufficient without the failure to satisfy desires for objects and the presence of unwelcome objects. What is primary is the *interest* which is *selective*: the infant's 'already present active trains—movement series, appetetive and impulsive process etc—which are selective and assimilative elements' (*op. cit.*, p. 49). Set against this is the *datum*— the sense perception of objects—failure to satisfy which (such as failing to re-encounter the breast with a head turn) is the first step in objectivising the world. Overall, the world of the datum is refractory and will not be moulded by the infant's primitively intentional movements; there is an inevitable mismatch between what the infant expects and wants and the behaviour of objects, an *embarrassment* is the term Baldwin employs. Also, at this early stage some notion of the difference between persons and things is germinated by the fact that

the movements of animate things are more capricious and unpredictable than of inanimate, indeed they come to him and 'go off like guns
on the stage of his panorama of experience.'

1.2.2 *Control, conversion and mediation*

To refer to the determination of psychic content by the objective
world, which the infant knows as the datum, Baldwin employs the
term *control*. This is an extremely important concept in the system for
it is taken to encapsulate the process whereby, in any way, our
freedom to act on the world or think about it is restricted by
something determinate. Without a system of controls there could be
no objective experience or knowledge.

Baldwin's next task is to give an account of the development of
those aspects of thought that are not directly concerned with the here-
and-now: image objects, which are constituted in both memory and
fantasy. Memory, first of all, can be free of the control mentioned
above to the extent that an image of the thing can be evoked. Yet, on
the other hand it is also a *conversion* mode, which means that if
something is memory rather than fantasy there must, in principle, be
the possibility of reconverting the image into a sense-object—of
seeing it again. That which is not convertible is subjective, inner. That
which is convertible constitutes the world of substance. Overall,
memory exerts *mediate* rather than immediate control over our
understanding, a concept which Baldwin employs to distinguish it
from perception, where the control is direct. Here again is a
fundamental proposition of Baldwin's thought: only in the most
primitive origins of perception (and in certain forms of aesthetic
judgment to be considered later) is thought not mediated; there is
always some kind of mediation between the concrete or personal
world and ourselves. Thus, cognitive development is essentially the
process of acquiring more and more sophisticated kinds of mediation the most general description of which would be 'ideas'.

Baldwin asserts, however, that this is only one means for the
conversion of the objects of memory; there is also 'secondary
conversion' whereby we validate our memory by checking it against
that of another person, thus laying the basis for a system of *common
meanings*. For example, the child's memory might be corrected by his
parents telling him whether something really did or did not take
place. Here we see the appearance on a primitive level of the main

Baldwinian theme: that the acquisition of knowledge is not a solitary enterprise because the world of knowledge is social and other people sustain the *truth* of our judgments. Furthermore, as the adult knows more than the child, this secondary conversion, a mediate control, is an extremely powerful influence on the child's world view, for he does not have an independent 'point of view' and is therefore inevitably subject to the authority of social constraint.

The failures of conversion set a limit on what we can think about the substantial world, just as at an earlier stage the dualism of self and not-self was germinated by the failure to assimilate the sense image into a current interest. 'In this the germinal opposition between datum and interest found in the sense mode has explicit development. The interest—directed now towards the memory context—again comes in to opposition with the stable and controlling sense coefficient' (*op. cit.*, p. 86). Thus, the real–imaginary distinction is originated.

1.2.3 *Imitation*

The important sustaining force in the separation of the inner and outer worlds is imitation, for in imitating another person the child is, in a sense, converting a perception into an action with the correspondingly inevitable degree of failure which this entails. Yet, memory and imitation are essentially divergent in that imitative objects are 'selectively and consciously produced and set up' (*op. cit.*, p. 88), and they are, to introduce two more Baldwinian terms, *experimental*, to do with trying things out on the world, and *semblant*, with playfully pretending something is what it is not because it resembles another thing in some respect. Nevertheless imitation has some kind of control, which fact distinguishes it from fantasising which lacks any.

In the development of the inner world the essential processes are familiar, with the inner failing to fulfil the criteria for being the outer: the inner fails in conversion, in persistence, has no context, has a 'carried-with-me-ness'. As regards the last criterion, the child's body is somewhat anomalous, for it is objective but not external to himself. Indeed, the body-concept is a kind of bridge between the worlds of inner and outer experience.

The body-concept is necessary to the development of the subjective–objective dualism but there is another major factor, that due to intercourse with others 'which discharges the electric spark into the mixture and releases the pure water of subjective life' (*op. cit.*, p. 99). The crucial interpersonal experiences are those when the child is made aware that other people have subjective experiences in their bodies, and the critical instances of this are when the child imitates somebody. (Note the 'bootstrapping' nature of the argument.) This occurs in two ways. Firstly the child becomes conscious of being an intentional agent by, as it were, artificially acting as an agent so that he can take over the subjective feelings of the other to his own body and thus delineate a class of subjective feelings as such (as in the dialectic of personal growth). Secondly, imitation serves as a means of making concrete what was previously a memory image of an observed event, so that he can now 'renew and extend' indefinitely this memory: imitation is an action-mediator for memory. By imitating, the outer experiences become more easily 'liftable' and transferable into the child's mental life. Yet he still lacks knowledge of the true dualism of the inner and outer because the child's self-determined action is controlled by what he has seen other people doing. Gradually, this control comes to be weakened by the following process, again familiar in form, which is a kind of embarrassment. The imitation of another's action makes the child's own body anomalous to himself at a higher level, because at the same time as he becomes conscious of the other person as an agent he is also becoming conscious of his own body as autonomous: the ability to consciously imitate, to do this at will, is literally a kind of 'self-control'. This is especially true when the imitation takes place some time after the original event, separate from the normal context or without the usual 'props'. In general, this process involves what Baldwin calls experimental control of action where the child employs 'actual selection, elimination and reduction' until 'the whole body becomes the tool of the mind' (*op. cit.*, p. 104).

1.2.4 *Play*

This kind of efficacy inevitably entails the freedom to employ the concrete world for one's own affective and imaginative ends, in short, to play. The play object, or *semblant object*, is an image object which the child ties to what is immediately in front of him, for example the 'brush' which the child pretends the stick to be. Baldwin claims that playing is of major importance in cognitive development for it develops the sense of reality. Through pretending the child is forced to distinguish *from* the real: 'consciousness, even while busy with the play objects, casts sly glances behind the scenes, making sure that its firm footing in reality is not entirely lost' (*op. cit.*, p. 112). Furthermore, it makes possible the determination of the mind–body dualism in that it continues the elaboration of inner–outer; likewise the dualism of self and non-self, as the controllability of semblant reality becomes further differentiated from the refractoriness of concrete reality. Play's alogical, willful nature helps develop logicality, judgment and truth by erecting a contrast, and further elaboration of the semblant, which play initiated, eventually produces the aesthetic mode of thought. At bottom play is a mode of experimenting, of trying things out on the real world, testing how far reality can be stretched and thus delineating it.

Baldwin calls the process whereby play aids in the elaboration of the mind–body, self–non-self dualism the *semblant progression*. This has two facets. One is the way in which experimentation enables the child to put reality to the test so that each semblant object becomes either a real object or an object of fancy. The other Baldwin calls *sembling*, which is the process of imaginatively construing an object as being what we choose, of 'reading into the object a sort of psychic life of its own in such a way that the movement, act, or character by which it is interpreted is thought of as growing from its own inner life' (*op. cit.*, p. 24). Animism is an instance of this. This also has certain implications for the development of the self-concept: the child is able to pretend to be in a certain affective state as well as knowledge state, which has much the same kind of consequences in the personal as in the cognitive sphere.

In sembling, the interest is over-determining the cognitive content, as against the datum, and yet this is, Baldwin argues, the primitive origin of the act of meaning. In meaning as in sembling, we must learn to distinguish between the thing and the act of signifying, the intentional treatment of the thing *as* a something, albeit, in this case, something that it is not. Furthermore, the interest is selective and thus can direct attention, for play purposes, to features of objects and abstract common elements so that the actual process of recognising a property or object and bringing it under one interest eventually becomes itself a kind of interest. Essentially, *anything* that arises out of the interest is a form of meaning: things 'have a meaning' for the individual who acts on the world under the determination of an interest.

1.2.5 *Commonness: Syndoxic meaning*

From what has gone before it is to be expected that Baldwin does not take the view that the development of meaning is something that just takes place between the child's mind and the concrete world. Other people are involved. Baldwin accepts the Kantian view that objective experience implies a corresponding awareness of oneself as the knower, but goes beyond Kant to propose that this could not be attained unless there was also an *awareness* of the commonness of meanings. Commonness, at this stage, implies the individual's knowledge that his awareness of things is shared. Otherwise we could never completely separate ourselves as meaners from the things meant. 'For it is evident that as far as conscious function departs at all from the simple direct and unambiguous apprehension of the present and immediate, the given, the projective, and develops any inkling of the separation of certain contents off into objects of the psychological sort, it begins to have a shading of meaning which we may call in some sense common, in contrast with the simple.' (*op. cit.*, p. 141). At this stage Baldwin sets out the role of common meaning, leaving the development of the full implications of this view to Volume II, and introduces the term *syndoxic* to refer to the kind of common meaning prior to the arrival of logicality. In syndoxic meaning the child believes that his meaning is actually held in common, that all people call these four-legged creatures 'dogs' for example; but he believes the commonness is a contingent fact rather than something which must be true *in principle* of all knowledge.

1.2.6 *From schema to general concept*

Having introduced these fundamental processes Baldwin goes on to demonstrate how the concepts of unity, class and group are elaborated, in a discussion which is rather more descriptive than dialectical. He again uses the term Kantian *schema* to explain how objects are individuated as things with enduring properties. The term refers to the embryo concept which is determined by the interest, as in play. For example, a spanner may have the schematic meaning to the young child of 'thing-to-throw' before it has the common meaning 'thing-to-tighten-nuts-with'. He specifically argues against any notion of concepts developing by a process of trial-and-error, for in early behaviour these processes are indissociable. (One might add in support of this that the ability to see an error *as* an error implies some previous concept or schema of what is to count as an error, hence a circularity.)

The experimental aspect of the schema is paramount. Before a child comes to attempt anything (say, the retrieval of a toy from behind some railings) he 'holds up before him an image-copy of an act, sound or anything else, and succeeds in getting it right by reproducing it in a variety of ways . . . Beforehand the copy is a schema, charged with possibilities; it is hypothetical and experimental' (*op. cit.*, p. 167). This radically diverges from what would later be called an S–R account, for Baldwin regards the image, determined by basic interests, as instigating and monitoring the action: before the action comes the action-concept. However, Baldwin refuses to conclude that this schematic action shares the same basic structure or function as later 'general' and 'singular' meanings—which we might call 'conceptual' judgments as opposed to intelligent action. *He accepts an analogy but not a prefiguration.* On this question he takes issue with the British psychologist L. T. Hobhouse, whom we shall be discussing later, for his use of the term 'practical judgment' to refer to this schematic, primitively intelligent action. Indeed he includes in his table of the 'Canons of Genetic Logic' at the start of this volume the 'Fallacy of the Implicit' which 'consists in treating something as implicitly or potentially present when it is not actual: so the fallacy of finding implicit logical process in the prelogical modes or a "potential" self in the impersonal modes' (*op. cit.*, p. 24). Reflective intelligence, Baldwin argues, requires an entirely different kind of control of mental content, not present in practical, schematic judgment. Only from the point of view of a final cause, teleological philosophy does the 'end overshadow the beginning.'

Much of the remainder of the book is concerned with the transition from schematic intelligence to the consciousness of what Baldwin calls *general* and *universal* features of reality. The schema is very powerful (and at one point he characterises it in language reminiscent of a contemporary advertisement for a surgical appliance! . . . it can 'aid reconstruction, induce accommodation, and relieve embarrassment'). But experimental intelligence is severely limited mainly because it is a set of means to an end, there is no notion of separate items in relation: 'it is in a *related whole* that generalisation finds a characteristic meaning' (*op. cit.*, p. 216).

In passing from the semblant schema to the general concept there is the stage of the disjunctive or alternative meaning which functions in the following way. By an awareness of the fact that there is more than one way of treating an object, the play and the functional, (an apple can be played with like a ball or it can be eaten for example) the child 'catches himself in the act' of applying a schema—it can be this, or that, or that—with the result that he becomes conscious of the classificatory activity essential to conceptual (*general*) thinking. The schema is hypothetical, and, to the extent that the child then goes on to treat the objects in more than one hypothetical way he will eventually discover that there is only one hypothesis that is constantly fulfilled: the spanner is for tightening nuts, the apple for eating. Thus, general and particular meanings develop together, such as all apples are for eating, this apple can be eaten. 'This inner determination of the whole and the parts, of general and particular meaning, is the *fruitful result of the experimental process*; for the schema, as an experimental forcast, is a meaning in which these determinations *are not yet present*' (*op. cit.*, p. 222). The final stage of elaboration of general meaning is when the child conceives of the law of classification as being a universal, necessary truth admitting no exceptions.

1.2.7 *Ideal meaning*

After following through some of the implications of the above account for the development of the concepts of unity, plurality, class and the individuation of the self, Baldwin distinguishes common from *ideal* meaning. Persons or things can be 'individuated as going to be something as well as being something', there is a 'further, unfulfilled meaning, the Ideal Meaning' (*op. cit.*, p. 233); or they can have common meanings as outlined above. As regards the personal sphere, personality can never be characterised as being static and objective in the same way as can an object. Similarly, to the extent that we erect abstractions of ideal states of things or imagine the world as being different from what it is we involve ourselves in the construction of ideal meanings. In fact, any semblant, experimental, hypothetical meaning is ideal. By including this category of meanings Baldwin does not have to commit himself to the *consensus* view of knowledge which his notion of common meanings suggests; there is now the possibility, indeed necessity, of extra-communal changes in the criteria of truth.

1.2.8 *Synnomic meaning*

Early in Volume II Baldwin returns again to the question of the commonness of knowledge and the development of common meanings. Previously we saw how prelogical, syndoxic commonness depended on the individual's awareness that other people were *as a matter of fact* employing meanings in the same way as he. Syndoxic meaning is a contingent affair which only functions when common meaning is actually going on, to describe which Baldwin uses the term 'catholicity'. He now contrasts this with judgmental commonness, which is *synnomic*. In synnomic judging, the individual knows that the objects of the judgment are common not because they are being commonly cognised but because it is in the nature of judgment that its objects are necessarily common. Rather than catholic, these meanings are 'appropriate', they are 'meanings held as fit for concurring function' (Vol. II, p. 79). Syndoxic meaning escapes privacy by, as it were, getting other people to join in; synnomic meaning conquers privacy through the individual knowing that what he judges can *in principle* be judged in the same way by other people, that this is a *universal* principle. As regards control, that of syndoxic meaning was external, mainly through secondary conversion and imitation. The synnomic control, however, although it arose through mediate control by other people, is *qua* knowledge, *independent* of what others do or say. Developmentally, Baldwin is saying that there must come a stage when the child judges that certain things are universally and objectively the case. Previously there would have been a kind of converging subjectivity rather than objectivity. To this we can apply the term 'intersubjective' in the way that Hamlyn applies it to Kant's categories (see p. 30).

Before synnomic control is attained, the child's syndoxic meaning is determined largely by imitation and coercion: 'meaning is enlarged and extended by two great agencies of accommodation or adjustment—*imitative absorption* and *disciplinary enforcement*' (*op. cit.*, p. 83). Imitation, Baldwin takes to be especially important, for here the child, as it were, gains a vicarious feeling of competence and efficacy through aping the adult's judgments. In disciplinary enforcement the child is cognitively socialised 'through certain recognised aids such as language, play, art, obedience, the contexts of established social recognition [which] are hammered onto the plastic surface of the child's mind.' However, Baldwin cautions, this is not effective unless the child is able to make these meanings his own 'by the essential process of assimilation; so that so far as this is not done the lessons are not incorporated into the body of meaning he is prepared to exploit' (*op. cit.*, p. 91).

Although Baldwin goes on to differentiate between the many ways in which judgments can be common to present a complex picture, his conclusions are very clear: 'So of knowledge. *It is not a private possession; it is public property*. It begins common, stays common, claims to be common, enforces its commonness. No knowledge confined in one private head, repeated in other private heads an infinity of times, would ever become an organic system of common knowledge . . . *The private thought is not a cognitive unit, it is a cognitive outcome.*' (*op. cit.*, p. 105).

1.2.9 *Predication: and language*

As Baldwin's overall task in this volume is to explain how judging develops he is, to a large extent, concerned with the act of predication—saying something about something—which is often taken to be a universal feature of all language. Therefore, as predication is a linguistic act, he is inevitably confronted with the problem of showing the place of verbal understanding in his system and to this end offers a theory of language which, typically, takes the form of a resolution between two opposing kinds of theory.

The first kind of theory emphasises that language evolves out of social intercourse and the exigencies of everyday life, the product of human cultures. The second stresses the formal aspect, that the language is an asocial, abstract, system of symbols which has a fixed structure varying only trivially between different societies. Baldwin's view is that neither the functionalist nor the structuralist account can do justice to the fact that language is the vehicle for the expression of common meanings: functionalist theories do not adequately reflect this because they concentrate on the schematic, experimental, prelogical kind of commonness, yet the commonness included in structuralist theories is that of the passive acceptance of an external system, not synnomic meaning. The fact is that language is both interpersonal and external for it grows out of private intercourse and yet is stabilised through public convention. It is an error to emphasise one aspect alone: the functionalist because the rule-system of language is, in an important respect, independent of the details of human life; the structuralist because what is at one time conventional can be changed by the 'development of appreciative and artistic consciousness. . . . The arts are such semi-socialised and in turn socialising systems of symbolic meaning' (*op. cit.*, p. 144). Anthony Quinton (1963) put this point rather neatly: 'Poets are the William Webb Ellises of language.' (William Webb Ellis is said to have invented the game of rugby by picking up a football during a match and running with it.)

Language represents the end-product of an historical process of the accretion of common meanings: the 'instrument of the development and conservation of psychic meaning. It is the material evidence and proof of *the concurrence of social and personal judgment*' (*op. cit.*, p. 148). Thus the general topic of predication—the *form* of the judgment—is treated not so much as the description of an abstract standard but as the explanation of its development out of social intercourse.

1.2.10 *Predication: elucidation and proposition*

In the discussion of predication Baldwin begins by stressing that not even the most universally accepted and elaborated propositions have entirely overcome their experimental nature. The idea then emerges, which becomes one of the motifs of the volume, that the establishment of truths, unless they are axiomatic or definitional within one system of meaning (for example, 'A scherzo is played in triple time'), is *dialectical*. The reason for this is that truth itself is achieved and maintained through the interaction of speakers and hearers. Although there is an *elucidatory* aspect to predication, and thus to truth, whereby both speaker and hearer share the same basic assumptions (for example, two musicians in the example above), most of the time the speaker is saying something *new*, giving substantive information, called by Baldwin the *propositional* aspect. Most of what we judge can in principle be discussed, so that 'the hearer joins the speaker in erecting the subject-matter into a schema of problematical meaning' (*op. cit.*, p. 152). Naturally this is not a one-way process and thus the development of truth is dialectical. Truth never abandons its experimental aspect. Even in the elucidation of a system of truths like

Kant's *a priori* principles of the understanding, the statements are only elucidatory so long as they remain within one closed system. Once we stand back far enough we can even treat a statement such as 'All *p* are *p*' as conceivably not being self-evidently true in some yet-to-be-invented system of formal logic; this axiom has been erected by past society for our employment and thus has no timeless certainty. The timeless, absolute truth of any judgment is inconceivable, Baldwin argues, because there is a 'comparative morphology' of meanings, not one meaning system—a notion basic to his genetic epistemology.

In the development of logical thought, therefore, there are two opposing but complementary tendencies which have to be synthesised: the experimental, functional, propositional aspect without which there would be no new knowledge; and the retrospective, structural, elucidatory aspect without which there would be no solid platform for the exchange of thought between individuals. Proposition cannot take place without an elucidatory framework and elucidation becomes mere circularity without practical interest. Baldwin points out that this general view arises out of the basic postulate that knowledge is common property not individual possession for in the genetic progress of thought individuals actively seek (proposition) to achieve the universal acceptance (elucidation) of their judgments—the synnomic progression.

1.2.11 *Abstract and general terms*

Thus, the development of predication can be construed as the progression towards the establishment of elucidatory truths that form the logical framework around which our thinking builds itself—what Baldwin calls the system of *implication*. There are three main stages in this progression: the establishment of the *term*, the *proposition* and the *argument*. As regards terms Baldwin distinguishes between *abstract* terms like 'red' (roughly properties) and *general* terms like 'horse' (roughly things). As would be expected, the development of the abstract term takes place by proposition moving towards elucidation which is never fully achieved. First there is the prelogical form of abstraction: selective interest. Next, a quasi-logical form in semblance; for here an image is 'abstracted' from its proper context. Conscious, logical abstraction arises as the end-state of the gradual progression of selective meaning, so that eventually through common control—mainly through language—the context and criteria for selective meaning becomes socially fixed—synnomic. In general Baldwin takes issue, as did Cassirer (see p. 184), with the standard Lockian account of abstraction which is that the individual isolates recurrent common elements from a given whole or sequence, thus forming an abstract concept (see p. 26). The argument, he says, is circular for if one is able to do this one must *already* have the abstract idea in order to select elements on the basis of it! The only way of destroying the circularity is by assuming that abstract meaning is a selective meaning in the course of development—'*it is not selected for abstraction, but abstracted by a process of selection*' (*op. cit.*, p. 186).

Baldwin gives some details of the specific dialectical processes which are involved in the growth of abstraction, and which will now be outlined in order to show how they relate to similar processes at a higher, more general level. Abstraction is the result of both erosion and accretion of meaning: abstract meaning is broadened by the individual's accretion of new instances to the primary schema and narrowed by the erosion inevitable in social experience where there will eventually be a mismatch with others' abstract categories. Moreover, the growth of the abstract term has itself an opposing, complementary relationship to the growth of general term, which relationship is represented in logic by the terms *intension* and *extension*—with abstraction being intensional and generalisation being extensional. To explain, general terms like 'coin' and 'horse' all have definitive extensions: they all apply to a specific number of instances at a given time. However, abstract terms like 'red' and 'fortitude' have intension: they determine what aspects of (say) an object or a personality are being cognised. The smaller the intension ('red' for example) the larger the extension (all red things); the larger the intension ('red and round') the smaller the extension (all red, round things). In this way generalisation is the attempt to erect a fixed category and then gather instances of it. But as this process goes on there is the complementary process of the development of intension whereby abstract categories multiply, thus checking the rise of general meaning. Then a new general category is established which develops until a further check is received from abstraction, and so on. To give an example of this, the child may have, on the one hand, the general, extensional category of tennis balls, together with the abstract, intensional property of being round. He begins by calling all round things 'tennis ball', but as his abstract meaning develops at the same time he (in this case correctly) increases the intension by adding the property of being bouncy, thus reducing the extension and excluding such round things as globes and pepper-corns. Then all round, bouncy things come to be called tennis balls until the intension increases again by adding the property of softness, thus excluding cricket balls . . . and so on (compare recent work on 'overgeneralisation' in semantic development by workers such as Clark (1974)). Viewed in terms of the broader distinction, intension is elucidatory and extension is propositional—these opposing and complementary relationships coexist at many levels, resulting in a truly dialectical system.

1.2.12 *Propositions*

With the establishment of the term we have the logical 'units of currency' but as yet no system of rules whereby they can be related to produce propositions. In outlining the development of propositional meaning Baldwin begins with the Kantian distinction between analytic and synthetic propositions. From what has gone before, his treatment of the distinction should hold a few surprises. He denies that they are watertight categories (at least within what he calls functional logic) as every proposition is both analytic and synthetic, with each aspect being differentially preponderant. Every proposition is analytic inasmuch as the acceptance of its truth is dependent on the prior elucidatory knowledge that a larger rule-system obtains; rules which a proposition such as 'women are more emotional than men' obeys and which one such as 'women are more circumscribed than three fish' violates. Similarly (compare the earlier point that there are no timeless *a priori* judgments) analytic propositions all have the characteristic that they produce a new relationship; for example, even 'All black cats are black' is *selected* from a set of possible obvious statements about cats; in a certain conversational context it might perform the task of reminding us of a relevant consideration; it also assumes the existence of black cats. Thus, from a purely philosophical standpoint (or in what he calls 'formal' or 'exact' logic) such a distinction might be useful, but in genetic epistemology, where we deal with the logicality *in vivo*, the distinction is distorting. Furthermore, the actual process of analysis and synthesis is continuous with the accretion and erosion of the term in the prelogical mode: synthesis is experimental and broadening like accretion, analysis is conservative and limiting like erosion. 'The two are the obverse sides of the one great movement of selective thinking, continuing as it does the processes that motive generalisation and abstraction. And we are to see that the same dual motive issues further in the great modes of reasoning known as Induction and Deduction' (*op. cit.*, p. 251). We see, then, that the dialectic changes its aspect with each level of the genetic progression of knowledge: proposition–elucidation; accretion–erosion; generalisation–abstraction; extension–intension; synthesis–analysis. At bottom, the same kind of opposing, complementary relationship is present.

It should now be made clear that the above defines by exclusion that class of meanings which Baldwin calls *singular*. The notion of uniqueness and the particular is, of course, primitive and had been introduced in Volume I. Although logic can be no respecter of individual cases (for when it loses its universality it loses its point) the singular sets the limit on the universal and vice versa; indeed, each kind of meaning produces the other. So, Baldwin does not wish to treat singular meanings merely as a kind of by-product of the main process, for to do so would be to ignore the fact that logicality is only one feature of our thinking—goodness and beauty as well as truth and validity are included in his system and considered in Volume III.

1.2.13 *Implication and reflection*

In moving from the proposition to the argument, to the establishment of the principles of implication, propositions come to be related to each other in a rulebound system. Prelogical actions and speech can be accurate or inaccurate; propositions can be true or false; but inferences are either valid or invalid. In the reflective knowledge of implication, Baldwin argues, we go *beyond* synnomic control because we know the validity of implication by *reflection on the relation* between the elements, not by the awareness of the universal principle. For example, we learn the truth of the judgment 'Snow is white' by the mediation of synnomic control, but the implication 'White implies not black' is something that we take to be valid by definition within the system (elucidatory). We can judge that some snow may not be white without changing the way we think, but in judging that the above inference does not hold we are challenging the rule-structure of the conceptual system. Inferences, once learnt, are never checked—only the permissibility of their application. Although, as we said before, once we 'step outside' the judging community even this has a schematic element to it.

There are again two opposing, complementary processes which form a 'bridge' between mediate common control and the 'inner' control of reflection. On the one hand there is the positive movement towards greater synnomic force for the propositions which include elements in given classes, for example, that being snow-coloured implies belonging to the class of white things. On the other hand there is the negative movement which excludes elements from classes by *limitation* for example, that being snow-coloured implies being excluded from the class of black things.

1.2.14 *Limitation*

It is worth expanding on what this process of limitation is. It is different from synnomic control because it is *not* a social process. It is, in a way, something which results from the relations between elements of the conceptual system. The prelogical origin of limitation is found in the infant's earliest consciousness of that which lies outside of his immediate span of attention; then comes selective action on his environment where, for example, in trying to grasp the rattle he does not try to grasp the ball. Later, as the child comes to form verbal judgments he realises that he is prevented, *by the nature of the system*, from linking certain predicates to certain subjects and thus develops a set of negative classes for himself—for example, mothers belong to the class of non-men. He learns, not from social control, but from the nature of the predication process, that certain things cannot be the case. Baldwin is careful to point out that the limitation thus derived is not a blind crossing out of propositions but that there is a definite control system of *presupposition* in the statement of negative meaning. Thus, in saying that 'This (cottage) is not a mansion' we do not leave open the possibility that it could be a turnip, but that it is nevertheless some kind of dwelling. By the same token we do not say things like 'Cabbages are not letters of the alphabet' because there is no conceivable system of control involved: a system of negation is 'wrapped about an envelope of belief'. The negative statement restricts presupposition to a certain sphere so that in the present example it implies that in the sphere of dwellings there are palaces and non-palaces. To use Baldwin's expression, the exclusion of the non-A class from the A class *exhausts* the content of the sphere involved. This exhaustion is taken to be the genetic foundation of the law of 'excluded middle' which lies at the heart of the system of implication. The law states that, for any proposition, either it or its negation is the case, that there is no middle state between something obtaining and not obtaining. Were it not for this principle anything could imply anything else.

Although much of what Baldwin has to say on this subject is not always perspicuous the main point should now be fairly clear, that the certainty of implication *cannot* be attained by continuing the process of social control, but must be formed out of the reflection on the necessary opposition between what can be and what cannot be the case within the system—just as the sculpture is formed out of the 'necessary opposition' between the stone and the chisel. As the knowledge of the principles of inference, once established, is not socially mediated, so the process of establishment of these principles must, at least partly, depend on an asocial factor, that of limitation, arising out of the nature of the relation between subjects and predicates. The genetic epistemological approach seeks to explain these 'laws of thought' by reference to their natural history and genesis in human development rather than by proposing them as *a priori*—independent of and prior to experience.

1.2.15 *Truth*

Much of the final portion of the volume is taken up with a general theory of truth and falsity. In the prelogical phase there was no question of truth, only of actions which did or did not succeed as means to an end. This, however, was the root of our knowledge of what is and is not the case, because here was the first control: a direct control of action by the environment. Later, as development progressed through social control it became less external, so that eventually with reflective control the truth became 'simply the body of knowledge *acknowledged as belonging where it does in a consistently controlled context*' (*op. cit.*, p. 361) —something distinct from accuracy, validity and goodness. Yet, Baldwin points out, this truth can be given a biological origin in that all thought has its starting point in the satisfaction of active, volitional, emotional interests which can ultimately be characterised biologically.

1.2.16 *Real logic*

At the start of Volume III, subtitled *Real Logic: Art and Interest*, Baldwin reviews the first two volumes as having been tracing the developing relation between the 'inner and outer controls': the outer control which holds the mind to the recognition of an external, stable rule-governed world; and the inner which actively frees itself by selection from the tyranny of the actual—a general statement of the dialectic. In this volume Baldwin is more concerned with the latter kind of control.

Real logic, the broadest conception of genetic epistemology, involves a comparison of the different kinds of reality which are known at each developmental and evolutionary level, standing back the farthest possible from human thought. It also involves a comparison between different kinds of thought because, up to this point, we have really only been concerned with one kind of thought, what Baldwin calls 'theoretical' knowledge (of truth and validity). It is time to discuss moral and aesthetic understanding.

If we go right back to the origin of the genetic progression of knowledge we re-encounter the interest which, as we saw, by the mediation processes involved in memory, the conversions, imitation, syndoxic and synnomic commonness and reflection, produced logicality. The motive force behind this was the schematic function, found in its purest form in play where semblant images are produced along with an understanding of concrete objects. Although it might have appeared from the description of logical development, that this semblant tendency was suppressed through the necessity of accommodating to the actual and the common, the semblant mode itself becomes elaborated into the aesthetic faculty, as we shall see. We shall also see how the instrumental, experimental facet of the interest which produced the propositions of theoretical knowledge is responsible for the establishment of the notions of worth and goodness. It will become evident that in no way are the developments of the semblant to the aesthetic, and the instrumental to the ethical, separate kinds of process from the progression of theoretical knowledge—the same principles operate.

1.2.17 *Mediate and immediate knowledge*

Beginning with the basic distinction between mediated and immediate knowledge. All knowledge of *truth* is mediated because we can never know things directly . . . 'Mediation, as here intended, may be described as the reference of an objective content away from itself, its "call" on some other experience to give it that aspect of its entire meaning which we call its "control" in a definite sphere or class' (1911, p. 36). As for immediacy this is found in the pure awareness in the prelogical phase and in states of aesthetic understanding.

Baldwin deals with mediated knowledge first and the kinds of reality which this engenders. The reality which is experienced in prelogical mediation is that of a world of existing things and of internal states, recognised by the stubbornness of the former and the strain of the latter; this being brought under mediate control mainly by memory, imitation and the conversions. In discussing the logical mediation in which the individual takes the true as the real, Baldwin distinguishes between two opposing accounts of our knowledge of reality. According to one kind of theory, the ultimate nature of reality is given by the relations which thought produces: nothing can be cognised outside of its relation to some other thing or class and nothing can be proposed or inferred unless through relational rules; nothing can be treated as real outside of a relation. Baldwin has the writings of the Hegelian idealist philosopher T. H. Green in mind here. Gestalt Theory, which this obviously resembles, came much later. Against this is the view that the construal of objects in relational terms obscures the original 'datum' of reality so that the real becomes *separate* from our thinking—the world of noumena in Kant's system. These theories go wrong argues Baldwin (and it is not difficult to see that they *are* wrong in some way) because they both neglect the genetic perspective. The following quotation gives a good, succinct statement of the genetic epistemological approach to this fundamental issue: 'It is a mistake to take reality as a "something", a term, rather than a predicate, a meaning that may attach to many terms or things with varying signification. Reality is a relative meaning—relative to the content to which it is attributed. Any content can have reality, no content is reality . . . The very question "Is it real?" is unintelligible, except as we make the fundamental distinction between the content and the control' (*op. cit.*, p. 49). What philosophical theories of this type do is to exploit the fact that reality is mediated in different ways—for each kind of mediation there could be a philosophical theory. Baldwin is not proposing any kind of subjectivism here: reality is not relative to the perspective of the individual or of the group but to the mode of control which confers objectivity on it.

1.2.18 *Value and worth*

However, the true is not the only mediated reality; there is also the reality of value and worth. This also is traceable to the interest but here the selective, instrumental aspect is predominant. The interest selects at the earliest prelogical stage what it wants—the fulfillment of a personal disposition instrumentally—for example, the rattle is 'good to shake'. The *content* of the interest (the rattle) is mediated by recognitive memory to produce objective knowledge and eventually the notion of truth; but the *intent*, to shake, to play for pleasure, is selected to produce what will become the idea of worth. The same object is being cognised in the former case as a means and in the latter case as an end. As to the broad question of the origin of the good and its relation to the true Baldwin says 'the answers to this question may all be comprised in one statement that *the good is simply and only the selective aspect of every determination of the actual*' (*op. cit.*, p. 63).

Later in making reflective judgments of value we cognitively 'stand back' far enough to predicate something of an object, act, or person, cognising our own interest rather than expressing it. (Often the verbal form of the value judgment will be the same as a truth assertion as in 'This chocolate is sweet'—statement of fact or expression of approval). Baldwin expresses the reciprocal relationship between truth and value judgments by saying that in the case of truth we attain knowledge through control, but in the case of value we attain control through knowledge. In the latter case this means that we develop our system of personal interests and purposes through increased knowledge of the world and skill in using the conceptual system—the means to satisfy the interests of the inner life. So here again is a symbiotic relationship, this time content and intent, which results in the conclusion that the realities of the world of fact and truth are the *means* and the values are the *ends*.

1.2.19 *Ethical judgments and ideal meaning*

The value judgments of ethics require a separate explanation. These grow not out of the interest alone but also from interpersonal conduct. He borrows the Kantian term 'Practical Reason' to refer to this (broadly) emotional rather than epistemic aspect of behaviour where conformity rather than validity is at stake. Ethical judgments are controlled by commonness of interest. First there is *syntelic*, premoral, conformity, a commonness of custom, with regard to which Baldwin stresses that although affective–conative states cannot attain the same kind of commonness as objective judgments they are not private in that it is not just 'up to the individual' whether he is (say) in a good mood or not, whether he feels sympathetic to the plight of some person and so on. There is some secondary conversion of affective states. The argument is not very clear on this point, but it seems to be that although this conversion cannot attain the commonness of theoretical knowledge the very fact that we communicate with each other on the assumption that such commonness is present establishes a kind of commonness. For example, we might say 'This fig tastes unpleasant—try it and see what I mean.' He gives a similar example of taste not because he holds that this kind of hedonistic judgment is at the heart of ethics but because *feelings* are fundamental to ethical judgments which cannot be directly related to the concrete world.

But Baldwin did not wish to argue that moral law becomes established by these syntelic judgments becoming synnomic and eventually reflective. He held rather that the affective organisation of *ideal meaning* was responsible for this. We have already seen how Baldwin contrasted ideal with common meaning: the ideal is a state of becoming towards a goal which has been schematically erected, an abstract idea of some end-state established by semblant, experimental, processes. Directed by the interest, the person produces an ideal self in which all the strivings of interest are fulfilled. What differentiates this from the pipe dream is that the child establishes this notion on the model of those whom he considers to be morally superior to himself: 'There arises indeed early in the development of the child's mind a shadowy presence, an indistinct reflection in the inner chamber of the self, of what its own ideal meaning is to be when the contradictions and hindrances of the active life are overcome. It is objectively embodied in the greater self of the parent, teacher, priest, God' (*op. cit.*, p. 137). We see here a return to the notion that value is the neglect of the means in the interest of the ends. These moral ends find their control solely in the development of an ideal self—an inner control analogous to that of logical reflection. Baldwin's explanation of how the feeling of necessity comes to accompany the moral imperatives is Humean: by reflection on our own feeling of impulsion to regard certain actions in a certain light, by 'catching ourselves' feeling that it is natural that certain actions should be praised or condemned, we come to believe that we feel it to be necessary because it *is* necessary.

1.2.20 *The moral as singular*

The surest way of differentiating the moral from the theoretical, Baldwin points out, is by reference to the fact that the theoretical has no place for the singular or unique, but concerns itself only with generalisations and instances. The moral, on the other hand, finds its complete fulfilment only in the singular. The fact that something cannot be both red and green all over is a conceptual truth, but the moral law has no instances, for no action unequivocally breaks or exemplifies a particular moral injunction—a fact to which existentialist thinkers such as Sartre have drawn attention. In codifying the moral law, says Baldwin, we destroy it, because 'moral life is a series of personal insights fed by single acts' (*op. cit.*, p. 148). Because morality is a system of ends it only realises itself in individual actions arising out of the individual's choice: the means (truth and validity) can exist independently of living people, as they do, for example, in works of science and logic, but ends cannot exist apart from individuals pursuing their own lives. One might add that arising from this is the proposition that no two actions can be morally equivalent and no action is completely free or completely determined; whereas two facts can be equally true and two inferences equally valid, and the question of the freedom or determination of their truth or validity does not arise. If Baldwin is correct about the singularity of the moral, this is a major consideration in rejecting theories of moral development which are generated directly from theories of cognitive development.

1.2.21 *Art*

Much of the remainder of the volume is concerned with aesthetic understanding. As would be expected, this is taken to have its roots in the aspect of the interest which develops into the semblant mode— play. And yet, artistic creation is not merely a more elaborated version of semblant experimentation further along the same continuous stream of development, because there are two important respects in which art is different in kind from play. Firstly, 'any old thing' will do to play with in as far as it satisfies the immediate interest—toys are instrumental—whereas the semblant activity which produces art has an ideal meaning. When we doodle or play charades we act to fulfil a present desire, instant satisfaction. But in producing a work of art, the individual at every stage erects an ideal of what he is going to produce: the doodle becomes a picture and charades become an imaginative construction. Play is free and capricious relative to art. Secondly, as regards the appreciation of art, there is the 'identification' of the individual's subjective life with the object, sound, or fiction, whereas in play we merely join in or amuse ourselves. In the enjoyment of art our emotional life is carried over into the artificial construction so that an impoverished emotional life makes for a restricted range of aesthetic sensibility.

When we come to consider the transformation of aesthetic feelings into the synnomic mode of aesthetic understanding we encounter a paradoxical feature of this kind of knowledge of some significance. It is that when an aesthetic judgment becomes synnomic it partakes both of the universality of a truth or value judgment and of the singularity of a moral judgment. The universality comes about through the fact that the work of art is produced, at least in principle, for all other people, for anyone who cares to see, hear, or read it. Each person who appreciates the work conceives it at some level as not for himself alone but as something which has a public, self-sufficient reality—unlike the moral act which in the instant that it seeks to draw attention to itself, and is carried out for its own sake rather than for that of the recipient, ceases to be moral. Another aspect of the same process is how the audience for a work of art colludes to treat the semblant make-believe object as if it were real, to take it seriously—another contrast with play which by definition is for fun: art is 'for real'. Yet at the same time the work of art has singularity for it is the creation of one person (or set of persons) and is the expression of an individual's inner life. Also, though the work of art can be reproduced there is originally only one: each is unique. It might be added that Baldwin does not take pains to distinguish the construction of the art work from the appreciation of it, although he does include a lengthy section on the 'springs of art'. One must assume that he regarded them as the active and the passive sides of the same psychological coin.

1.2.22 *Immediate knowledge—reconciliation*

At the end Baldwin returns to the distinction between mediate and immediate understanding. It should now be clear that everything which we normally think of as knowledge is mediate: 'When reduced to its lowest terms mediation consists in a "reference" of a content away from its own mere presence to some other experience or bit of meaning' (*op. cit.*, p. 227); the reference system being essentially that of commonness. Ideas mediate truths, and ends mediate values by the same basic process. But what of immediacy? There are three kinds. There is the primitive immediacy of pure experience before even self and world are differentiated. There is the immediacy of *completion* which is attained when we have a flash of complete understanding, when we feel that we are not understanding through the medium of ideas but have become one with that which we are trying to know, as in mystic ecstasy. There is here achieved the same state as in primitive immediacy but through *transcending* ideas rather than by regressing to a pre-theoretical state. The third kind, the immediacy of *reconciliation*, is of the most importance to the general theory. What is being reconciled are the fundamental dualisms which we have followed throughout the work, which, from the broadest perspective are: interest—control; value—truth; end—means. This state is essentially one of aesthetic contemplation: the realisation of the earlier statement that this was both universal and singular. What Baldwin is saying is this: aesthetic appreciation bridges the apparently irreconcilable opposites of mental life—thought and feeling, reason and emotion, truth and goodness, the discipline of the intellect and the capriciousness of the imagination.

1.2.23 *Kinds of reality*

This genetic approach to the theory of knowledge produces in the end an account of the different kinds of reality that we apprehend, their origins in the life of the individual and their genetic interrelations. In the final chapter are set out the three main species of reality. The first two are mediate: the reality of truths and worths and that of imagination and assumption. The third is immediate: the realities of contemplation—the playful semblance and the aesthetic semblance of truth, values, hypotheses and ends.

The reality of truth and worth is what we normally judge to be the field of 'things as they really are'. But, Baldwin stresses, this should never be thought of as an achieved stability for 'how can [one] continue to acquire [truths and worths] and go on progressing in the achievement to which this store of results bears witness? Only by the use of imagination, the vehicle of prospecting, trying, assuming, schematizing, postulating, desiring functions' (*op. cit.*, p. 246). Thus, the motive power by which objective knowledge develops produces a reality of its own (type two) of imagination and assumption—a world of ends rather than facts. The first type is mediated by ideas by way of factual controls; the second by ideas also but not controlled by facts; rather controlling fact in the interest of ends, neglecting facts to erect an idea of the good. The other difference between the two realities is that in the former case to mediate a control is to generalise, to produce an eventually universal truth; whereas in the latter the mediated control is of the single affective, conative, agentive act.

The third type, that of the immediate reality of contemplation produces the 'sheer acceptance of things in their own interest—not merely in that of their truth or that of their values, according as one of the motives of life requires one or the other—this is the manner in which the actual procedure of the mind produces the "realest" real' (*op. cit.*, p. 253). Baldwin arrives at this conclusion because this appreciation of reality forms a balance between the objective and personal understanding. It is the 'realest' real not because something 'extra' is being revealed but because distortion is not engendered by focusing on either the control by the actual or by the semblant activity of the interest.

Conclusions are set out in detail in a later book, *Genetic Theory of Reality* (1951), with which Baldwin saw his work as completed, but are anticipated in the final section of Volume III of *Thought and Things*. The general view of knowledge is, of course, a dynamic one—'While a given immediacy of the aesthetic represents the equilibrium of motives then at work, still as such it is reconstituted at each of the modes of progressive experience' (*Thought and Things* (1911), p. 258). This not only applies to Baldwin's notion of the place of aesthetic understanding in knowledge but also to a theory of science. Science is both positive and hypothetical. Viewed from within it appears to be a stable set of truths, but once we stand back far enough from the progress of science, as far as we do from the individual in cognitive development, we see that each science at one time 'expresses the static and "a-genetic" aspect of organisation present in the particular mode with which it deals (mechanical, chemical, vital etc). But science rests on postulation and assumption, in as much as the truth of each mode is relative to the movement of genesis and progress as a whole; thus science is always fundamentally hypothetical' (*op. cit.*, p. 259). He echoes the Bergsonian evolutionary theory when he states that the level on which each science functions represents a mode of organisation *sui generis* which must presuppose the science which preceded it. Thus, the attempt to reduce one level to another—sociology to psychology to biology to chemistry to physics—is inherently nonsensical: psychology, for example, exists to explain psychological phenomena and rests on a coherent conceptual system different in kind to that of biology.

Standing back from the system one can view it as an original synthesis of Darwinian, Pragmatist and Kantian influences. The Darwinian influence is found in the developmental approach; Pragmatism is revealed in Baldwin's emphasis on the functional origin of conceptual thinking and in his social functionalism (which became in Mead social behaviourism) which views concepts as originating from socially efficacious processes; the Kantian influence is realised in the fundamental assumption that certain forms of self—world interaction are *necessary* for the acquisition of any objective understanding and that this is why cognitive development must be seen within a philosophical framework.

There were other reasons why Baldwin's work did not have the influence he had hoped for, apart from its difficulty and intellectually hybrid nature. One was his emigration from the USA in 1909 to live in Mexico and France, but the other involved historical forces beyond his control. As the influence of Wundt began to wane in psychology Watson and Freud appeared and remained for many decades as the opposite poles of the main axis of contention on which Baldwin could not be located. Specifically, 'Watsonian and positivistic Philistinism drove Baldwin's work into oblivion in a way that Hall neither could nor would' (Kessen, 1965; p. 180).

It would be a great error to suggest that Baldwin was the only psychologist before Piaget to have had genetic epistemological interests. The British psychologist L. T. Hobhouse (1864–1929) was certainly labouring in the same vineyard as Baldwin, especially in his *Mind and Evolution* (1901). Although there are many respects in which they diverge (Hobhouse was a comparative rather than a child psychologist, his philosophical and psychological concerns were kept more distinct, he underplayed the prelogical phase in the child's mental development) he believed like Baldwin that the role of mind in evolution was active and made great use of the concept of assimilation. He saw evolution as working towards a greater and greater degree of organisation within the organism. 'There is a development in organic unity or "organicity" as parts and wholes come to be more and more completely interdependent. And there is an increase in scope, as the life and purpose of the organisation becomes more and more comprehensive.The lower phases of the movements are worked out by biological forces. The higher are worked out by Mind' (Hobhouse, 1901, p. 378). Just as the nervous system integrates the functions of the different parts of the body so the mind is seen as *correlating*—'bringing things together so they have a bearing on each other' (*op. cit*., 2nd ed., 1915, p. 6). There is a gradual emergence of mental correlation out of biological correlation through various stages rather than a Bergsonian insinuation of a vital impulse. As regards consciousness, this is for Hobhouse neither a result nor an epiphenomenon of evolution: it plays an active, determining role in the emergence of the higher mental functions by apprehending the uniqueness of the stimulus formation at any point in time and relating this to a pre-existing schema. Also, when he talks of linguistic and social forces Baldwin is strongly suggested: 'from the dawn of language the action of mind on mind is the leading factor in development and . . . *any phase of thought may be regarded as a social product and as a cause of further social effects*' (*op. cit*., p. 94; my italics).

Hearnshaw (1966) has indicated the degree to which Hobhouse made specific anticipations of Piagetian theory . . . 'let us note the underlying resemblance between their systems of genetic epistemology, both aiming to link the most elementary beginnings of dawning mentality to the highest levels of rationality through a series of necessary intermediate stages of development. In both there is an emphasis on what Hobhouse calls "consilience" and Piaget "groupings" on the gradual achievement of system, and on the underlying drive towards cognitive equilibrium' (p. 17).

Unlike Baldwin and Hobhouse our third example of a theorist offering a genetic explanation of knowledge did so from within philosophy. The German philosopher Ernst Cassirer (1874–1945) was fundamentally a Kantian but unlike Kant took the view that the principles by which we order our sense-experience to construct an objective world are not static categories but developing structures. Kant's mistake, since indicated by many others, was that he assumed that the science, mathematics and geometry of his day, specifically the Newtonian and Euclidian systems, offered unchangeable, absolute truths. He could not, of course, foresee the projective and topological geometries, quantum mechanics, the theory of relativity, and indeed the genetic view of science as a continuous process of enquiry.

Another movement that Kant could not have foreseen was the growth of the human and social sciences in the nineteenth century. Although Kant taught a course on anthropology and produced a volume *Anthropologie* in which he revived the Galen model of personality types, he did not view the scientific study of man as relevant to his epistemological work. However with the emergence of sociology, psychology, linguistics, comparative religion and the continuing influence of Darwin and anthropology, the form of man's thought about the world could be regarded as the outcome of social and biological forces. Man was seen as existing *within* cultures which were subject to more or less lawlike change. In order to reflect the cultural basis of the human conceptual system Cassirer focused on the role of symbolisation, as this he took to be the function by which cultural conditions and rulebound structures codetermined man's understanding of his world. Symbols, like Kant's concepts, do not reflect the state of the world but structure it, transcending sensible experience and ordering it spatiotemporally.

Cassirer gave three levels of symbolic representation: the primitive, mythical symbol, the *expressive* function, in which the sign and the significance merge (for example, the thunder is a sign of God's anger and *is* God's anger at the same time); the symbolic representation of the everyday world in time and space is the *intuitive* function; and the *conceptual* function of science wherein relations between substances are considered rather than the attributes of substances, as in the intuitive function, and where the aim is to subsume particles under principles of ordering—to represent ordered structures.

Thus far it can be seen that Cassirer shares with Baldwin a developmental, stage-bound view of knowledge, though with the emphasis more on phylogeny than the ontogeny. But this is not the only justification for calling him a genetic epistemologist. Like Baldwin, he explains the development and evolution of knowledge in terms of two opposing but complementary principles, one conservative, the other innovatory. In the expressive function the primacy of the conservative principle is seen in the myth whereby present events are subsumed under arcane principles and events in the far distant past; the corresponding innovatory principle being the movement towards some notion of individual responsibility and self-determination (for example, contrast the treatment of this theme in Classical Greek drama and existentialist literature). In the intuitive function the fixed rule-structure of grammar represents the conservative principle, with linguistic (especially semantic) change being the innovatory. Cassirer draws a parallel between the ontogeny and phylogeny of language in these terms. Similarly in the development of the arts there is a tension between conservative imitation, both of the thing and of past creations, and inspiration. Finally, in science we see a tension between the necessity for working within fixed principles and procedures and the equally necessary freedom to effect what Kuhn calls a 'paradigm change' (see p. 10).

Thus the parallel with Baldwin is clear, although it is one of general principle rather than detail. In Piaget, however, although regarded outside (and even inside!) psychology primarily as a theorist of stages in child development, not only do we find Baldwin's ideas clarified and extended, but we find a theory with a broad empirical base and one fundamentally divergent from Baldwin's regarding the nature of human knowledge and the role of social factors in its acquisition: Piaget is almost as unique as it is possible for a theorist to be.

Part 2

Piaget's Theory

2.1 1910–1930: THE EARLY QUEST FOR STRUCTURES AND STUDIES OF INFANCY

Baldwin and the other theorists considered in the previous section did more than provide an elaborate fanfare for the appearance of Piaget's theory, yet at the same time Piaget did much more than extend or resurrect what had been done by them. He was able to produce an account of cognitive development which was more intellectually and empirically 'tangible' and in which the child was more than the hero of a set of anecdotes produced to illustrate abstractions, within the context of a genetic epistemological system clearly different from that of Baldwin.

By and large Piaget has been well served by his commentators* (though systematically misinterpreted by those with an axe to grind) so it would not be fruitful to attempt a very detailed summary of his work. Rather, we will take something of a bird's eye view, centring more on the genetic epistemology than the experimental aspects, and following the theory through the stages of Piaget's intellectual development instead of the child's. Perhaps this way it will be more evident that Piaget himself is not insulated from the genetic process in that his theory is constantly developing.

Jean Piaget was born on 9 August, 1896 at Neuchâtel, Switzerland. From his earliest years he was passionately interested in natural history. Indeed he was publishing articles in learned journals, mostly on the subject of mollusks, in his early teens. 'These studies', Piaget has written 'premature as they were, were nevertheless of great value for my scientific development; moreover they functioned, if I may say so, as instruments against the demon philosophy' (Piaget, 1952, p. 239). He was not able to resist the demon for long. Sometime in his

---

J. H. Flavell (1963) has written an authoritative and readable account of Piaget's theory and Ruth Beard (1969) has produced a lucid and more brief summary of his child psychology. A very useful introduction to the fundamental concepts of Piaget's system is given by Furth (1969) with the aid of a set of extracts from Piaget's own writings. The difficulty of reading Piaget in the original is often overemphasised: he has written a short overview of his system in Mussen (1970) and a synthesis of his work in child psychology up to adolescence with Bärbel Inhelder (1969), and a very accessible account of his genetic epistemology (1970).

sixteenth year Piaget's godfather introduced him to Bergson's evolutionary theory, which came to him as a profound emotional and intellectual shock . . . 'It made me consecrate my life to the biological explanation of knowledge' (*op. cit.*, p. 240). And yet he found Bergson frustrating because between the biology and the philosophising there seemed to be nothing, no experimental basis—a gap which psychology was later able to fill. He began to read voraciously in philosophy and, not surprisingly, in the list he makes of his philosophical reading at this period, Kant is mentioned first.

Already the teenage Piaget was laying the foundations of a system, often writing during the more boring of his school lessons. Like Baldwin, the young Piaget saw Pragmatism as providing some kind of bridge between philosophy and biology and to this end he concentrated on the functional 'unit' of the action. In an early unpublished paper which he called 'Sketch of a Neo-Pragmatism' he propounded the theory that action possesses a logic and that the root of our logical thinking is the spontaneous organisation of acts. But where was the link with biology? The insight arrived when he became acquainted with arguments for and against the 'reality' of the species in zoology: what was indeed the reality of *any* biological unit vis-à-vis the total system of life? 'I suddenly understood that at all levels (viz., that of the living cell, organism, species, society, etc., but also with reference to states of consciousness, to concepts, to logical principles etc.) one finds the same problem of the relationship of the parts to the whole; hence I was convinced that I had found the solution. There at last was the close union I had dreamed of between biology and philosophy, there was an access to an epistemology which seemed to be scientific' (*op. cit.*, p. 242). This embryonic system contained the following main principles: (1) in organic, mental and social life there are totalities qualitatively distinct from their elements and imposing on them an organisation; (2) there are two inferior forms of equilibrium between the parts and the whole (predominance of the whole with alteration of the parts; predominance of the parts with alteration of the whole) and one form of complete equilibrium (reciprocal preservation of the parts and of the whole) and (3) stable equilibrium of the totality corresponds in psychology to normative states of consciousness such as awareness of logical necessity and moral obligation and the inferior forms correspond to such functions as perception. Thus, Piaget's first and continuing quest was for the *structures* of mental life. Some of these notions Piaget set out in the final chapter of a philosophical novel *Recherche** which he published in 1917.

So right in this early teenage period Piaget diverged from the functionalist path on which Pragmatism had set him. His interest came to be not in the purpose and function of actions but in the relations between them (and within their subroutines) as parts of whole structures.

In 1918 Piaget left for Zürich with the intention of working in the psychological laboratory at the University. Here he attended Bleuler's psychiatric clinic and Jung's lectures on Freud, which made him 'sense the danger of solitary meditation; I decided to forget the system lest I should fall victim to "autism"' (*op. cit.*, p. 244). Overall he did not find Zürich very intellectually nutritious, and left for the Sorbonne in 1919 where Simon, at the Binet laboratory, suggested to him that he should standardise Burt's reasoning tests with Parisian children. Thus occupied, he found himself less interested in the quantitative aspects of the successes and failures of the children than in the wrong answers which they tended to give. Consistent patterns began to emerge. He employed the clinical expertise gained with Bleuler to engage the children in conversations which revealed that even the simplest reasoning task involving the inclusion of a part in a whole or the coordination of relations, or finding a part common to two wholes presented fundamental difficulties to children below 11 or 12 years age. Logic, he could see was not inborn in children but developed towards a state of *mental equilibrium*.

Having duly reported such findings in journal articles, Piaget was invited by Eduard Claparède, an eminent child psychologist of the time, to join his department at the Institut J. J. Rousseau at Geneva with the result that these researches were continued in earnest. He had decided to spend just another two or three years studying childrens' thinking, then to turn to the origins of mental life in the human infant and then to go on to construct his psychological and biological epistemology. The outcome of these early studies are contained in Piaget's first five books: *The Language and Thought of the Child* (1942a), *Judgment and Reasoning in the Child* (1924b), *The Child's Conception of the World* (1926), *The Child's Conception of*

---

* Piaget has spoken of his desire to analyse Proust's *À la Recherche de Temps Perdu* from genetic epistemological principles (interview in the *Times Educational Supplement*, 1972).

Casuality (1927) and *The Moral Judgment of the Child* (1932)*

Apart from the first which deals in part with conversations within groups of children these books mainly report the answers which children give to questions presented *in vacuo* as in an IQ test. Although this might appear to be the perfect recipe for an unmanageable clutch of disconnected data, Piaget is able to blend reporting with interpretation in such a way that a coherent picture of childish thought emerges. At the focal point of this picture we find the notion of *egocentrism*. This is an epistemic egocentrism which exists as a result of the child having no way of cognising the thought of others in relation to his own; he is at the centre of the cognitive world and the only 'point of view' is his.

Egocentrism is reflected in a number of ways in the various volumes. In the early (4–7 years) conversations of the child it is revealed in the inability, according to Piaget, to exchange information, in the sense that his speech is not adapted to the listener but is a kind of 'spin-off' from his own train of thought, for example, he may ask a question without waiting for the answer. 'Collective monologue' is the term Piaget uses to refer to this. Similarly, because he cannot put himself in the other person's place the child is incapable of coherently explaining the functioning of a piece of apparatus such as a syringe (Piaget, 1924a). This same egocentrism is said to make thinking unadapted to any 'external' system such as logic and causality for if he is only capable of conceiving the relevance of his own thought, then he will feel free to make connections between judgments and events in any way he pleases simply because there is no notion that a contradictory thought might invalidate his own—a cognitive fools' paradise. This is shown in Piaget's study of childrens' use of logical connectives such as *because*, *although* and *therefore* (Piaget, 1924b). One child says, for example, 'I had a bath because afterwards I was clean' (p. 17), as logical implication for her is the juxtaposition of two states of affairs on the grounds that *she* sees them as going together. Furthermore, as there is no idea of contradiction there is the consequence that, for Piaget, nothing can be called 'reasoning' before the age of 7 or 8 years, for this relies on the principle of the necessary contradiction of certain propositions (the law of excluded middle mentioned above). Because the child

---

*English Publication dates will be given throughout. Swiss publication was normally very much earlier.

freely assimilates experiences to his own egocentric schemes he can
have no understanding of the objective generality of the class and
thus cannot produce deductive (general to the particular) or inductive
(particular to the general) reasoning. Piaget borrows a term from
Stern, 'transductive reasoning', to refer to the aspect of childish
thought whereby a move of implication is made from particular to
particular or general to general. For instance we can see how one child
of 8 years links particular occurrences as if they constituted implications in: 'I can shut my [cardboard desk] if I want to. That is why it
doesn't stick. Afterwards [if it sticks] I shan't be able to shut it' (p. 184).

Egocentrism is plainly seen in the fact that children will assert that
they have a brother but deny that their brother has one: the child
cannot see himself from another point of view. Also, the state of
egocentrism does not allow him to distinguish between causality and
intentionality. As the consciousness of his own psychological states
of willing, feeling, wanting and so on is immediate, this, as it were,
spills over into causal judgments about the concrete world: knowledge of causality entails an objective rather than purposive point of
view. Thus, in the case of one child, although he no longer judged that
the clouds moved of their own volition, he still related their
movement to the intentional world by saying that people walking on
the ground (purposive behaviour) made them move.

In the volume on morality Piaget is not so much interested in
ethical conduct as in the judgments that children make about moral
questions insofar as they involve rule-following, responsibility and
justice. To this end he studied children's attitudes to rules by
questioning them about the game of marbles, and in order to examine
the notions of fairness and moral responsibility told them stories
about which he then asked them to pass moral judgment. Inevitably
this aspect of morality cannot be dissociated from cognitive level.
Egocentrism is found in the early moral judgments because they do
not involve a recognition of the *reciprocity* of behaviour vis-à-vis
other people. The essence of moral understanding, according to
Piaget, is the knowledge that the moral law establishes mutuality
between people: I cannot do to you what you cannot do to me and
vice versa. However, because the child is socialised in his early years
(of necessity) mainly through constraint, epistemic egocentrism does
not result in the child just doing what he likes; rather he develops an
egocentric view of the moral sanctions, regarding them as unchangeable, absolute injunctions, and this because he cannot cognise their

conventional nature—the lack of reflexivity inherent in the egocentric view.

This view of moral development is of course quite different to that of Baldwin, and Piaget does set out their points of disagreement (Piaget, 1932, pp. 392–401). Baldwin, according to Piaget, did not appreciate that egocentrism would be the consequence of the child beginning with an adualistic concept of the self. Furthermore, the imitative process of the dialectic of personal growth between the self and others is not sufficient to overcome egocentrism he argued. 'But imitation will never enable us to perceive in ourselves anything but what we have in common with others. In order to discover ourselves as a particular individual, what is needed is a continuous comparison, the outcome of opposition, of discussion and of mutual control' (*op. cit.*, p. 400). The egocentric state of mind is destroyed by the child being forced through the necessities of his social life to take into account the other person's point of view. Conflict *between equals* is, for Piaget, the main energiser of reciprocity in the moral and cognitive life. For similar reasons Piaget attacks Baldwin's account in *Thought and Things* of how knowledge of morality develops. He says, against Baldwin, that general acceptance of a principle is not at the heart of morality for there are many modes of conduct which are generally accepted and yet still irrational or immoral. Piaget does less than justice to Baldwin here because he ignores the fact that Baldwin's main aim in his account of morality was to explain how moral judgments developed *from mere syntelic* commonness to the status of laws (see pp. 74–5). Piaget does not mention that Baldwin's theory of the moral law depended on the construction of *ideal meaning*.

Just as there must be reciprocity between persons in morality so must there be *reversibility* between actions and between thoughts for the establishment of mental equilibrium and objective knowledge. Piaget defines equilibrium as the reversibility of cognitive *operations*, on the model of reversible operations being performed on a set of scales such as adding and subtracting weights to produce a state of balance. He gives a broader explanation as to why egocentric thinking cannot result in objective knowledge by highlighting the nature of the mental disequilibrium which it produces: it is one between *assimilating* reality to the self and *imitating* reality (Piaget, 1924b, pp. 169–180). Childish thought represents the primacy of assimilation of experiences to personal, subjective schemes alternating with the primacy of blind imitation of others without understanding (without assimilation) as if weights were being randomly exchanged from one pan of the scales to the other. In order to equalise the cognitive weight and make the mental scales balance, assimilation must become more imitative and imitation more assimilatory—opposing, complementary processes as we found in Baldwin. To explain how this eventually comes about Piaget again cites social interaction, especially epistemic conflict, with other children and later with adults. Assimilation and imitation cease to be antagonistic and come to balance each other as a result of the progressive socialisation of thought—through the 'clash of perspectives' and the necessity for taking in the other person's point of view in social cooperation.

These studies brought Piaget an unexpected acclaim but one that was not entirely welcome; for they were received as if they represented facets of a completed system ready to be contended. Indeed, still today one finds these early books discussed as if they had been written *after* Piaget had developed his theory of stages and criticised for lacking an experimental sophistication to which they did not aspire. He was aware of their shortcomings: 'I well knew that thought proceeds from action, but I believed that language directly reflects acts and that to understand the logic of the child one had only to look for it in the domain of conversations and verbal interactions. It was only later by studying the patterns of intelligent behaviour in the first two years that I learned that for a complete understanding of the genesis of the intellectual operations, manipulation and experience with objects had first to be considered' (Piaget, 1952, p. 247).

The second shortcoming, according to Piaget, was that he was looking in vain for structures-of-the-whole relative to logical operations by concentrating purely on the social aspect of thought and neglecting the fact that the source of the mental operations was also to be found in concrete experience, producing what he later called *concrete operations*. Nevertheless, social experience of the kind outlined above, is still taken to be necessary for cognitive development by Piaget; although social factors came to be given progressively less weight as the theory developed.

We might add a third problem which exists within the early work, and which stirs up a hornets' nest of epistemic dilemmas. It is the question of the role of specifically verbal, especially semantic, misunderstanding in the wrong answers which the children were giving. For example, is it not possible that children might use a form of logical connective in thinking but lack the linguistic competence to use the correct one in speaking? Could they be using a word in a systematically different way to the adult due to an immature semantic rather than cognitive system? And yet is such a distinction between linguistic and cognitive abilities philosophically tenable? I shall be returning to this fundamental problem in Section 3.3.

It was not until this period that Piaget became acquainted with Gestalt psychology and found clear echoes within it of his structures-of-the-whole notion. However it was evident that Gestalt principles suited only one of the inferior forms of equilibrium—when the whole dominates the parts, as in perception. In a logico-mathematical structure, on the other hand, like the number system, there is a complete two-way equilibrium between the parts (the numbers) and the system: numbers are created by rules of the system which is itself constituted of numbers so that there is a stable interdependence between elements and the totality.

The next period, 1925–1929, was perhaps Piaget's most fruitful. He undertook heavy teaching duties in philosophy, and returned for a period to his research on the evolution of mollusk morphology. Also by this time he had married (Valentine Chatenay, one of his earliest research collaborators) and in 1925 their first daughter was born, to be followed later by another girl and a boy. This confluence of academic, scientific and domestic circumstances produced three of the most remarkable and original documents in psychology, based largely on the observation of and experimentation with his own three infants (Piaget, 1953, 1955, 1962). Piaget was, in fact, carrying out phase two of his programme, studying the sensorimotor basis of thinking in the infant.

The philosophical and biological concerns appear in the introductory chapter of *The Origin of Intelligence in the Child* (1953). Organic life parallels intelligence—and phylogeny ontogeny—insofar as they are both biological functions involving *adaptation* and *organisation*. Taking adaptation first, every living thing must be adapted to its environment in order to survive. To this end it must both assimilate the environment and accommodate to it. Biologically, assimilating can mean taking in such things as food, water and sunlight—all the materials which maintain life. Naturally this would be impossible if the organism were not able to make use of them towards the appropriate end, if, for example, the animal could not masticate the food, digest it and transform it into energy, if the plant could not take in water by osmosis or utilise sunlight in photosynthesis. This means that the structure and functions of the organism must be adjusted, or accommodated, to the job of assimilating: the organism must have the working apparatus to assimilate. Moreover accommodation must involve the ability to modify the assimilatory process in accordance with immediate environmental contingencies. For example, all types of food cannot be chewed or digested in the same way, and plants must be capable of responding to different degrees and conditions of sunlight. Very generally, assimilation is what the organism has to do to remain alive and accommodation is how it does it. Yet it must be emphasised that these are only concepts, for in practice the two processes can never be separated. Adaptation prevails when there is a state of equilibrium between these two such that an organism, or species, has its assimilatory needs balanced by its accommodatory capacities.

Intelligent behaviour and understanding also involve a two-way interaction between organism and environment controlled by assimilation and accommodation. For example, a continuing piece of behaviour is incorporated (assimilated) into a general strategy of action, yet at the same time the present action differs from previous actions in that individual features of the objects acted on and immediate contingencies force the actor to modify his behaviour (accommodate) in order to complete the sequence successfully. By way of illustration, when we set about knocking a nail into a plank of wood the task is assimilated into a general plan, a category of tasks, whereby the point of the nail is placed on the wood, the hammer is brought down onto the head of the nail and so on. Yet at the same time the behaviour has to be accommodated to the actual length of the nail, the grain and thickness of the wood, and also to each position of the nail after every blow so that if the nail is tending to one side the next hammer blow has to be angled to correct for the bias. Consideration of these processes should tell us that intelligent action is not automatic for it does not run through preset sequences without regard to environmental variability, but is actively correcting and restructuring its plans and categories—accommodation. Neither is intelligence pragmatic and empirical as it relates each piece of behaviour to the categories and plans developed from past experience so that things are never known nor actions performed independently from their similarities to other things and actions—assimilation. On a conceptual level, the process of understanding is essentially relating a new idea (such as decimals) to what we already know (fractions for example) by altering our present arrangement of knowledge in order to make sense of it (changing our conception that numbers less than one must be expressed as fractions). In this way assimilation and accommodation are always pushing in opposite directions: assimilation is conservative, structuring the present in the light of the past, whereas accommodation changes present behaviour and thereby future structures. These concepts help us to understand why our performance at nail-hammering improves with practice and why we are unable to comprehend an idea when it is totally new to us or when we do not make the effort to rearrange our previous knowledge. All this implies a fundamental unity between the organism and the environment such that the environment is structured by the mind insofar as it treats present reality as classifiable under previously constructed categories and the mind is structured by the environment as it continuously produces novelties to challenge the old categories to change or fail to adapt. Intellectual adaptation begins with assimilation and succeeds by virtue of accommodation.

In explaining intellectual adaptation we were forced to employ two kinds of example: those involving sensorimotor actions (the hammering) and those involving conceptual understanding (decimals). This is because intellectual adaptation can take place either on the plane of action or on the plane of conception, so that in the former case equilibrium between assimilation and accommodation means practical success and in the latter it means knowledge. The central idea which develops out of these three volumes on infancy, which can be construed as being at the heart of Piaget's theory and explaining the importance of infant development within it, is that sensorimotor adaptation is the foundation and prefiguration of conceptual adaptation.

The second parallel between biology and intelligence was found in the notion of organisation, without which adaptation would not be possible. Organisation involves the relating of parts to the whole in such a way that one constituent is responsible for the successful functioning of the totality and the continued functioning of the constituent is made possible only by the functioning of the whole (compare Spencer, p. 41). This is best understood by considering the case of a vital organ in the body which, if it is removed, eventually causes death yet which only functions itself if all the other organs cooperate to support it. Every organ is related to every other organ with varying degrees of directness such that the life of the organism is dependent on the interrelations between its parts. Similarly with intelligence, every piece of intelligent activity, from drinking a pint of beer to calculating its specific gravity, is interrelated with other pieces of behaviour so that the world is mentally structured by the coordination between these behaviours. How inconceivable it is that we should have ever developed the use of the hammer if we had never coordinated the act of lifting a heavy object with the act of bringing it down, or developed our notions of number without coordinating addition and subtraction, treating them as quite independent activities.

The parallels with Baldwin (and with Hobhouse) are certainly evident but it must be stressed that Piaget is not merely taking over Baldwin's terminology and concepts. As regards assimilation and accommodation, for example Piaget's use of assimilation implies an active incorporation of the environment and experience, not the somewhat passive association of one past imitation or habit with another or the existence of a 'conceptual net' as found in Baldwin. Conversely with accommodation, this is a more active principle for Baldwin; but in Piaget, although it is an innovatory principle, it is one which produces change in the organism only to the extent that the organism is trying to assimilate. Also, Piaget has little place for the Baldwinian interpretation of 'habit' (though his use of the reflex was similar) and so his theory can be said to involve a more radical rejection of fixed neonatal patterns and instincts than Baldwin's.

Piaget then goes on to reject four psychobiological theories of intelligence in order to posit a fifth. He rejects Lamarckism and its psychological analogue associationism (from Locke to Pavlov) because it entails a passive organism being determined by the environment. Development proceeds, on the contrary, with an actively assimilating, accommodating organism. Secondly, vitalism (presumably from Bergson) and the psychological analogue of 'intellectualism' (it is unclear whom Piaget intended here) is inadequate simply because it is unable to account scientifically for the origin of the vital impulse and gives, in psychology, an agenetic view of the mind which blocks further explanation. The third pair of theories, preformism and Gestaltism, present an innatist view of intelligence which sees physical and mental development in biology, and perceptual and cognitive structures in psychology, as fully determined by the form (molecular structure of the genes or the electrical organisation of the cortex). If structure did completely determine function the assimilation–accommodation model would be redundant: Piaget's concern is with genetic not static structures. Finally, mutationism, or Darwinism, finds its psychological counterpart in Thorndike's trial-and-error learning (and of course in Skinner, though Piaget could not mention this for reasons of chronology); both theories see the organism as generating forms or behaviours from which the environment selects the more advantageous after the event—again the active structuring of the organism is absent.

Piaget now makes explicit the phylogenetic implications of his assimilation–accommodation model by reference to the research he had recently undertaken on the acquatic mollusk *Limnaea stagnalis*, a creature of elongated shape found commonly in the stagnant waters and marshes of Europe and Asia. In order to adapt to the more turbulent water of lakes like Neuchâtel and Geneva which are exposed to strong winds, the species has produced a shortened, globular variety (because of the need to clamp itself to stones in rough water) which resulted in a stable morphology obeying the laws of Mendelian inheritance. Piaget takes us through each of the five possible explanations of this adaptation to show that only the fifth is tenable. First, laboratory experimentation shows the Lamarckian solution to be inadequate: breeding of the elongated variety in an agitator to produce experimental contraction revealed no genetic transmission of this acquired characteristic. Vitalism, even apart from its practical implausibility, cannot explain why the primitive 'intelligence' of the species took so many centuries to manifest itself and why it has not done so in all the other lakes. These problems are also encountered by proposing the preformation of adaptive characteristics in the gene: why the delay and why the geographical restriction? But what of mutationism? Is not this the inevitable solution? Piaget gives two reasons why selection after the event is inadequate. One of them deals with a characteristic of *Limnaea's* mode of inheritance which is rather technical, but the other sets out an objection in principle to mutationism. It derives from the fact that, although the elongated variety cannot survive the rough waters of the lakes, the globular contracted forms seem to be perfectly well adapted to stagnant locations. Why then are these mutations not scattered everywhere if the elongated variety has no particular advantage over them? This is an objection to Darwinism that is commonly encountered: why do populations not tend to contain a scatter of individuals who have biological advantages which are redundant?

The Piagetian solution admits selection of some kind but not for a rigid, fixed morphogenesis which develops independently of the environment but rather for a modified assimilatory capacity which enables the organism to react to environmental contingencies and which can later become fixed in the genotype. The new globular form is not independently preformed but represents the genotype's *response* to the environment—its assimilation of and accommodation to it. One of Piaget's concerns in the book was to show that intelligence also was not an independent, preformed absolute. With this explanation we re-encounter Baldwin's principle of orthoplasy, which regards evolution as producing not advantageous fixed forms but an increased accommodatory capacity—a plasticity. It was not till much later that Piaget was able to give a precise account of this, having himself assimilated Waddington's theory of 'genetic assimilation' (see below).

Contained in the main body of the three works are a set of detailed observations and simple experiments, performed mostly with Piaget's three infants, interwoven with a complex tapestry of interpretation to produce something of richness and precision. Although the first two books of the trilogy cover the same territory there is the difference between them that *The Origins of Intelligence in the Child* follows the developing interrelationship between assimilation and accommodation which produces sensorimotor adaptation, whereas *The Child's Construction of Reality* examines the consequence of this development for the infant's knowledge of object existence, space, causality and time.

In the first book Piaget traces the gradual separation of assimilatory from accommodatory activity and the development towards a complementary rather than an antagonistic relation between them; which we might compare with a similar development already sketched above for conceptual intelligence. He follows this through six stages which are distinguished in terms of the utilisation (or lack of it) of circular reactions. Piaget borrows Baldwin's term here, but although he employs it towards much the same end, his usage is less diffuse and he distinguishes between three types of circular reaction—primary, secondary and tertiary—which are best illustrated with reference to the stages. Stage 1 (0 – 1 month) is distinguished by a lack of circular reactions and the presence of

relatively fixed reflexes—sucking, blinking, swallowing, bodily movements for example. Although assimilation and accommodation
cannot really be distinguished in the reflex, to the extent that the
infant treats objects (such as nipples, fingers) as 'coming under' an
action (sucking) there is the beginning of assimilation and to the
extent that this can be successful (nipples are sucked) there is
accommodation. Moreover, although the two processes are hardly
distinguishable they are fundamentally antagonistic: the infant's first
assimilation is completely egocentric, indeed autistic, because the
virtual absence of accommodation implies no distinction between the
self and the world, yet on the other hand the world is refractory for it
keeps imposing experiences on to the infant to which it cannot adapt
without further accommodation. The infant tries, the world resists;
the world imposes, the infant fails.

Stage 2 (1–4 months) sees the arrival of the *primary* circular
reaction. This differs from the reflex in that there is a definite element
of accommodation to the contours of the immediate environment. In
the case of sucking for example, reflex sucking meant sucking
anything that came into chance contact with lips, but this early
circular sucking comes about through coordination between the
hand and the mouth, with the infant bringing the hand to the mouth
in order to suck the thumb and then going on to repeat this for its own
sake. Assimilation can also now be distinguished clearly because the
infant extends the range of things which can be sucked, from thumbs
to rattle to blankets and so on, which in turn brings accommodation
into play as different things come to be sucked in slightly different
ways. Piaget employs the, by now familiar, term *scheme* in quite a
technical way to refer to the existence of a sensorimotor 'concept'
such as 'sucking things'. (The French word *schème* was originally
translated as 'schema' but as Furth (1969) has pointed out, Piaget
uses *schéma* to refer to something quite different, thus 'scheme' is the
translation now favoured. To further complicate matters 'scheme'
can also be used at the conceptual level.) So the primary circular
reaction is essentially the coordination between parts of the body and
between modalities (mutual assimilation of schemes) and the circular
repetition of actions for their own sake. Some other examples are:
following moving objects with the gaze, examining stationary
objects, early attempts to grasp seen objects, repeating sounds (like
coughing) for their own sake, and turning the head in the direction of
a noise. In general, development is seen as coming about through the

interplay, within the circular reaction, between conservative repetition (assimilation) and the necessity for changing the action in accordance with environmental novelties (accommodation). In the beginning is the action and its repetition; the world affects the repetition; the scheme is altered and the whole process begins again.

However, the primary circular reaction is still relatively autistic in that it is concerned with the repetition of actions rather than the production of an effect in the world *through* actions. This comes in Stage 3 (4–8 months) with the *secondary* circular reaction. We might here give one example of this type from each of the three kinds of assimilation which Piaget takes these circular reactions to be representing. In *reproductive* assimilation the infant reproduces an initially fortuitous effect, such as systematically striking dolls to make them move after having first done so accidentally (Piaget, 1953, pp. 167–8). In *recognitory* assimilation the infant shows by his actions that he perceives what something is or that one event is the sign of another. For example Laurent (at 0;7) cried in the morning as soon as he heard his mother's bed creak; Jacqueline (at 0;8) smiled and said 'aa' as soon as the door of her room opened, before seeing the person enter (*op. cit.*, p. 195). *Generalising* assimilation, or 'procedures to make interesting sights last', is found when the infant is confronted with new objects and events; indeed the older he gets the *newer* novelties seem to him. For instance, Lucienne was accustomed to shake her bassinet by waving her arms and legs in order to make dolls move that had been attached to the hood. At the age of 0;7 months she applied this scheme to make her father repeat things she saw him doing for the first time and which she liked, such as unfolding a newspaper and rumpling it, or peeping round the hood of her bassinet (*op. cit.*, p. 205).

Stage 4 (8–12 months) sees the coordination between secondary circular schemes by way of the reciprocal assimilation of one to another, and the application of the resultant combination to new situations. An example of this process is where Laurent (at 0;10) developed the scheme of releasing his grip on objects intentionally so that they would fall to the ground. Piaget then, in the sight of the infant, struck a tin of shaving cream against the side of a wash basin to make a sound which interested Laurent. Let us take up Piaget's own account of the result and its significance

(Observation 130 continued) Now, at once, Laurent takes possession of the tin, holds out his arm and drops it over the basin. I moved the latter, as a check. He nevertheless succeeded, several times in succession, in making the object fall on the basin. Hence this is a fine example of the coordination of two schemata of which the first *serves as a 'means' whereas the second assigns an end to the action*: the schema of 'relinquishing the object' and that of 'striking one object against another' (*op. cit.*, p. 225, my italics).

The *tertiary* circular reaction (Stage 5, 12–18 months) develops accommodation to the point where the infant not only applies old schemes in his means-end behaviour but actually invents new schemes by active experimentation; he 'lies in wait for a new experience'. This ability arises out of the interest he now has in repeating actions not just in order to reproduce old effects, but altering them slightly each time to see how the effects change (for example, dropping objects in different positions). As regards the invention of new schemes in means–end behaviour Piaget gives an example of Lucienne (at 1;4) wanting to grasp an aluminium flask which is too far away from her (Observation 158, p. 98–9). She sees a stick lying alongside so decides to use this to bring the flask nearer. At first she just strikes it with the stick (an old scheme) then 'most attentively' comes to push it from left to right till she learns how to bring the flask towards her (a new scheme).

Stage 6 (18 months onwards) finds the infant coming to perform mentally what he had previously been doing in action. The infant is *interiorising* action schemes to perform them in imagery; what some would call the first appearance of thinking. A famous example of this is Jacqueline (at 1;8) arriving at a closed door in the house with a blade of grass in each hand. She puts the grass on the floor in order to free her hands to turn the door handle, but when she comes to open the door she sees that this would chase the grass away, therefore she carefully picks up the grass and places it outside the range of the door's movement (*op. cit.*, p. 338–9). There is now no need for her to experiment in order to understand the consequences and advantages of an action.

It is not easy to appreciate the developing relationship between assimilation and accommodation, partly because there appears to be a paradox inherent in the proposal that they begin by being antagonistic yet almost indissociable. To illustrate this, if an infant of 0;2 attempts to grasp all objects—string, rattle, blanket—in the same way this implies little distinction between assimilation and accommodation and an antagonism because of the fact that each crude assimilation lessens the possibility of accommodation and the very variability of the to-be-accommodated world reduces the chance of assimilation. However, if the infant comes to grasp the objects each in a different way and thus succeeds in prehending them, one can observe an element of accommodation distinct from assimilation and see cooperation in that accommodation aids assimilation and without assimilation there would be nothing to become accommodated. One way of expressing their relationship is that they begin by inhabiting, and thus competing for, the same motor 'territory'; gradually they find their own sphere of application and thus cooperate to construct an objective world-view. This very process explains the gradual dissociation of the self from the world. The self and the world are, to the egocentric infant, the same yet they are in competition: the infant assimilates everything to itself and the world is too refractory to be thus assimilated (compare Baldwin, p. 54). As assimilation and accommodation become dissociated so do the self and the world. The cooperative element is found in that knowledge is the result of an interaction, or dialectic, between the self and the world.

In *The Child's Construction of Reality* (1955) Piaget gives a stage-wise account of how sensorimotor intelligence entails the infant's constructing a model of a world in which objects exist independently of his own perception of and actions on them; in which these objects are related in a space which includes his own body; in which causal relations obtain between objects and between the infant and objects that are independent of his perception of object—object relations and of his feelings of effort towards the objects; and a world in which temporal succession is independent of temporal duration and sequences of events are independent of the order in which they were perceived. Each of these concepts (object, space, causality, time) mutually entails the others, and the object concept can be regarded as the pivot for the other forms of understanding. For this reason, and because its stages of development are relatively easy to observe, this has been the most widely discussed of the sensorimotor developments. In Stages 1 and 2 there is no special behaviour towards vanished objects. In Stage 3 however there is the appearance of accommodation in that, for example, the infant will retrieve one object from behind another so long as part of it remains visible, will anticipate the trajectory of a falling object, look away from and return to a stationary object and actively search for objects. But if he is reaching for an object which is then completely occluded he will act as if the object has ceased to exist. For instance Jacqueline at 0;8:

(Observation 29 continued) . . . while she watches I place her little bells under the coverlet, rolling them up into a ball to facilitate her search. I shake the whole thing to make the bells ring. No reaction. As long as she hears the noise she laughs but then her eyes follow my fingers instead of searching under the coverlet . . . I then raise it in order to reveal the object; Jacqueline quickly stretches out her hand, but just when she is about to get it I cover it up again and Jacqueline withdraws her hand. I repeat the experiment but this time hide the bells behind a fold in the sheet; same negative reaction, despite the sound. Subsequent attempts yield nothing more. (Piaget, 1955, p. 37)

Piaget's explanation for this phenomenon is that the infant is trying, by her actions, to bring sensible items into existence; assimilating their appearance to her visual and tactile schemes. As to the counter-theory which might be offered by a nativist, that the baby believes in a substantial world but only pays attention to things on which he can act, disregarding and forgetting all others, Piaget says (*op. cit.*, pp. 41–2) that this would involve attributing knowledge to the infant completely without justification. Also, one might add, the observations are *consistent* with 'innate ideas' but they are also consistent with a theory which holds that the infant fears growing up and thus shams incompetence in order to gain prolonged nurture from his mother—this is 'consistent' too! Nevertheless, there are problems of interpretation here which we will examine in Section 3.1.

In Stage 4 the infant can retrieve completely invisible objects but if an object which he has been used to finding behind one particular occluder (A) is transferred before his eyes to behind another occluder (B) he will return and search behind A. This, according to Piaget, is because the existence of the object is still not separated from the action which the infant has to take to find it, nor from the context in which it was found: not therefore 'watch chain' but 'watch chain-found-behind-this-cushion-when-I-lift-it-up'. That is, assimilation and accommodation are still competing for the same territory: the child assimilates the object to the movements it makes to accommodate to it and the movements accommodate only to past assimilatory schemes.

Even at Stage 5, if the infant does not perceive the movement from one hiding place to another he will not search in the correct location. At 1;0 Lucienne played the game of finding her father's watch chain in his closed fist. When Piaget passed his fist containing the chain beneath a cloth, left the chain there, brought the fist out still clenched and let Lucienne discover it to be empty she looked all around her but did not lift the cloth (Observation 57, p. 69). Cognising invisible displacements depends on the ability to construct a mental image of movements, which is the acquisition of the final stage.

One particularly relevant feature of Piaget's account of the growth of spatial understanding is the use to which he puts the reversibility principle and his introduction of mathematical 'group' theory* in this context, upon which his later account of concrete thinking in middle childhood would be reliant. The reason why Piaget employs group theory is that it offers a formal account of a system in a state of equilibrium (a 'structure-of-the-whole') which is of particular importance to action in the spatial field. A group can be anything which consists of elements and operations and which forms a closed system such that none of the operations applied changes or disequilibrates the system. In the spatial field movements of objects are the elements and ways of relating the movements are the operations. For example, if we make a movement in relation to a thing (we look to the left of a table lamp), cognising the stable relation between the thing and ourselves as two objects in space entails understanding that the operation of reversing this movement (turning the head an equal distance to the right) will recover the thing's original location in our field of vision. If the original location is not recovered then either we or the object have moved, and to discover which we have to use other objects as references. It is instructive to compare this with Kant's argument in the Second Analogy (see p. 32); indeed Piaget often makes reference to Kant's theory of space—though more often to criticise its apriorism.

But, as group theory shows, reversibility is not the only characteristic of a system in equilibrium. There must be at least three other characteristics: composition, associativity and identity. *Composition* (A & B = C) in this instance would involve the possibility of combining actions to make one continuous action. If we wish to move from the fireplace to the garden we can go from the fireplace to the kitchen, then from the kitchen to the garden. If this did not hold we could not in principle predict where we would end up. *Associativity*

---

*For an account of group theory which is not too technical the reader might consult Part IX in Vol. III of J. R. Newman's *World of Mathematics* (New York: Smith and Shuster, 1956).

$((A \& B) \& C = A \& (B \& C))$ implies that there is more than one way of combining the elements of an algebraic expression. So in action there is, in principle, more than one way of combining the elements of the route from A to B and thus we are free to take detours. So what limitation there might be on the combination of elements in the possible fireplace—garden routes is due to the presence of brick walls not logical necessity. *Identity* (I & A = A; I & B = B; and so on) can mean, in the spatial field, that if we stay still the same relations between objects and ourself will hold—unless the objects move. All these characteristics, argues Piaget, must be possessed by the infant's actions if he is to separate his own movements from relations between objects in space (including his own body as an object); and thus if he is to overcome his sensorimotor egocentrism.

In Stages 1 to 3 the infant's groups are *practical* in that his actions and relations between objects are fused, as evinced by the inability to retrieve completely occluded objects. Stage 4 sees the transition between practical and *objective* groups which Piaget calls *subjective*. For example, Laurent (at 0;9) showed some evidence of reversibility when, on being handed his feeding bottle with the teat pointing away from him, he was able immediately to rotate it and suck for milk (Observation 92, p. 163); but in other areas this is lacking. By Stage 6 there is complete objectivity of the spatial groups.

In the third book of the infancy trilogy *Play, Dreams and Imitation in Childhood* (1962) Piaget's concern is with states of disequilibrium rather than equilibrium. He sees imitation as reflecting the primacy of accommodation over assimilation and play as reflecting the inverse disequilibrium. Again he takes us through the genesis of each mode of functioning in six stages, but this time extends the analysis beyond infancy into middle childhood. As regards play and dreams one particularly interesting feature of the book is Piaget's discussion of the relation of his theory with that of Freud. In some ways Piaget adopts quite a Freudian view: he makes use of the distinction between 'primary' and 'secondary' symbolism in play and dreams, accepts a wish-fulfillment element in dreams and a catharcic element in play. But in many essentials Freud's theory of cognitive development is opposed to Piaget's. As regards the development of symbolic thinking for example, Piaget criticises Freud for treating it as the outcome of unconscious processes when it should be seen as the result of a *conscious* attempt at comprehension.

In fact the original title of the book was *La Formation du Symbole* and this gives a clearer indication of the main theme. Piaget is offering a theory of how the infant comes to *represent* reality after the sensorimotor stage by means of mental images and symbols, these being modes of signifying reality not immediately present to the senses. When the infant comes to imitate the actions of others by movements of his own that are not immediately visible to himself (around Stage 4), he does so by means of a primitive kind of signification which Piaget calls the *index*. For instance Jacqueline was able to imitate her father's blowing of a 'raspberry' by relating what she could see of his tongue and lip movements to her own tongue and lip movements via a sound index, that is, she could imitate the movement because she was already able to relate the sound the movements made to movements she herself could make—a sound thus 'signifying' certain movements. However imitation does not become truly representational until Stage 6 when action schemes are becoming interiorised. Here we find deferred imitation in which the child imitates an event that occurred in the relatively distant past. An amusing example of this, again from Jacqueline, is when she imitated the tantrum of a playmate a whole day after it had occurred (*op. cit.*, p. 63). Piaget argues that this kind of imitation involves the distinction between the signified—the original tantrum—and the signifier, the mental image of the tantrum which Jacqueline uses as a 'draft for exterior imitation'. The mental image is thus interiorised imitation, in which accommodating to the thing or event is put above assimilating it to existing schemes; although of course there has to be some assimilative element.

At the assimilative end of the spectrum, play originates as early as the first dissociation between assimilation and accommodation, when, for example, the infant might play with his voice for functional pleasure. Later, in Stage 4, when removing an obstacle to prehension he might break off and start taking the obstacle away for the fun of it. Representation in play appears at Stage 6 when the child uses one object (a cardboard box for example) to 'stand in for', to symbolise, another (a plate) and thus plays symbolically (pretends to eat from it), implying a definite separation between signifier and signified but showing an opposite disequilibrium from the imitative image.

What then is the relationship between the representative facility—by image and by play (and dream) symbolism—which is achieved at the end of the sensorimotor period, and the growth of conceptual intelligence? Piaget's account is somewhat confusing here because he refers to 'the symbolic function' as equivalent to the total significatory system *including* mental imagery, but the general picture is as follows. Language consists of a system of collective *signs* which are symbolic in that they 'stand in for' things and events yet which involve imitation and imagery in that there has to be an element of imitation in language learning and words can evoke mental images. There is a mutual dependence between the language system and representation: words could not be learned without the representative facility and representation would remain totally disequilibrated were it not for the socialising influence of a collective, shared system of meanings which functions as a medium by which to dissolve egocentrism.

Yet, as Piaget showed in the early books, this disequilibrium takes many years to be resolved. It results in the appearance of what Piaget calls the 'preconcept' between about 2 and 4 years of age. A famous example of a preconcept is when Jacqueline was walking in the garden with her father and they encountered a series of slugs which she kept referring to as 'the slug'. When Piaget asked her if it was the same slug that they kept seeing she replied that it was and when she was asked if it was a different slug each time she also said that it was (*op. cit.*, p. 225). An object is thus assimilated to an evoked representation (one slug assimilated to the set of slugs seen) without a corresponding accommodation to its individuality; and when its individuality is recognised this destroys the assimilated set—the primary antagonism between assimilation and accommodation. One also finds a similar disequilibrium between generality and particularity in the transductive reasoning mentioned above (*cf.* Baldwin, p. 61).

2.2 1930 ONWARDS: LOGICO-MATHEMATICAL SYSTEMS IN CHILD AND ADOLESCENT THINKING; GENETIC EPISTEMOLOGY

After 1929 Piaget resumed his experimental work with children at the Institut. He now had a large number of collaborators—of whom Bärbel Inhelder is still the most notable—and with them he undertook an exhaustive series of studies which, as before, involved 'clinical' interviews with children about their judgments, but which now called on the child to make a decision about a *concrete* matter, such as whether or not a beaker still contained the same amount of liquid as before, and to justify this decision. The fruits of these labours began to appear in the early years of the Second World War and by the mid-1950s studies had been completed on the child's concept of quantity, number, logic, time, movement, speed, space, geometry, chance, and on adolescent reasoning.

The usual pattern of these books is for each chapter to tackle one aspect of the topic with the use of a concrete problem, for the method and general results to be stated first, and then verbatim extracts given from the testing of individual children grouped in three of five stages: Stage I, IIA, IIB, IIIA and IIIB. These can largely be viewed in terms of the age of the children. Let us take the example of one of the earliest books which has only recently been translated, *The Child's Construction of Quantities* (1974). The first chapter presents a test of the child's knowledge that the amount and weight of a substance remains the same throughout changes in its shape. He is presented with a ball of modelling clay and a lump of the same material and asked to make a ball 'as big and heavy' as the first. Once the child is satisfied the balls are identical, the experimenter changes the shape of one of them by flattening it into a disc or by rolling it into a coil. The child is then asked a question such as 'Are they still the same?' and then always asked to *justify* his answer. Stage I children (about 4—5 years) say that there is now either *more* (because it is wider for example) or *less* (because it is thinner); Stage IIA children (about 6—7 years) give answers that veer between conservation and non-conservation and Stage IIB children (about 7—8 years) affirm conservation. However if the question is 'Do they still *weigh* the same?' Stage II children rely on the visual appearance and say, for example, that the coil is heavier than the ball because it is longer. At Stage IIIA (about 8—10 years) there are intermediate reactions and only at Stage IIIB (about 10—12 years) is it confidently asserted that both shapes weigh the same. Only very rarely is one told in these books how many children were tested or the proportion of successes or failures. Nevertheless it is fair to say that replication by other workers has largely found the same kind of pattern.

Piaget was here concerned with the process whereby the child's thinking about concrete phenomena attains a state of internal equilibrium, with this concept now being applied to the relations between the thoughts of the child rather than between the child's thought and other peoples' thought. He had developed from his study of sensorimotor intelligence the belief that thinking is essentially the manipulation of interiorised actions, so each thought could now be seen as an *operation*, for example, thinking that one pencil is longer than another. But thoughts do not attain the status of concrete knowledge until they are coordinated with each other in an equilibrated system. Thoughts which are unequilibrated have no fundamental advantage over perceptions: the mind centres on how things look but this information remains unstructured—every thought is a separate entity rather than an element within a structure-of-the-whole.* The Stage I child *centres his thought* (Piaget's term) on the appearance of the lump of clay, sees that it is longer and then immediately concludes that there is more clay; another child centres his thought on the decreased width and judges the quantity to be reduced. A Stage IIA child alternates between the two; which is just as if weights were being added to one side of the mental balance and then to the other in an uncoordinated fashion. Naturally, Piaget employs his notion of the necessary reversibility of thought to characterise what is required for equilibrium. Metaphorically, for thought to attain reversibility in the first child there must be added simultaneously to the other side of the mental balance 'but thinner means less', and in the case of the second 'but longer means more', and in the case of the third, this balancing of gain against loss is made a logical rather than a pragmatic process.

Naturally Piaget did not wish to explain the development from what he called *intuitive*, (or 'perception-like') thought to *concrete operational* thinking by a metaphor. The aim was to give a formal, algebraic account of the mental structures which become established between about 7 and 11 years of age. The reason why he deemed a structural account to be necessary rather than one which treated matters such as conservation as contingent and having no necessary connection with other concrete truths, or one which regarded the eventual belief in conservation as due to the maturation of an innate predisposition, should be evident by now. But Piaget did more than just state that the knowledge the child acquired around this age was structured as a group. He held this also to be a model of the child's actual mental structures, which were developed by *his own constructive activity, not from internalising rules used by the adult*. Thus

---

*Piaget wrote a short synthesis of his work up to 1949 published as *The Psychology of Intelligence* (1950) which contains an excellent discussion of the growth of concrete operational thinking and its relation to perception.

each child was seen as constructing logicality anew: a consequence of Piaget's coming much closer to recapitulation theory than ever Baldwin did.

Piaget had already extracted the characteristics of equilibrium in mental structures from the mathematical group which had been previously used to explain sensorimotor space development, but a model of the actual structures was required. To this end Piaget and his associates, around the late 1930s, developed the *grouping**('groupment') which contains properties of the group but also of the lattice, as the model had to cover relations as well as operations.

Viewing what was required of the grouping model in an *a priori* fashion, it had to encompass the following facts about concrete thinking: it deals with (1) either classes or relations by (2) either adding or multiplying them in (3) either a symmetrical (one-one) or an asymmetrical (one-many) manner; which makes $(2 \times 2 \times 2 =)$ 8 groupings. (There is also a ninth possible grouping; see Flavell (1963)). Taking each one of them in turn, Grouping I, the symmetrical addition of classes, is the relating of subclasses to the total class. One task which Piaget has used to test for this grouping is known as the 'class inclusion problem' (see Piaget and Inhelder, 1964). A typical example of this is when the child is shown a set of 17 brown beads and 3 white beads and is asked 'Are there more brown beads or more beads?'. The usual answer below about 7 years of age is that there are more brown beads. The reader might try to analyse for himself the disequilibrium represented by such an answer and by some of the other examples of concrete operational tasks which will be described. In this case there is lack of reversibility (centration of thought on the major subclass cannot be reversed), associativity (the thought is not 'free' to detour from the major to the minor as well as minor to major subclass), composition (the subclasses cannot be composed to make the class) and so on. Notice here, as throughout preoperational thinking, the domination of thought by perceptual appearance: the child is asked about something being 'more', he sees more brown than white beads and judges on the basis of what is perceptually obvious.

Grouping II, the asymmetrical addition of classes, means that there is in principle more than one way of dividing a class into subclasses. Although no test of this has been designed this would

---

* A fifth quality, of *tautology*, is found in the groupings: A + A = A (see pages 103–4).

involve the child knowing that, for example, when faced with a group of red and blue squares and red and blue triangles that there could be two simultaneous classifications of 'red and blue things' and 'square and triangular things'. Grouping III, the symmetrical multiplication of classes, refers to the cognitive ability to establish a matrix of correlation. Psychological studies of this have often involved the establishment of a one-to-one correlation in seriation, such as matching a series of dolls graded in height against a similarly graded series of walking sticks (Piaget, 1952). Grouping IV, the asymmetrical multiplication of classes is like the former but that the type of correlation is one-many. Tests of this are conceivable but have yet to be constructed. Grouping V, the asymmetrical addition of relations involves what is generally known as *transitive* reasoning ($A > B$; $B > C$ therefore $A > C$). Here the child can be shown that a red stick is longer than a green stick ($A > B$) then shown that the green stick is longer than a blue stick ($B > C$) then asked about the relation between the red and the blue stick ($A?C$). Transitive relationships can also be extracted from Grouping VI, the symmetrical addition of relations, but this time the relations would be such as 'equals' ($A = B$; $B = C$ therefore $A = C$) or 'brother of' (X is the brother of Y; Y is the brother of Z; therefore X is Z's brother). In this context it is worth recalling that Piaget had shown in *Judgment and Reasoning in the Child* that young children cannot appreciate symmetrical relations such as 'brother of' and will affirm that Johnny has a brother but deny that his brother has a brother.

The structural model of the *conservations* (substance, weight, quantity, length, area, volume) is found in Grouping VII, the symmetrical multiplication of relations. Increases in one dimension are compensated for by decreases in another so that some property perdures ($A \downarrow \times B \uparrow = k$). For Grouping VIII, the asymmetrical multiplication of relations, no psychological tests have been constructed.

The groupings are also meant to characterise the child's knowledge of space and time on the conceptual plane (in this context usually referred to as the 'infralogical' groupings), for this too must possess an operational structure. For example, if when the preoperational child is asked to select a photograph of what a model landscape looks like to another child he selects the photograph that shows his *own* viewpoint (Piaget and Inhelder, 1956), we can do more than call this 'egocentrism', and relate it to an assimilation–accommodation disequilibrium. This child's thought lacks fundamentally the same kind of structural properties as does that of the child who fails problems of class inclusion, conservation, transitivity and so on.

The system of concrete operations has the major disadvantage that it can only deal with actualities, not possibilities, with what *is* the case rather than what *could be* the case. The concrete operational child is still unable to think hypothetically, to construct a system of propositions which enables him to project his thought into the future. The system of *formal operations* which gets underway during adolescence can be construed as the performance of operations *on* operations—manipulating the various states of concrete reality that could obtain. In *The Growth of Logical Thinking from Childhood to Adolescence* (1958) Inhelder and Piaget presented children and adolescents with a set of problems to test their ability to construct and test hypotheses by holding one factor in a situation constant and varying another, that is, to manipulate sets of propositions. One problem was to discover the factor or factors determining the speed of oscillation of a pendulum: it could be the heaviness of the weight, the length of the arm or some combination of both. They were given two weights and two lengths of string and told to proceed. In order to perform this task it is necessary to hold one of the factors constant, vary the other and then do the inverse. Concrete operational children fail at these kinds of tasks because they tend to try unsystematically various combinations of factors (heavy weight plus short string for example), and when they *witness* a fast swing they judge immediately that the combination of factors which produced this determines speed, without testing whether only one of them is responsible. Thus, there is still at the concrete stage a strong perceptual influence on thinking. (In fact, speed is independent of weight and increases with decreasing length of the arm.)

We will do little more than give the flavour of Piaget's structural model of formal operational thinking. Piaget employs propositional logic to give the set of the combinations of propositions which can be mapped onto the world and then employs a different kind of group to characterise the state of equilibrium which must obtain between these combinations. Propositional logic has two terms to denote different propositions which can be combined in various ways: p (for example, 'it is raining') and q ('it is wet'). Naturally more than two propositions can be combined at one time but two are sufficient to show the principles whereby propositions relate to each other. Given p and q

and their negations, not p ($-p$) and not q ($-q$) there are four possible associations of the propositions ($p\&q;$ $p\&-q,$ $-p\&q;$ $-p\&-q$) and there are sixteen states of reality that these combinations could produce, ranging from the impossibility of any of them obtaining to the possibility of any of them obtaining. These are known as the sixteen binary combinations and in them the associations are combined *disjunctively* (by the copula 'or') so that each of the combinations presents the alternatives that could hold in reality. Only one of the sixteen combinations can obtain given that p and q refer to real propositions. If we take the case of the pendulum problem and make p the heavy weight $-p$ the light weight, q the long piece of string and $-q$ the short then the only one of the 16 combinations that gives us what we want is '($-p\&-q$) or ($p\&-q$).'

According to Piaget, that the adolescent is able to come up with this answer implies that he can not only map the set of binary combinations on to the world but that he can relate them in a group, just as the concrete operational child was able not only to centre his thought on the total set of dimensions in the concrete situation (increasing height, decreasing width and so on) but could coordinate them in a reversible system. Testing possible combinations of propositions systematically entails the ability to coordinate them in a lawlike manner. Piaget used the mathematical *four-group* to characterise this state of equilibrium, the details of which need not detain us. The main point is that, like the groupings, the four-group consists of a system of transformations which retain the equilibrium within a system: the identity (I), negation (N), reciprocal (R), and correlative (C) transformations. These transformations are interrelated within a closed system such that the application of any two of them to a propositional operation is equivalent to the solitary application of only one of them.

Piaget did for a number of years become so enmeshed in the logico-mathematical implications of these structural models that he seemed to lose sight of their proposed relation to cognitive processes. Much of his writing on logic has not been translated into English. This almost obsessive excursion into the rarified heights of formal logic might almost be regarded as Piaget's becoming a victim of the intellectual 'autism' which he had so long feared; but it must be said in defence that Piaget's epistemology is so dependent on logico-mathematical structures and the claims he makes in this area are so far-reaching that it was necessary to examine the formal foundations of the system to ensure that they could support this weight. Certainly Piaget and his associates have produced a wealth of material since 1960 which is of much wider interest and which consolidates, clarifies or extends the system. The experimental volumes on perception (Piaget, 1969), mental imagery (Piaget and Inhelder, 1971), and memory (Piaget and Inhelder, 1973), the work on theoretical biology (Piaget, 1971a) and the three short books on genetic epistemology (Piaget, 1970; 1972a; 1972b) will be briefly mentioned in rather a catalogue fashion to give something of a cross section of the relatively recent developments in the system. Broader aspects such as Piaget's views on structuralism (Piaget 1971b) and on European philosophy (Piaget, 1972c) will be mentioned in Part 4.

In *The Mechanisms of Perception* Piaget reports research carried out with a large number of collaborators on visual illusions, size constancy and on movement, speed and time perception in children and adults. As regards the relation between the growth of perceptual abilities and intelligence Piaget presents his view that intelligence develops autonomously out of action and that the operations of intelligence enrich the structures of perception. Yet perceptual activity *prefigures* the mental operations in that seeing things as they really are is achieved by a preoperational, perceptual centring, decentring and recentring to counterbalance the deforming influence of fixating on one part of a figure. In these terms he also offers a general theory of the visual illusions. The prefiguration of functions at lower levels is, of course, fundamental to Piaget's theory; with another example being the sensorimotor prefiguration of the notions of space, time and causality not acquired on the conceptual place till the concrete operational stage. In an important final chapter Piaget characterises his theory as a Kantian resolution between associationism ('geneticism without structure') and Gestalt theory ('structuralism without genesis').

Mental imagery, which Piaget studied on the operational level in *Mental Imagery in the Child*, is in a sense, intermediate between perception and intelligence. The main result of the set of experiments presented here is that it is not until the concrete operational stage (after about 7 years of age) that the child can form mental images of the successive states of transformations of a set-up such as a square rotating on a pivot through 360°, a row of three coloured beads rotating around the middle one, a straight line falling through 90°. The child's ability to form the images was usually assessed by his reconstructing or drawing the display. The main reason for the dependence of mental imagery on operations is that only through operations can the child imagine transformations or displacements of static states: transformations are precisely what the operational structures deal in. Yet at the same time images are necessary for full operational functioning: anticipatory imagery completes the understanding of physical transformations, and imagery provides, in the spatial field, a kind of rough sketch (a 'schema') on the basis of which the operations can extend understanding. Piaget further stresses the necessity for imaginal symbolism in the functioning of the language system and the inadequacy of language as a representational medium without symbolic imagery. In the final section on the epistemology of the image Piaget deploys his operational arguments against the Platonic view, found amongst some mathematicians and logicians, that knowledge is a kind of copy of abstract ideal entities not of perceptible reality. Imagery, he argues, is necessary for knowledge.

It might be regarded as somewhat surprising, especially in view of the current state of cognitive psychology, that one rarely finds Piaget using the word 'memory'. This is obviously not due to neglect on Piaget's part, but to the fact that a theorist who regards the individual as constructing a model of reality through active interaction with the world rather than by coming to record and store in his brain information about an already structured reality, is not going to treat memory as a distinct field from intelligence: by studying the latter one is *ipso facto* studying the former. Piaget puts the aim of his study *Memory and Intelligence* concisely: 'The central idea of this book is that the memory is not simply a mechanical function of successful or unsuccessful coding and decoding processes, but that it is basically dependent on the nature of the code which, far from being static, changes in accordance with the preoperational or operational structures, and hence with the schemes proper to the intelligence' (Piaget and Inhelder, 1973, p. 62). Thus Piaget and his associates were able to present evidence of children's memory for displays *improving* over a period of months with operational development (for a serial row of sticks for example) and of systematic distortions of memory in older children not found in younger (for two matchstick configurations for example) so long as cognising the original display clearly involved operative processes.

One of Piaget's main criticisms of contemporary psychologists who would consider the volumes just reviewed purely in terms of their relevance to 'experimental psychology' is that they have lost sight of the fact that knowledge is a biological phenomenon. In *Biology and Knowledge* he reiterates this point and levels a similar charge of isolationism against biologists and philosophers. This is a work of vast scale and far-reaching intellectual significance which sets out Piaget's position more definitively than any of his publications in the past ten years.

One concept which is now absolutely fundamental to Piaget's system is that of *autoregulation*. Autoregulation is what all levels of biological and cognitive life share; it is the ability of a biological, behavioural or cognitive unit to maintain equilibrium between itself and the environment. 'Life', Piaget says 'is essentially autoregulation' (1971a, p. 26). The genetic system enabling the species to adapt to the environment, the embryo developing, the manifestation of more or less instinctive behaviour in animals, the infant acting on objects, the perceptual system centring and recentring, the equilibration of operations in middle childhood and adolescence, the scientist developing a theory, *any* kind of biological or intellectual function or structure involves autoregulation, an equilibrating interaction with the environment. Although this idea should be familiar we now have a term to encompass what these equilibrations have in common and to state the hypothesis boldly. From this position we might separate the two derived themes treated in the work: phylogenetic adaptation is an interactive process between the genome and the environment; there are functional and structural isomorphisms between the different levels of biological and cognitive processes.

As regards the first theme, we have already seen how Baldwin's orthoplasy principle (for a discussion of the 'Baldwin effect' see V. Grant's *The Origin of Adaptation* (1963), pp. 137–39) and Piaget's arguments in *The Origins of Intelligence in the Child* attempted some kind of resolution between the mutationism of Darwinian theory and Lamarckian theory which held that characteristics acquired during the organism's lifetime could become heritable. (This was seen as an aspect of the genetic epistemological concern to resolve innatism and environmentalism—rationalism and empiricism—by an inter-actional theory.) In this regard Piaget makes extensive use of the evolutionary theory of the British geneticist and embryologist C. H. Waddington (1957) who presents a very similar account to Piaget's. The central idea is that one of the results of natural selection is to increase the probability that all members of the same species will develop in the same way regardless of minor environmental variations during development. To ensure this, the reactions of the embryo to its early environment are 'canalised' by *regulative* processes. To give an example of this, there must be regulative processes at work which ensure that although all the cells of the body are similar in genotype they develop into distinct phenotypical categories of bone cells, nerve cells, muscle cells and so on. Therefore natural selection not only acts on mutants in an all-or-none fashion, but also cuts from the genotype to the phenotype pathways along which development flows. This is because the production of one definite end result (for example, male or female rather than hermaphrodite) is of selective advantage.

How would this apply to a case like that of the mollusk *Limnaea stagnalis*, which Piaget studied, to explain how it came to develop a morphology which was adapted to two kinds of environment? The evolution of the mollusk would have become canalised in the following way. When the elongated variety was exposed to the rougher water it proved of selective advantage to contract efficiently and at a low stimulus threshold and that there should be one specific kind of contraction to deal with the new environment. Therefore, natural selection modified the regulative processes in development so that a contraction of a *uniform character* would be produced to a wide range of stimuli. But this contraction would still be a response to the environment, not genetically fixed. To explain how this could occur Waddington introduced the concept of *genetic assimilation*. In this case it would work by random mutation taking over the role of a contraction-causing stimulus so that the shortened, globular form became part of the genotype; a process which one geneticist referred to as 'being comparable to being sewn into one's winter underwear'.

Waddington's principle means the organism accommodating to the environment and assimilating the results of this accommodation to its genetic structure. The principle is also cybernetic: the genetic system of the embryo receives feedback from its immediate environment in order to regulate its development. The relation between the phenotype and the environment is interactional, not only because the responses it makes lead to canalisation of development from genotype to phenotype, but also because the developed organism is able to *select its environment* (if there is no food in one location the herd may move to another). It should be pointed out however that Waddington's theory is certainly controversial and that there might be a mutationist explanation for his demonstration of genetic assimilation in the laboratory (see Maynard-Smith, 1966). What Piaget does is to extend these ideas to present a highly speculative account of how the genetic system of the organism might be regulating growth in accordance with environmental features and contingencies.

As regards the other theme of the book which involves the presence of functional and structural isomorphisms between the biological and the cognitive levels, Piaget writes 'while these functional correspondences we are going to talk about will supply some indication of effective continuity in functioning, the structural isomorphisms that we may single out will not necessarily be a proof of direct or lineal filiation. Rather, they are likely to be a disjointed series of convergent reconstructions, which will, moreover, *be much more interesting* as far as relations between life and cognitive functions are concerned' (*op. cit.*, p. 147, my italics). We saw before that organisation and adaptation are common to both biological and cognitive phenomena. As regards *organisation*, one example of a functional isomorphism is that there is a factor of conservation present in the organisation of the genome from generation to generation, a constant, regulated part—whole relationship which is also present in cognitive functioning, as we have seen. An example of a structural isomorphism in organisation is inclusion, or the hierarchical structure, which is found in such biological phenomena as the organisation of the genetic system, the succession of embryonic stages, physiological assimilation, all behaviour, and is at the same time at the heart of the coordination of logical operations (for example class inclusion and Grouping I). Other examples of structural isomorphisms include order and multiplication structures. As regards the isomorphisms of *adaptation* there is assimilation and accommodation, the 'two functional poles set in opposition to each other' and the presence of schemes at all levels. The regulations themselves, of course, represent another aspect of organic/cognitive isomorphism from the regulatory genes or 'repressors', the regulation of the endocrine system by hormones, to the regulation of centrations of thought by a system of concrete operations.

Two other examples give an indication of the radical nature of Piaget's use of the notion of isomorphisms between levels. We have seen how the equilibration of mental structures enables the child to anticipate the result of transformations, allied to anticipatory imagery; there is also logical anticipation in the development of deductive foresight. Here we have an isomorphism with organic anticipations similar to the appearance of calluses in the ostrich embryo* in the rump area before the animal ever sits, and the patterns of instinctive behaviour, first studied by such ethologists as Lorenz and Tinbergen, which are more dependent on the genetic programme than on acquired information. There are also isomorphisms between levels of behaviour, the neural and the cognitive for instance. Here Piaget cites the work of McCulloch and Pitts who showed that the nervous system functions in accordance with the structure of an algebraic lattice. An analysis of neuronal connections revealed that their functioning could be characterised in terms of the 16 binary combinations of propositions which we encountered in Piaget's model of the formal operations appearing during adolescence.

Much of the book presents the biological face of Piaget's genetic epistemology: that man's cognitive capacities represent *reflective abstraction* of lower level functions and structures, which extends and completes them but can never become independent of them—in general that what we know and how we come to know it exists in the biological world rather than in some autonomous world of thought. The philosophical face of his genetic epistemology is represented in three short books which at first blush seem almost identical (one reviewer suggested that Piaget had been caught up in a circular reaction!)—*Genetic Epistemology*, *Psychology and Epistemology*, and *The Principles of Genetic Epistemology*. Although their themes are identical they diverge in style of presentation and in the aspects emphasised: the first contains the substance of four lectures (delivered at Columbia) so the style is relatively untechnical and the outlines bold; in the second Piaget is more concerned with the role of genetic epistemology in encouraging interdisciplinary cooperation in science, in employing developmental psychology as a 'supplementary instrument' for tackling fundamental conceptual questions in the exact sciences, and in disposing of 'static' philosophical epistemology; the third is perhaps the most austere and contains a summary of the psychological and biological aspects and a fairly formal investigation of the epistemology of logic, mathematics and physics.

*This is Waddington's main example of the evolution of a character that it is not feasible to explain by mutationism, but which can be explained by genetic assimilation.

As we saw in the Introduction, the philosopher has approached the explanation of knowledge by asking type (1) and type (2) questions (p. 2). Piaget treats the various answers, from Plato to Bergson, as being of historical interest but obsolete and suggests that the reason why philosophical epistemology developed as it did is to be found in the theories themselves—Plato's transcendent realism, Descartes' innate ideas, Kant's *a priori* limits and so on. Such conceptions became outdated, argues Piaget, since it came to be realised that knowledge is a process and not a state. Thus the current state of the sciences should be regarded as an episode in the progressive acquisition of knowledge by the race and should be studied as one aspect of the movement from lesser to greater knowledge, of which developmental psychology and biogenesis are the others. Just as there is structural and functional parallelism between biogenesis and psychogenesis so there is a parallelism between psychogenesis and the acquisition of knowledge by the race. In this way the study of cognitive development extends beyond psychology insofar as it reflects the resolution of fundamental scientific problems in the mind of the developing individual. Furthermore, because knowledge is a process, an understanding of its nature cannot be attained by armchair reflection but must be set against hard data on how the individual develops in the real world rather than how he reasons in some transcendental world. This is hardly a new position for Piaget for it dates back to his childhood dissatisfaction with Bergson. It can also be seen as early as 1952 in *The Child's Conception of Number* where he takes issue with the Russell and Whitehead definition of number in their *Principia Mathematica*; with Russell again and with the logical positivists in *The Psychology of Intelligence* (1950).

It is a mistake to construe Piaget as holding that the basic assumptions of *scientific and logico-mathematical* theories can be validated or invalidated by developmental data. He is saying rather that because there are developmental processes which are universal in the human mind and in the scientific community in their adaptation to, more correctly 'construction of', reality, the resolutions of problems on the child level may prefigure or illuminate their means of resolution on the scientific level (see the horizontal arrow in the figure on page 2). The rather 'stand up–knock down' style of some of the arguments in *Genetic Epistemology* may suggest this misinterpretation, but Piaget's treatment of number, space, time, velocity and chance in *Psychology and Epistemology* (pp. 6–16) presents the position less ambiguously. Moreover the rejection of Russell's definition of number does not arise out of empirical findings but begins from general logical considerations as to the necessary place of serial order in number which is reflected in his work on the role of seriation in number development. There is, however, the suggestion of invalidating purely *philosophical* theories in this way. He rejects the logical positivists' viewpoint that the rules of logic are nothing other than the rules of language in the light of his discovery of sensorimotor logic in the human infant which precedes language use and also in the light of work which others have carried out on the logical capacities of profoundly deaf children. Piaget's point is not so much that the logical positivist doctrine contains implicit empirical assumptions which came to be invalidated but that it is, in principle, fruitless to speculate about the relation between logic and language without reference to the development of actual logical behaviour and language use.

Although Piaget denied that there are two separate, watertight compartments of epistemological and of genetic issues he did not contend that the distinction simply dissolves. For the consequence of this would be that no distinction between philosophical and psychological issues *could* be made and that there would exist a grey area of issues which came under neither field. Piaget's aims (though not his conclusions) in his genetic epistemology were much the same as Baldwin's. Baldwin said that the genetic logic of the real does not distinguish between thought and reality but 'studies the actual movement of thought as a genetically built up and evolving reality'. If thought and external reality are viewed as counterpoints in a developing dialectic then a distinction between the genetic course of the dialectic and its results at any one period will be an *intellectual convention* rather than a fundamental logical division. However, as we shall be discussing at length in Part 4, this convention forms part of the framework within which we try to understand ourselves and is thus far from arbitrary.

In conclusion one notable feature of the development of Piaget's theory is that the basic hypotheses and the concern with structures were present from the start. It might be viewed as consolidation and extension rather than as cumulative grouping, as dialectical interchange or as progressive revision (as in Freud for example). Piaget likes to say that he himself is the main reviser of Piaget's theory, yet it is significant that he has never actually recanted on the earlier work and he still refers to books written over 40 years ago in his current studies. Thus, the overviews that he has presented of his theory in the past 10 years may differ on points of emphasis from the original development of the notions (little use of circular reactions in Piaget and Inhelder, 1969; emphasis on the distinction between figurative and operative thinking and between simple and reflective abstraction in Piaget, 1970), but the theory has not really changed. Also Piaget does not revise the theory so much as assimilate elements into it which are presented by others as contradictory (for example, the Russian psychologist Vygotsky's work on the socialised nature of 'egocentric' speech); and this with surprisingly little need for accommodation!

I shall present a critique of genetic epistemology in Part 4 and comparisons between Baldwin's and Piaget's genetic epistemologies will also be left until then. But first I shall examine the wide interface between Piagetian theory and present-day psychology in order to show how genetic and epistemological issues interdepend within empirical research.

Part 3

Experiments

This part is not intended to be a review of experimentation testing Piaget's theory, which would be a mammoth undertaking, neither does it always give an up-to-the-minute report on the current state of the field. The aim is rather to present certain recent studies as exemplars of fundamental problems encountered in testing hypotheses about the acquisition of knowledge.

Genetic epistemology proposes that philosophical and developmental issues are mutually dependent. If this is the case, then, to the extent that the psychologist sets out to study the growth of *knowledge* rather than the progressive accumulation of *skills*, no matter how empirical the spirit in which his research is undertaken he should not only encounter epistemological dilemmas but should find himself almost willy-nilly assuming or even proposing epistemological theses. Among the epistemological problems I shall consider are the interpretation of behavioural criteria for states of knowledge; the role of memory, imagery and justification in knowledge; the differentiation between efficacious information-processing and the knowledge that something is the case; the relation between having a cognitive capacity and having conscious knowledge of a truth; the relation between structure and function within an account of language and the forms of knowledge required for, and expressed within, language use.

3.1 OBJECT PERMANENCE

The two problems that will be discussed here are the nature of the justifications that we have for attributing to the infant knowledge of the continuing existence of an invisible object, and the degree to which we can use weakness of 'memory' to explain the infant's failures on object permanence tests.

We have seen that, on the basis of research with his own children, Piaget proposed that only after about 8 months of age, or during sensorimotor Stage 4, does the infant retrieve objects that are completely hidden. His explanation for this was that previously the infant took the existence of the image (of an object) to be a result of the movements which he made to keep it in sight. The advance after 8 months is due to his having learned that this 'tactile image' can be retrieved by moving the thing which had, as it were, swallowed it up, through the coordination of secondary schemes; thus representing a higher degree of accommodation to the object's independent existence.

In his book *Development in Infancy* (1974) T. G. R. Bower has reviewed a number of experiments, mostly his own, which he takes as suggesting that there is also an important advance after about 5 months. It should be said at the outset that, no matter how the studies are interpreted, Bower's book demonstrates the exciting results which can be obtained in infancy research by employing sophisticated apparatus, results which could not have been achieved by the more homely techniques available to Piaget. Yet the technology is only at the service of the experimenter's skill and creativity and in this book ingenious experiments abound, linked in a tight network of argument. After about 20 weeks, he argues, the infant knows of the continuing existence of an object *behind* an occluder but not *inside* an occluder. Let us first examine the evidence that Bower gives for his conclusion and then attend to the question of whether it allows us to attribute knowledge of object permanence to the infant. Here are the experiments, with the relevant controls and some of the intermediate steps omitted (see Bower, 1974, pp. 180–211).

(1) Infants much younger than 8 months were more surprised (index: drop in heart rate) when an object that they saw move behind a screen did *not* reappear on removing the screen than when it did (Bower, 1966), thus indicating that they 'did believe that the hidden object still existed even though it was out of sight' (*op. cit.*, p. 189).

(2) Infants as young as 8 weeks will anticipate the reappearance of an object from behind a screen, tracking the movement with their eyes to the exit side of the screen.

(3) When infants between 12 and 20 weeks see a moving object stop, they continue to track along the same path of movement; these infants continue to track along the expected path of movement when an object moves off in a new direction and continue to track the same path of movement when the object is 'magically' transformed (by an arrangement of mirrors) into another object. Bower argues that the infant below 20 weeks thinks that one object is the same object so long as it keeps moving along the same path; if it changes direction or stops it is a different object. However, because the infant above 20 weeks does not produce these behaviours he is taken as not believing this.

(4) Infants between 12 and 20 weeks also believe that an object is the same object so long as it stays in the same place irrespective of

changes in its appearance. The clearest demonstration of this is that they will not look for their mother when a replacement object appears in her place. Similarly, when presented with multiple images of the mother (one real and two virtual for example), the infant above 20 weeks is disturbed, but the younger infant quite happily interacts with each of the mothers in turn because he does not know that an object can only be in one place at a time. Overall, the infant above 20 weeks has coordinated the 'place' and 'movement' criteria for object identity.

(5) Mundy-Castle and Anglin (1969) employed a piece of apparatus which consisted of a large board with four portholes in a square formation. A round object appeared at each of the portholes in turn as if it were moving behind in a clockwise rotation. The aim was to see whether infants could track the invisible, curving movement from place to place. Twelve-week-old infants could perform simple side-to-side and up-and-down tracking, but the older ones could actually interpolate an invisible, curving trajectory whose form was dependent on the latency between appearances. For example, for a long latency between the top two holes the infant looked in a high, steep curve, and for a short one the curve was low and flat.

Therefore by the end of the first 20 weeks of life, although he fails the standard object permanence problem, the infant 'as judged by his eye movements and startle responses knows a great deal about objects. The infant knows that objects exist when occluded by a screen. He knows how to identify objects by their features as well as by their location. He knows seen objects are tangible and he can infer how an object gets from one place to another' (*op. cit.*, p. 203). Why then, if the infant knows all this does he fail the standard test? First, Bower produces evidence that simple inability to organise a motor response for the purpose is not responsible. He considers an explanation in terms of the Piagetian notion of *déclage* (in this case, horizontal *déclage*) which refers to the repetition of a function on a different developmental level. Thus he may know of the existence of the object on the level of eye movements but not on the level of hand movements: 'The conceptual knowledge that controls eye movements may have to be reformulated at a different level in order to control hand movements' (*op. cit.*, p. 205). At Stage 4 there is a similar mistake at a higher level where the infant will look for an object where it was last found irrespective of its recent movement to another location which he witnessed—the 'place' error. Bower suggests that the *déclage* between success at 5 months and at 8 months can be accounted for by the fact that before 8 months the infant can appreciate the occlusion of one object *behind* another but not *inside* another, because not until this time does he have the rule 'Two objects cannot be in the same place at the same time unless one is inside the other'. He quotes two pieces of evidence for this: infants who fail the standard object permanence test succeed in grasping an object if the room is plunged into darkness before they begin reaching for it; and that similar infants can retrieve an object from behind a screen if the screen is exactly between infant and object rather than in the same place as the object (*op. cit.*, pp. 207–10).

Bower supports Piagetian principles overall and later presents a very interesting training study in support of some form of assimilation–accommodation model of learning in infancy against an S–R account, but the explanation he is presenting here is radically different from Piaget's. The main difference is that he, quite unequivocally, talks about *knowledge* the infant possesses of the object's continuing existence. For Piaget, however, the infant has not separated existence from his own action till the *end* of the sensori-motor stage. Of course it is often convenient to talk about what an infant or an animal 'knows', 'understands' and so on as a kind of shorthand description of what it can do, and in such a context it is mere semantic nit-picking to take exception to it. But in the present case it looks very much as if the ascription of knowledge is determining the form of explanation offered, which thus proves to be more of a description than an explanation.

Let us go through each of the peices of evidence in turn to see whether we are justified in ascribing knowledge of object permanence. In (1), the fact that the infant is more surprised at non-reappearance minimally implies that he is anticipating reappearance of an *image*. When, in the past, one image had dissolved into another, movement of the remaining image had resulted in the reappearance of the first image. In (2) anticipation of reappearance on the other side of the screen is just that; it has no necessary implications for knowledge of invisible, enduring existence. As regards (3) and (4) the fact that the infant above 20 weeks has coordinated place and movement as criteria for (to us) 'object' identity surely has no implications for his knowledge of existence when the object is invisible; rather two broad schemes have been coordinated. Now (5) (the demonstration of trajectory interpolation) is really a remarkable finding. It even appears to imply a primitive creativity on the part of the infant in producing a trajectory which could be responsible for an appearance—reappearance sequence and is the strongest of the five pieces of evidence for knowledge of object permanence. And yet there is a more parsimonious account which would view this on the model of (3), (continuing to track along the path of movement of a stopped object). In the present case the much older infant is applying a piece of information which he has assimilated to the scheme of watching the occlusion of moving objects: the longer the interval of occlusion the longer the occluded path. For example, he might see that daddy takes longer to reappear from behind the garden wall than from behind the garden shed; thus he interpolates a long path of trajectory for long intervals and vice versa. Of course, as adults we tend to regard it as nonsensical that there could be conception of movement without corresponding conception of a solid, enduring thing moving, but this is because we live in a world of solid enduring things. What the infant's continuing failure at object permanence problems tells us is that we *cannot* assume that he does. If, as Bower has himself shown, the infant below 20 weeks of age will follow the nonexistent trajectory of a stopped object, why should not an older infant construct a trajectory of *only movement* without any implication of his believing that there is a thing moving? In fact this looks like a *déclage* of an *error*: separating movement from the object at a higher developmental level.

It is precisely because Bower prematurely ascribes knowledge of object permanence to the infant that he is then faced with 'an apparent contradiction between the *knowledge available* to the infant to control his eye movements and the *knowledge available* to the infant to control his hand movements' (*op. cit.*, p. 206; my italics). This contradiction is insoluble by explanation; only a description can encompass the difference because, as knowledge has been assumed, its explanation has been short-circuited. To say that the difference between the 5 to 8-month-old infant and the 8 to 12-month-old infant is that the latter knows that one object can be inside another as well as behind it is to give the most parsimonious description available of the developmental data. It implies nothing about how the infant might move from one plane to another. However to say as Piaget does, that the 8-month-old infant has acquired a procedure, through the coordination of schemes, for making tactile perceptions reappear *is* an explanation: it is what the infant *does* which results in the acquisition of the ability. As soon as we ascribe knowledge however, albeit in a relatively primitive form, we have blocked further developmental explanation simply because knowledge is what has to be explained.

However Bower does support Piaget experimentally and theoretically in agreeing that conflict between schemes, as a spur to accommodation, is an energiser of sensorimotor development—conflict rather than the cumulative acquisition of experience. But for Bower this conflict has to be (because of what has gone before) not between behaviours '*but is entirely inside the infant's head between incompatible ways of understanding the event*' (*op. cit.*, p. 236; my italics). Again a behavioural interpretation in terms of success and failure rather than a cognitive one in terms of truth and falsity is infinitely more parsimonious. We *can* characterise movement between the stages in terms of beliefs (for example, that two objects cannot be in the same place simultaneously) but we can also characterise it behaviourally in terms of the infant acting so as to recreate a 'tactile image' (to us: 'object'): intentions can be ascribed rather than specific kinds of understanding. The conflict is brought about by the inevitable failures to which this leads (such as the place error)—as Baldwin says, by the *refractoriness* of the real world—leading to accommodation. As regards the general question of the ascription of mental states to nonverbal creatures it is well to bear in mind Lloyd Morgan's canon that one should always aim for the lowest level of explanation for a piece of behaviour and never introduce reference to psychological states which are not needed by this explanation—a kind of psychogenetic Occam's Razor!

✎ As Bower's epistemology certainly tends towards the rationalist it would be relevant to insert at this point something about the *a priori* possibility of innate knowledge of object permanence. First of all no one would wish to quarrel with the notion that there may be innate predispositions in the motoric or perceptual repertoire to acquire object permanence. One such perceptual predisposition seems to be revealed in the finding that very young infants display surprise when the elements of a symmetrical figure break up after moving along together (Bower, 1965) which suggests that the infant may be preset to cognise the 'common fate' (a Gestaltist principle) of the elements of an object. But for object *permanence* to be innate would entail the infant's being programmed to immediately evince the knowledge—

not acquire it—that objects exist independently of his perception of them. The question is: can such a programme be established prior to any experience? Berkeley did not even believe that it existed after cognitive development was complete! It is at this point that a traditional philosophical dilemma arises and the wrangling between rationalists and empiricists appears to be of more than 'merely' historical importance.

Specifically, the reason why Piaget does not ascribe knowledge of object permanence to the Stage 4 infant is, of course, the existence of the place error: his searching for an object in its previous location, although he has witnessed its transformation to another location, which implies that he has still not separated existence from the movements he makes to accommodate to it. Now it is quite possible to argue, indeed it is, given the current state of cognitive psychology, an inevitable objection, that these errors can be accounted for by failures of *memory*. Even the Stage 3 errors, some would argue, may be explained by saying that as soon as the object disappears from sight it is being forgotten. In the case of the Stage 4 error the infant is only remembering the location where the object was found last—after all, do not adults make the same kind of mistake in moments of absentmindedness? Might infants just be more 'absentminded' than adults?

Harris (1973) performed an experiment on the place error which presented a version of the memory objection. Infants of 10 months were shown two hiding places. A on the left and B on the right, which were curtained compartments. They were allowed to retrieve a stop-watch from behind curtain A a few times and then saw it hidden at B. Harris found that returning to A was especially common under the following condition of hiding the object behind B: both curtains were open, the watch was put into compartment B and the curtain closed, *then* the curtain was closed over the empty compartment at A. His interpretation was that the infant's storage of the information that the object had been hidden at B is especially susceptible to interference and the most interfering experience in this situation is seeing the empty compartment at A after closure of B, because this location had previously been associated with correct search. This experience proactively interferes with storage of the new conceal-ment. Why is the information so vulnerable? Harris suggests that immaturity of the frontal cortex is responsible for this.

This hypothesis receives some support from the findings that the place error is very rare if the infant is allowed to search immediately after the object has been hidden at B (Miller *et al.*, 1970) and that the error is much more likely if there is a delay of a few seconds between hiding and letting the infant search (Landers, 1971). In another study, Gratch *et al.* (1974) pointed out that the crucial distinction is between forgetting the placement at B and failing to 'register' this placement (for which Piaget argues) and set out to test the differential predictions. Firstly, they too found that with an 0 second delay between hiding and search the place error was practically non-existent, suggesting that maybe placement at B *was* being registered. However they also looked at the attentiveness of the infants during the delay period as another index of something akin to registering. They found that of those infants who were at all attentive to the display, they tended to err who immediately returned their gaze to A and maintained this orientation. Those who alternated their gaze between A and B were more successful and those who maintained their gaze at B were still more so—these tending to be older than the A-gazing infants. Those who were just generally inattentive were highly likely to err. The authors say that the younger infants had their gaze drawn to B and that this 'motor set' was held only for a fraction of a second, during which time if they were allowed to search they would go to B. Thus, so many infants succeed with immediate search because of such tendencies rather than because they registered the disappearance at B; if they had so registered it, why do they turn at once to A and thus fail? It certainly does not seem justified to call the maintenance of a motor set for a fracton of a second 'registering' in 'memory'.

An interesting finding of Harris (1974) suggests that the memory hypothesis is certainly incorrect. When transparent Perspex doors were used instead of curtains so that the object was actually still visible at B, infants would still return to A. The door was locked so that when they failed to get at the object behind the B door they returned to A and tried persistently to get in *although no object was visible*, with the older infants being the more persistent in their efforts. All this is quite congruent with Piaget's hypothesis: in trying to get into the empty compartment the infant is attempting to produce what we call an 'object'; the fact that he has seen 'an object' (no notion of '*the* object') at B should not affect this. Also, the more used he is to finding objects on removing obstacles (that is, the older) the more persistent he will be.

Harris's alternative to the Piagetian account of this result is of some interest because it reveals the same assumptions we found in Bower. He says that the infant fails because he does not 'acknowledge' the alternatives 'at A or at B' as mutually exclusive; he has to acquire this knowledge by application of a rule such as 'if an object moves, delete prior locations from memory as possible locations of the object'. The problem is, as before, that this rule ascription about objects is not justified. The whole point of the observations is that they do not allow us to assume that there is an object concept established, so we should start from this point rather than assume that there is some object concept and then treat the failures as if they were mere errors in *performance* which can be overcome by the establishment of rules. The infant cannot come to resolve conflicts between appearances and form rules about the relation between appearances *until* he has established their independence from his actions. Similarly, it is misleading to ascribe to Piaget, as Harris does, the hypothesis that the infant 'thinks he can recreate the *object*' (my italics). Piaget's position is rather that the infant's actions and the visual and tactile *perceptions* of solidity to which they give rise are still not dissociated.

The general point here is that memory explanations are wrong for epistemological not for empirical reasons. As Piaget points out, if the infant's memory were really so ineffectual that it did not retain a record of displacements for more than (in this case) a fraction of a second: 'its universe would consist in a series of total pictures whose coherence would pertain to the action itself and not to the relations sustained by the elements of the different pictures with each other . . .: the construction of objective groups of displacements presupposes time and memory, just as time presupposes a universe spatially and objectively organised' (Piaget, 1955, pp. 64–5). That is to say, a memory *this bad* would imply the infant's cognising the world in just the way Piaget supposes: the inability to retain perceived displacements in memory but only displacements brought about by his own actions is just what Piaget is arguing for. The infant is taken only to 'know' to the extent that he acts.

This kind of misapprehension seems to arise from a treatment of 'memory' as a compartmentalised cognitive facility, a tendency which must have originated in the old 'faculty' psychology which in turn came from ordinary usage, but which has been strengthened within experimental psychology in recent years due to memory being regarded essentially as a skill or a capacity. Obviously, in one sense, memory is a skill which can be discussed in terms of concepts such as storage, coding, retrieval and so on. But the notion of memory *qua* storage can only be employed in an agenetic context, that is, if we are taking cognition as a developed constant (in adults) rather than making comparisons between levels of intellectual functioning and trying to explain cognitive progression. In the latter case we have no choice but to treat memory as a *result* of intelligence or at least as indissociable from it, not as a construct which we can use to explain how intelligence is functioning. If we do not, we end up explaining why the infant fails to retain perceived information in terms of failures of memory, that is, explaining a failure of memory by saying that it is a failure of memory. The argument is circular, therefore, in very much the same way as saying that the infant knows that an object continues to exist in one kind of situation but not in others and that he eventually learns about existence in these situations by the use of abstract rules: we begin by assuming knowledge and explain the difference between the failing and the succeeding infants in terms of the fact that the latter knows even more.

It should be pointed out that the spirit of the present objections is rather more skeptical than Piaget's own presentation. Indeed, one does find in his writings on the object concept statements such as that the Stage 4 infant 'succeeds in conceiving of objects as existing behind screens' (*op. cit.*, p. 92). However more usually he says something like: 'during the fourth stage the object remains a practical object rather than a substantial thing . . . it is a reality at the disposal of a certain context itself related to a certain action' (*op. cit.*, p. 65). The fact is, when Piaget occasionally talks of 'conceiving of' and 'belief in' the existence of occluded objects it is due to the employment of the kind of shorthand usage mentioned above, or to using the word 'object' in a special sense. The attribution of cognitive states does not determine his explanation, which is in terms of the coordination of schemes and the establishment of tertiary circular reactions and imagery.

At the fifth stage when the infant no longer makes the place error, the object appears to have for the first time an autonomous trajectory and thus a spatial permanence. Keeping track of visible displacements carried out by another person means that the perceived movement is cancelling out actions that the child has made himself. Thus when he succeeds in searching at B (even after a delay) we cannot explain this in terms of his acting to bring about the perception of a solid object because the object has itself been endowed with a life independent of and taking precedence over his own actions.

But *now* (at Stage 5) does the infant know or believe that objects continue to exist when not perceived? This brings us to the nub of the problem. There is an obvious difference between the adult and the infant of 12 months in that the adult can say what he believes and what his states of knowledge are, and thus we have from him direct evidence that he knows objects have an independent existence. The only *behavioural* difference vis-à-vis objects is that the child of this age cannot represent invisible displacements (see p. 102). So what is more significant in the attribution of the object concept, the verbal competence of the adult or the final behavioural acquisition of the sixth sensorimotor stage? Or, put another way, is there a difference in kind between Stage 5 and 6 brought about by the employment of mental imagery to represent reality, independent of language use?

Let us begin to answer this question by looking again at Piaget's view of the infant's state of knowledge at the end of Stage 5. He says that until the sixth stage the infant has only utilised a system of signs linked with actions; searching behind screens implies 'simply that he has understood the relation of the two objects *at the moment he perceived it* (at the moment when the object was covered) and that he therefore interprets it as a *sign* of the actual presence of the object. It is one thing to assume the permanence of an object when one has just seen it and when some other object in sight *recalls* its presence, and quite another to imagine the first object when there is nothing in sight' (*op. cit.*, p. 85; my italics). The infant's consciousness is dominated by perceptions in a way that is analogous to the *intuitive* nature of the 4–7-year-old child's cognition on the conceptual plane. But what is the nature of the advance in Stage 6? Is being able to cognise, by the use of mental imagery, that objects can change their location unobserved just carrying out internally what had previously been carried out externally, or is it doing something different in kind?

Although the Stage 5 infant has acquired something beyond procedures for recovering objects, his reliance is perceptual where before it was motoric: on what he has seen rather than on what he has done. Therefore, we are justified only in restating our skepticism about the infant's object concept in terms of sights rather than actions. At Stage 6 however there does not appear to be a foothold for any kind of skepticism. This can be appreciated by comparing the representation of invisible displacements with the finding of the Mundy-Castle and Anglin study (p. 127) which it was possible to interpret in terms of disembodied movement. We cannot give such an interpretation in the present instance. If Piaget's daughter could deduce that her father had released the watch chain from his fist beneath the cloth, this can only be a case of conceiving of the movement of a solid, tangible thing which remained there having been *acted on*.

If the child can now cognise invisible transformations there does not appear to be any alternative but to ascribe this to the mental representation of the movements of solid objects, as Piaget does. Mental imagery seems the best contender for this representational device as language is hardly underway at 18 months. Thus the progression after Stage 3 is from action to perceptions to images. This should not, however, be regarded merely as a gradation, in view of a fundamental discontinuity between perceptions and images: actions and perceptions are forms of the object's *dependence* on the infant's experience, whereas images should be regarded as evidence of *independence* from what he has done and seen—the first two involve weaknesses and the last a strength. The upshot of this must be the conclusion that when there is nothing to prevent us from ascribing to the child knowledge of the independent existence of objects we have at the same time to introduce representation. This has clear implications for the development of memory because representation must act as a medium for the encoding and storing of information about invisible states which must in turn enrich knowledge of the concrete world—another example of the indissociability of memory development and cognitive development.

There are still a host of empirical issues to be met, not the least of which is the construction of a precise model of how mental imagery arises out of sensorimotor equilibrium. But as regards a broad conclusion, it might be that knowledge of object permanence is representational. This is a conclusion which has both epistemological and genetic elements because it is the result of having to coordinate both kinds of question. It is genetic not only because it is based on developmental research but because it is open to further empirical refinement: for example there may be discovered a seventh stage because the 2-year-old child may be found to lack some form of sensorimotor understanding of object permanence which is possessed by the child of $2\frac{1}{2}$, and which might entail specifying the necessary representation further. Also, it is epistemological because it is open to criticism on the grounds of purely philosophical coherence, on the grounds of how knowledge is being characterised. And furthermore these philosophical and psychological theses interdepend because of the dialectical nature of knowledge *qua* process.

It would be possible to construct a still broader theory on the basis of some form of representation's being a necessary feature of all knowledge. In fact this is very close to Baldwin's notion that all knowledge involves mediation, with control of thought by the world only being 'direct' in very early infancy and in certain kinds of aesthetic experience.

3.2 TRANSITIVITY

We have already seen (p. 110) that the asymmetrical and symmetrical addition of relations (Groupings V and VI) are of fundamental importance to Piaget's account of the concrete operations. For example, at around the age of 7 years, Piaget argues, the child can deduce from the premises $A \geqslant B$ and $B \geqslant C$ that $A \geqslant C$. What is essential to the transitive inference is the employment of a middle term (B) by utilising the fact that it has a relation to both A and C such that their relation can be inferred.

There are two ways of testing transitivity, although Piaget does not always make the distinction explicit: the *spontaneous* inference and, what we might call, the *elicited* inference. In the spontaneous inference the child is encouraged to work out for himself the relation between two terms (A, C) by actively employing a third (B), which typically means using some form of measuring implement to deduce the length relationship between A and C. For example (see Piaget, Inhelder and Szeminska, 1960) the child is shown a tower made of large bricks on a table and is asked to build a tower of the same height using smaller bricks, and to do this behind a screen so that direct visual comparison is not possible. Although he is also given a set of paper strips and sticks which can be employed as measuring implements he is 'on no account' told how to use them. The child may begin by using his arms or trunk as a measure, but typically succeeds after 7 years in employing a standard to equalise the heights. A similar situation is one in which he is asked to judge between strips of paper pasted in a variety of linear arrangements onto a board to see whether they are equal and, if not, which is the longer, and is then given other strips with which to verify his judgment by measurement. On the other hand, in the case of the elicited transitive judgment the child is presented with the premises and asked for the relation between the two end terms, rather than encouraged to manipulate the middle term. As regards weight for example (Piaget and Inhelder, 1974), if he is asked to weigh two bars of metal to find that they are equal (A = B), and then to do the same for bars B and C (B = C), he will not conclude that A and C weigh the same until he is about 7 years old.

As to the experimental objections, memory is again the main factor involved, specifically the memory element present in the elicited but not in the spontaneous inference. For example, in order for the child to conclude that A > C he has to recall the A > B and the B > C relations. It is at least a fair point to make that in situations like the weight test given above Piaget did not include a control to insure retention of the premises. Bryant and Trabasso (1971) focused on this weakness and employed an experimental design which did insure this retention. (However, their neglecting to make it clear that they were not questioning the studies of spontaneous inferences, and their making reference only to Piaget's work on these inferences, caused added opposition to their study from Piagetians.) They also controlled for another weakness of the traditional design, which had been pointed out by Smedslund (1969), that it was possible in principle for the subject to succeed with an *absolute* response, without performing any logical deduction. For example, if the comparisons are between the sticks in descending order of size, A is always bigger and C is always smaller so when asked about A, C he need only judge the absolute 'bigness' of one and the 'smallness' of the other, which he might do by parrotting the verbal labels that he had attached to them. First of all to control for the absolute response it was necessary to make the end terms both smaller and bigger than other items in the presentation of the premises. Thus four comparisons were used of sticks where A > B, B > C, C > D and D > E. The main concern was with the child's understanding of the relation between B and D, for B was both smaller than A and bigger than C, and D was both smaller than C and bigger than E. In order to control for forgetting there was a training series to insure that the child had learned all of the four relations, then a testing series to test for their retention as well as the ability to make the transitive inferences including the critical one B > D.

The materials were five rods each of a different colour presented on a stand in which holes had been bored to different depths so that the sticks all protruded by one inch. The child was shown one pair of rods at a time, asked which was longer and shorter, then given visual feedback as to the correctness of his choice by the sticks being drawn from the stand so he could see which was the longer. Thus he learned that red > white; white > yellow; yellow > blue and blue > green. In testing he was given *no feedback* and was tested for his retention of the pair relationships (premises) and for transitive pairs including the critical one B, D. The clear result was that children from 4 years of age could correctly infer that the white rod was longer than the blue (B>D) well above chance probability. However one objection to a conclusion that children so young were performing what Piaget would call a concrete operation was that in training they had been shown the full length of the rods which could have enabled them to remember their absolute size, for example, that the white one looked about 6 inches and the blue one about 4 inches. Bryant and Trabasso controlled for this in a second experiment by giving only verbal feedback in training. The results of this experiment were essentially the same.

Here we have then what appears to be very clear evidence that children who are only just entering Piaget's intuitive substage can perform a concrete operation. In developmental psychology a difference of 3 years is not one that can be dismissed as merely a matter of timetabling! Moreover the presence of transitivity so early must affect the kind of explanation we give for other facilities and the explanation for the acquisition of transitivity itself. But were the children really performing a genuine transitive inference in Bryant and Trabasso's study? de Boysson-Bardies and O'Regan (1973) argued that there is another way of explaining the result, in terms of verbal labelling. In the training series the child would be labelling the sticks in terms of whether they were *big* or *small*. Thus the end sticks A and E would consistently receive the labels *big* and *small* respectively, but all the others would be labelled inconsistently both *big* when compared in one direction and *small* when compared in another so that no useful labels could be retained. The authors said that if a stick to which the child has not been able to attach a label is paired with one to which he has (A with B; D with E) it acquires the label of that stick (B—*big*; D—*small*) and so when asked about B, D he can succeed absolutely in terms of labels rather than by utilising the middle term C.

Harris and Bassett (1975) did an experiment to test a prediction which they claimed to be implicit in de Boysson-Bardies and O'Regan's objection. They argued that if only consistent labels were retained then giving preoperational children the information that A = B; B > C; and C = D should lead them to conclude erroneously that A = D. This is because B would be both *same* and *big* and C would be both *same* and *small* so they would lose their labels and A and D would retain theirs of *same*. In both a simultaneous rod-matching and a verbal version of this design they found that children of 4 and 5 years correctly inferred that A > D rather than A = D. Therefore the authors concluded that de Boysson-Bardies and O'Regan were wrong and that they themselves had produced another example of a transitive inference in preoperational children when forgetting is controlled for. However, neither conclusion is justified. Firstly, there is no necessary inconsistency between something being the same as something else and its being big or small at the same time; at the very least there is no inconsistency such as where an item is both big and small at the same time. Thus de Boysson-Bardies and O'Regan do not have to predict an incorrect inference from these children. Secondly the Harris and Bassett task is not a transitive inference because a middle term does not have to be utilised for success. A child may successfully infer A > D by linking A with B and C with D, then focusing on the difference between them. In A = B; B > C; C = D, the information can be parcelled into two without a common term: (A & B) > (C & D). Now, the terms B and C are, of course, common on either side, but (compare the Smedslund objection above) they need not be employed transitively. That is, when told that A = B and B > C, the child can conclude A > C simply by recalling that C is small. D is on the small side of the fence with C, and by the same process A is on the long side of the fence with B. What the child has to do therefore is to associate A with a big item and D with a small item, by treating the sizes of B and C absolutely.

Nevertheless there are problems with the de Boysson-Bardies and O'Regan interpretation. The first one is relatively minor. The authors's explanation relies in part upon the children encoding *bigger* and *smaller* as *big* and *small*, because there are no circumstances in which a thing can be both big and small whereas something can be bigger and smaller than two other things at the same time and thus there is a clearer conflict between the absolute terms. This assumption is in line with Piaget's (1928) claim that children of this age interpret a comparative as a class term, and with children's spontaneous verbalisations about unidimensional properties. But is the misencoding inevitable? In a stringent test of the ability to carry out an instruction containing *bigger* it was found that 45% of a sample of 4 and 5-year-olds interpreted the instruction in a relational rather than absolute manner (Russell, 1973).* Thus the competence for correct encoding may be present in many children at this age, although there certainly may be a tendency to misencode.

The second difficulty is that the authors' claim that pairing an unlabelled item with a labelled item causes it to acquire that label, is not only an unwarranted assumption but a counter-intuitive one. We have no reason to believe that such a carry-over takes place. Also the items A, B and D, E are not so much paired as set in opposition. It is much less counter-intuitive to claim therefore (though still unjustified) that this opposition *resolves* the *big/small* conflict (for example, if B is small compared with A which is always big then it *must* be small) and makes the child retain only the label *small* for B and *big* for D!

But more crucial than these points about rationale is that the implicit predictions of de Boysson-Bardies and O'Regan regarding the role of label conflict are not fulfilled when the degree of conflict is manipulated experimentally. Their prediction would have to be that if preoperational children are energised to make the transitive inference by label conflict then increasing the degree of conflict should increase the probability of making the inference. Riley and Trabasso (1974) found the opposite to be the case in a study that was not carried out specifically to test the de Boysson-Bardies and O'Regan interpretation. They were primarily concerned with the way in which the kind of questioning in the training series might have been encouraging the preoperational child to encode the *reversible* nature of the stick lengths, that is, that A > B and B < A. They point out that

---

*The child was presented with five cardboard squares graded in size. The experimenter took the second largest and instructed the child to pick the card or cards that were bigger than it from those remaining. The biggest card was then removed and the experimenter's returned. The same thing was done twice. All the cards were returned, the experimenter took the third largest, and likewise once more. The cards were returned and he took the fourth largest. Competence was recorded if the child could carry out all six of these instructions.

the Bryant and Trabasso experiments made this reversible relation explicit by asking both comparative questions: for each pair 'Which is bigger longer', 'Which is smaller shorter?' on different trials. Thus the child was helped to encode $A > B$ and $B < A$, and so on. Now this should have the effect of decreasing the conflict because, insofar as there *is* a tendency to encode comparatives as class labels (for example, bigger as big), this condition would reduce it by focusing on the relational rather than absolute nature of length. This would be operative particularly if, as the results of Russell suggested, many 4 and 5-year-old children do have the competence to interpret a comparative relationally. Therefore, according to de Boysson-Bardies and O'Regan, giving both comparative questions *within* a training pair should *decrease* the probability of the $B > D$ inference.

Using a situation similar in essentials to Bryant and Trabasso, (but which further examined the role of visual feedback in training and the possible utilisation of spatial ordering cues from the display stand in the Bryant and Trabasso study) Riley and Trabasso used the above questioning condition in their initial experiment. In a second experiment the more traditional procedure was employed of using only one comparative. Here one group of children were asked 'Which is longer?' and another 'Which is shorter?'. This was taken to be encouraging the children to encode A (long), B (not long); B (long), C (not long) and so on, or A (not short), B (short), B (not short), C (short) with a high degree of inconsistency resulting. The authors report that the contradiction was very obvious to the children, so much so that in the training series many of them seemed totally baffled and told the experimenter that she was 'crazy'. One child said 'You have two sizes of stick, long and short, and you keep changing which ones are which!' In the third experiment the children were given both comparatives but *across* pairs, rather than within them as before. There were two groups trained on two of the four pairs using *longer* and two of the four pairs using *shorter*. For one group the *longer* pairs were A, B and C, D and the shorter pairs were B, C and D, E, and vice versa for the other group. There was consequently less encouragement here for the subjects to encode the length relations in a reversible way.

The results were the opposite to what de Boysson-Bardies and O'Regan would have predicted, in that the first experiment gave the best evidence of transitive inference with $B > D$ being deduced above chance probability level. However the children in the second experiment had great difficulty even in attaining criterion on the training series due to the encouragement of absolute encoding. Also these did not perfom the B > D inference above chance level. Likewise the children in the third experiment did not perform the inference although training was easy. As regards the results of the third experiment the authors conclude that either the reference to ordinal relations has to be made explicit in training by using both comparatives within a pair, or the children had been attaining criterion in training without learning anything about length relations, which, as it turned out, was possible on their design. The general conclusion can be fairly clearly drawn however, which is that the use of *both* comparatives is necessary for preoperational children's successful performance of a transitive inference and that increasing inconsistency in labelling the B, C and D terms decreases rather than increases the probability of transitive inference, contrary to de Boysson-Bardies and O'Regan.

Up to this point we have only been concerned with points of experimental rationale and detail. But there are those who would deny that a training study of the kind we have been considering can in principle test a logical capacity. Youniss and Furth (1973), who have themselves produced evidence of what they called sublogical inferences in young children (Youniss and Furth 1965; Furth and Youniss 1966), made a set of objections to the Bryant and Trabasso study including this one. They said that certain extra controls should have been run and mentioned the importance of spontaneous inferences in Piaget's theory which are not open to the memory objection—although not mentioning that elicited inferences are required in many of his procedures. However, their crucial objection was one of principle concerning the nature of the mental processes which could have produced such a result. They say that the children in the study were not presented with premises from which they had to deduce a relationship but were merely taught a series of size discriminations between coloured rods so that all we need conclude is that they 'performed consistently in judging new pairs in an organised system dictated by old overlearned pairs'. Of course the onus is on Youniss and Furth to indicate the nature of this 'organised system' and say how it was 'dictated'.

They suggested that the inference may have been arrived at by 'perceptual generalisation and consistency', making their suggestion more explicit by referring to the work of Huttenlocher (1968) who has shown how adults construct spatial images in their performance of different kinds of transitive problem to aid solution. From their introspections of how they went about solving transitive problems Huttenlocher concluded that spatial ordering was the mental strategy and tested this by comparing the differential difficulty of ways of ordering the terms in the instructions by measuring errors and reaction times. When coupled with the fact that Youniss and Furth, in the work cited above, had reported that children order colours in this way, it does seem likely that mental imagery was being employed by the children in the Bryant and Trabasso study. Within Piaget's theory, as we have seen, mental imagery comes to be organised by operational structures and mental imagery enriches the concrete operations, but the operations themselves are not dependent on imagery because part of their general significance is that they render imaginal representation redundant in epistemic judgments. This mental imagery need not have been organised in a reversible system: the child would have a picture before his mind's eye of a series of colours red, white, yellow, blue, green, constructed by an additive fusion of units red, white, and so on. Success would thus be independent of utilising the yellow stick as a middle term.

In his answer to this objection Bryant (1973) makes the point that the employment of mental imagery does not make us any less justified in calling the inference logical, and this *especially* in view of Huttenlocher's work. Riley and Trabasso presented a similar argument regarding the rather circular nature of the Piagetians' objection: they refuse to call anything a transitive inference that could have been carried out by mental representation because within Piaget's system transitivity is a concrete operation, thus ruling out the relevance of certain kinds of mental process *a priori*. The following quotation shows the philosophy behind Riley and Trabasso's empirical approach to cognitive development: 'Our view is that science is inductive and we prefer to infer the mechanism underlying the behaviour from empirical evidence. This means that our interest is in any process that the child uses to solve a problem and that is why we have stressed the role of memory ' (p. 201). The authors themselves posited a model of transitivity in (at least) preoperational children based on imagery in which the child coordinates the premises into a spatial array—again based on the work of Huttenlocher. They admit that if this is the case (Trabasso, Riley and Wilson 1975) then the Bryant and Trabasso procedure is irrelevant to Piaget's theory but very relevant to the general question of the cognitive processes underlying transitivity.

To an extent we have to agree with this position in that the 'hard line' Piagetian view of transitivity as *a priori* a concrete operation blinkers the psychologist against giving processes like mental imagery their full due. Taking Piaget's account as a theoretical base must produce an experimental 'tunnel vision' in which one form of problem solution is written off as being of less developmental significance than another. But how then are we to regard the logicality of the transitive inference? For the other extreme is to call any inference logical where a middle term is *present* regardless of how the child is using it. On this account transitivity would begin around 18 months. In some of his observations in the sixth sensorimotor stage Piaget superimposed a series of occluders around objects in order to see whether Jacqueline could remove them in turn to retrieve an object. In one, he put a pencil into a box, wrapped it in paper, wrapped this in a handkerchief then covered the whole thing in a beret and then a coverlet (Piaget, 1955, p. 81). She succeeded, Piaget argued, by virtue of her *mental image* of the occluded pencil. Each of these occluders can be regarded as a middle term: A behind B, B behind C, therefore A behind C. Another sensorimotor example comes from a study we shall be discussing later by Greenfield, Nelson and Salzman (1972) who showed that children of 3 years can nest cups in a transitive way. One cup is put inside another which is then put inside another: A inside B, B inside C, thus A inside C. (Indeed there is something of a paradox within Piagetian theory that Piaget (for example, Piaget 1970) stresses the logical nature of sensorimotor acquisitions and yet his supporters—in this instance—do not wish to call the use of mental imagery in a transitive problem logical!) Also, on the verbal plane, very young children sometimes reveal an informal kind of transitive understanding in their everyday judgments. Here is an observation of my daughter Charlotte at 2 years 8 months. She came into the house carrying a new toy. On being asked how she had come by it she said 'Liam gave it to me'. As this answer was received somewhat dubiously she further said 'Clare gave it to me. Liam gave it to Clare'. Although her first statement was accurate only as to the origin of the toy her replies show that 'Clare' was being used as a kind of middle term in two sequences of handing over. Also there is very persuasive evidence for the employment of perceptual inferences by preoperational children from Bryant (1974) in his book

Perception and Understanding in Young Children. Bryant presents an original synthesis of developmenal tasks which are usually treated separately, arguing that transitive inferences function to enable young children to make relational judgments about orientation, position, size, number, invariance and comparisons across sensory modalities, in order to overcome their immature ability to code absolute values.

In general, we are faced with the difficulty that the 'logical' form of inference only seems to be defined in terms of the *absence* of something—mental imagery. Given these transitivities, are we justified at all in saying that there is a special kind of inference which is truly logical and which is established around the age of 7 years. In answering this let us look first at the empirical justification for there being this fundamental change: there is the fact that up to this age the child fails both spontaneous and elicited transitive inferences when no precautions are taken against his forgetting the premises. If we accept that the child is failing the elicited inferences because of a weak memory we have to explain why he improves so drastically after this age.

Let us focus on the nature of these failures. Supporters of the memory account would have to say that, in the weight comparison example given above, the child failed to conclude that bar A weighed more than bar C because he had forgotten that $A > B$ and $B > C$, although he had been presented with the information immediately before. Typically, in testing for transitivity without memory precautions, there is a delay of only a very few seconds between the presentation of the first premise and asking the inference question. Although it is well, in this context, to resist the temptation to appeal to the common observation that the memory of children between 4 and 6 years is just not this bad, we can press the question as to *why* the information is forgotten before this age and retained thereafter. In the discussion of the memory explanations for the place error it was suggested that the infant who could not retain a perceptual concealment for one second would *ipso facto* have the action-dominated, insubstantial universe which Piaget ascribes to him. Similarly, one might argue, if a child of 4 to 6 years cannot retain the perceptual information that a blue rod is longer than a red one which is longer than a white one for more than a very few seconds he must lack the ability to structure relationships which Piaget says is acquired in the concrete operational period. To adopt the position that the preoperational child fails because the premises do not remain in memory is quite different from arguing that the two relations were never taken in as 'raw material' for a transitive inference in the first place—like the Stage 4 infant failing to 'register' placement. Proposing that the failure is one of *organising* the premises in short term memory at the outset is to admit a basic deficit in cognitive structuring rather than just a weak memory.

Now if this were stated in the information-processing terminology of input, encoding, storage, retrieval and so on, it would end up rather similar to Riley and Trabasso's process model of preoperational transitivity. But that the child fails to encode the premises at input, or fails to coordinate them in such a way that they can be efficiently retrieved implies that preoperational failure is not just a failure of memory. Encoding and coordinating relationships are active, structuring functions not just subprocesses within the larger process of memory. Thus there is the same kind of basic circularity in a memory theory as in the hard-line Piagetian: anything that involves the retention of information is assumed to be fundamentally a question of memory, and the encoding, storage, retrieval processes are just the cognitive small print. But the preoperational child succeeds with the Bryant and Trabasso procedure not just because the design insures against forgetting but because he is *trained to structure the information*. Hence the Riley and Trabasso finding that the giving of both comparatives in the training question was necessary for success; calling this 'encoding' does not make it any more a 'memory' phenomenon. In general, science is not as inductive as Riley and Trabasso are suggesting in the above quotation. Using memory as the cornerstone in their conceptual framework is determining the nature of the explanation prior to any experimentation.

If the preoperational child can be trained to encode the premises this is of considerable interest in itself but does not, as Riley and Trabasso themselves point out, challenge Piaget's theory except insofar as it shows how Piaget's neglect of such procedures leads him to miss important phenomena. On the other hand the significance of Piaget's observations of elicited inferences is that before a certain age *without training* the inference is not performed and after this age it is automatic. We must return therefore to our original question of whether the concrete operational inference is truly logical in a sense in which success with the Bryant and Trabasso procedure is not. We also return to the problem of when we are justified in ascribing knowledge to the child—on a higher level than that of object permanence this time. The knowledge with which we are concerned here is of a logical principle and our genetic epistemological problem is one of distinguishing inferences based on such knowledge from contingent success due to expeditious processing insured by careful experimental manipulations.

In order to escape the circularity of the Youniss and Furth position which establishes the logical nature of the inference after 7 years by reference to its status in Piaget's theory, it is necessary to establish criteria for knowledge of the principle independently of any theory of how the competence arises. This knowledge might be seen as the making use of an abstract rule or procedure as we do, for example, when we perform a piece of mental arithmetic such as $216 \div 3 = 72$. In this case we may well construct a mental image but this is not something that *happens to us*; it is something which we *do* on the basis of an abstract rule which we know: we construct the image for a purpose. It must be stressed that we need not rely on introspection to distinguish knowledge from success. For the point is that if someone were *entirely* reliant on his imaginative faculty for thinking logically or for carrying out mathematical procedures and gave no other evidence for knowing these basic principles we would not be entitled to say that he knew the principles of logic or mathematics. We know that adults employ mental imagery when faced with even simple logical problems but what is important is their *construction* of the image on a principle, not the mere fact that imagery occurs. Transitivity is not a task but a principle which can be known and used to justify performance. What we have to do is establish a set of criteria for knowledge of the transitive principle without relying on the fact that after a certain age elicited inferences can be performed without training the premises. These criteria fall naturally into two kinds: those which refer to what the child can do and those which are about what he can say.

One of the first set of criteria would be the possible development of a test of an elicited transitive inference which could only be performed by utilising a middle term and could not be performed by mental imagery alone. Nobody has been able to develop such a task. But what we can of course have, is a test of *spontaneous* inference which fulfills these conditions. Indeed in the performance of the spontaneous inference we can actually see the child utilising the middle term (measuring stick) so we need have no doubt that success is dependent on it. Until recently it was widely accepted that spontaneous inferences could not be performed by preoperational children, but we now have evidence, again from Bryant, that children of five years can manage them.

Bryant and Kopytynska (1976) criticised Piaget *et al.*'s (1960) experiments on spontaneous transitive inference on the grounds that they leave open the possibility that the children knew how to use measuring sticks but did not know that a direct comparison by eye between (say) the towers would be unreliable. They tested this by making the A and C terms invisible so that children were forced to use an intermediate measure to work out their relation. The materials were two identical black wooden blocks presented side by side, each of which had a hole in the top whose depth could not be seen. The hole was either 6 or 4 inches deep. On two of the trials the holes were the same depth and on two they were different. Between the blocks was a 10-inch long stick the central 2-inch portion of which was yellow and the surrounding 4 inches at either end were red. Thus the middle band of yellow was visible when in the 4-inch hole but covered in the 6-inch hole. The children were instructed to find out whether or not the holes were the same depth. The authors found that the majority of a group of 5 and 6-year-old children who had failed the Piagetian measuring task with the towers used the stick as a measure without prompting and that most of their judgments were correct. However, as the tendency fell short of significance for these children *not* to use the stick when the blocks were of transparent perspex (with the holes only differing by $\frac{1}{2}$ inch), it cannot really be concluded that they had failed the standard Piagetian task because they did not know that a comparison by sight alone would not be reliable.

This is an interesting result but, like the Bryant and Trabasso experiment, really concerns an ability on which knowledge of transitivity is based rather than transitivity itself: practical success not a practical judgment. The stick had to be employed more as an aid to perceptual comparison than as a logical middle term, and is further along the continuum on which the sensorimotor skills evinced by Jacqueline at 18 months (see p. 145) are treated. A comparable situation would be one in which a child sees two opaque beakers of drink on a high table, he wants the one with more though he cannot see the level so he pokes a finger over the tops of the beaker. My daughter Charlotte at 3;5, for example, was able to perform a kind of aided comparison intermediate between the finger-poking and the Bryant and Kopytynska situations. She was shown two large opaque mugs of water well above eye level one of which was much fuller than the other, given a straw and then told to find out which contained more by using it. She could feel the larger amount of water by its greater resistance against the straw.

Again, as in the Bryant and Trabasso experiment, the present study *structures the task for the child*: the stick is put between the blocks and is tailor-made for the job in hand. Remember that in the Piagetian testing situation the child is on no account told how to use the measuring stick; thus he has to apply the transitive structure himself. Experimentally the differences in the extent to which the child is given information in the form of hints of how to use the measuring implement is one of degree; psychologically it is a difference of kind. As both Baldwin and Piaget stress, there is a fundamental difference between success and truth, a difference therefore between knowing how to get the answer and knowing that a principle holds. To say that the practical success cases involve a 'transitive inference' is justified in a way, but let us recognise that our use of the term is parasitic on its proper use in characterising a logical judgment.

We have to turn to our second criterion, in terms of what the child says, to his justification of his answer, for the criterion of full-blown knowledge of the transitive principle. Piaget reports that justification was usual for children who make the inference in the weight problem above. It is too much to expect the child to be able to verbalise the principle in its abstract form, but minimally he should evince some awareness that $A > C$ holds *because* of the relation between the premises and that using the $> B >$ relation is a necessary step. Mental imagery could not enable the child to do this: the aliment of imagery is perception and thus an answer acquired through imagery alone cannot be justified by reference to a rule that is independent of any particular visual, auditory or tactile procedure for reaching it. The ability to use a measuring stick could not by itself enable the child to justify the answer arrived at: it is a technique which can be applied without necessarily having conscious knowledge of a rule. Closely related to justification is the ability of the child to understand how he went wrong if told of a mistake made in a transitive task. One way of testing this understanding would be to determine whether pointing out the mistake leads to improved performance.

In fact, placing the burden of ascribing (conceptual) knowledge on to justification goes back beyond Piaget to Plato and his discussion of the *logos* (see p. 18). But there is some novelty in the further proposal that justification is not a *post hoc* verbalisation of a success gained by constructing mental images or manipulating measuring sticks. Linguistic justification, it is suggested, comes from conscious knowledge of a rule which the child has learned to be universally applicable within the conceptual system into which he is being cognitively socialised: it is a *synnomic* judgment. Only with language can this common, conventional knowledge be revealed by the child and, initially, *to* the child.

Also, having this rule in consciousness will determine the performance on transitive tasks, so the following empirical hypotheses can be proposed on the basis of this notion. First, success on Piaget's more difficult version of the spontaneous inference is due to conscious knowledge of the rule at 8 years as revealed by the justifications made at this age. Second, returning to the question of why the premises are not forgotten by the concrete operational child in elicited inferences, we can turn the memory hypothesis on its head and propose that the child remembers them *because he knows the rule*. As soon as he is informed that A > B and that B > C he orders the relations transitively because he is aware of the transitive nature of the middle term. Third, the prediction is entailed from this proposal that if the recall of the premises is varied independently of making the inference there should not be found a gradual improvement in recall between 4 and 6 years (as in the processing theory) but that recall should become perfect as soon as the inference can be made: a 'quantum jump' in memory capacity with knowledge of the principle.

As regards this prediction Bryant (unpublished data) in a recent study tried to get an index of memory independent of inference ability by showing children A > B; ... D > E, then immediately asking about the test pairs and about B, D. Similar trials then followed so that trial-to-trial memory plus inference ability could be assessed. The procedure was found to be too difficult for 4 and 5-year-olds. All of the 4-year-olds and many of the 5-year-olds could not make the inference. But of those children who could perform at all none was found who could remember B > C and C > D without being able to infer that B > D. This is in line with the present suggestion because (1) the extreme difficulty of the task would be due to the fact that preoperational children generally lack the knowledge of the principle and thus did not 'take in' and coordinate the premises spontaneously,

(2) only those few who did know the principle could recall that B > C and that C > D and (3) if memory gradually improves towards preoperational success one would have expected there to have been children who recalled B > C and C > D but could *not* make the inference.

Overall, the topic of transitivity demonstrates not only how a few relatively simple but absolutely crucial experiments can disturb 'dogmatic slumbers' but how experimental evidence forces us to delineate what is from what is not the acquisition of knowledge that something is the case.

3.3 CONSERVATION

Many laymen who know nothing of Piaget's theory have heard of his experiments on conservation, and developmental journals are still chock-full of investigations into the acquisition of conservation. One reason for this must be the striking nature of the phenomenon: a child who a few months previously had judged that a quantity of lemonade was more to drink when poured into a taller, thinner glass might now respond to the conservation question as if his intelligence were being insulted! There is surprisingly little variability in the ages at which the various conservations are attained and in the order of their attainment. It is an extremely robust phenomenon relatively independent of the materials used, testing situation and other 'performance' factors—and when non-conservers trot out the same kind of answer to the question 'Why do you think there is more now?' it is difficult to suppress the suspicion that they have been reading Piaget! Yet although Piaget's reporting may be accurate this implies nothing about the truth of his explanation for the knowledge nor of his assumptions regarding its status in cognitive development.

Basically the conservation experiments tap the knowledge that there are properties of objects and arrays that remain unchanged through transformations. Here are procedures that can be used for testing the conservation of continuous and of discontinuous quantities—of liquid and number. The child is presented with two identical glasses one of which is filled with a fruit drink. He is instructed to fill the empty glass till it contains the 'same amount to drink' as the first, thus equalising the levels. After he has done this the liquid in one of the glasses is poured into a third glass of clearly different width and height; into (say) a taller, thinner glass. Typically, children below about 6—7 years judge that the amounts are no longer equal saying that there is now more in the third glass because it is taller or less because it is narrower. In testing for the conservation of number, two rows of the same quantity of sweets might be used. If these are aligned in one-to-one correspondence like ranks of soldiers the young child will easily judge there to be the same amount of sweets to eat in each row. But when one of the rows is bunched up or spread out the preoperational child will change his mind and say that there is now more or less in the transformed row, employing the same kind of unidimensional justifications—the shorter of the rows having less sweets.

For something to qualify as a test of conservation the following mutually dependent conditions have to be met: the crucial information about the relation between the standard and the transformed items comes from having witnessed a transformation from a state of perceptually obvious equality; and that there is no direct perceptual evidence of the relation between the standard and the transformed items available after the transformation—otherwise a test of conservation is reduced to one of a perceptual skill because the child is not having to cognise a perduring property but only attend to a perceptual attribute.

In order to clarify the importance of these conditions and to indicate some of the pitfalls of research on this topic, two studies which failed to meet them should be considered. A study of number conservation by Mehler and Bever (1967) received considerable notice when it appeared because the authors were purporting to show that children as young as 2 years can conserve number, that this ability is then temporarily lost during the third year and reacquired in the fourth. In fact they were not testing for conservation at all. The initial display was of two rows of four elements (clay pellets or sweets). However the transformation was not merely the bunching up of one of the rows, but was this together with a real change in quantity: one row was bunched up and two extra elements were added at the same time yet leaving it shorter than the other. The children had to judge that the bunched-up row had more. Thus, all they had to do to succeed was to notice this addition, to utilise what must be a very primitive rule that one quantity is made more than another if some is added to it. What Mehler and Bever found was that this rule is indeed present very early but that seduction by perceptual attributes is strongest at the age of 3 years as these children chose the longer, less numerous row. This is an interesting finding which conflicts some-what with Piaget as he takes the intuitive stage as beginning at the age of four; but the conservation of a perduring property was simply not being tested. Interestingly, the authors seemed rather coy about the addition and referred to it as a 'modification of the array'.

By way of contrast the second experiment is by a Piagetian, Hans Furth, whose work on the cognitive capacities of deaf children is well known. Furth's aim was to show, in support of Piaget, that as language is only one way amongst others of representing reality symbolically the deaf child's conservation of weight should not be grossly handicapped relative to the hearing child. The standard weight conservation test is to present two perceptually identical quantities such as balls of clay, to weigh them to show that they are equal, to transform one of them into a sausage or a pancake shape and then ask the child if they will still weigh the same. This is one of the later conservations and is not usually acquired before the eleventh year. However what Furth (1966, pp. 117–21) did was to teach deaf children a response with which to indicate a judgment of equality, which involved holding a lump of clay in each hand and making horizontal movements of the arms. The judgment that one of the lumps was heavier was indicated by lowering the hand holding it. After one of the clay balls had been deformed they were both returned to the child's hand and he was encouraged to judge whether one weighed more or if they weighed the same. Forty-five per cent of the deaf children were successful at age 8 and deaf children lagged behind the hearing children by a mean of only 1 year 7 months overall. Again this is an interesting result but cannot be considered a test of conservation because the subjects were provided with direct per-ceptual evidence of weight equality rather than having to deduce it from a transformation from previous equality: they had to make a *response* to the substances rather than a judgment about them. Indeed a child could have succeeded with his eyes closed! Doubtless the failures were due to some children making the weight response to shape or size, which, ironically, does have a judgmental status.

If we now compare the cognitive demands of conservation with those of transitivity we will be in a better position both to appreciate the special status of conservation judgments as well as the general nature of concrete operational thinking. In transitivity the child has to relate unidimensional relations by an *abstract* rule and in conservation he has to correlate at least two dimensions in an *abstract* judgment. Abstraction is involved in both to the extent that there is no direct perceptual evidence for the judgment. The abstract judgment in each case is made by relating what we might call *perceptual* judgments. The essential nature of the perceptual judgments might be illustrated by the following example. If we are shown

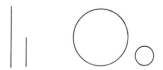

and told to choose the larger of the two items there is no possibility of justifying the judgment other than by say something like 'Well it just *is* bigger, look': there is a relatively 'direct' relationship between what is seen and the judgment. However, to contrast this with length conservation, we are here shown two sticks in a formation like

then one of them is moved up to produce

and we are asked whether they are still the same length. This can be *justified*. We might do so by saying that the stick has been transformed from a position of previous equality, that although one of the sticks protrudes above the other this is cancelled out by the end of the other stick trailing below it, and so on. Thus one criterion of demarcation between perceptual and abstract judgments is that only in the latter case is there the possibility of justification. Another criterion is that abstract judgments involve the correlation of unidimensional relations—of perceptual judgments in fact. In transitivity the premises are correlated; in conservation an increase in one dimension is correlated with a corresponding decrease in another. However, the abstract judgments can be made perceptual by showing the A, C relation or, in weight conservation, by allowing direct estimation prior to judgment as Furth did.

These criteria rest on the essential feature of the concrete operations and the abstract judgments which they require: in every case *rules* of application are involved. Abstract concepts, as characterised above, are *rulebound* and perceptual concepts are *non-rulebound* (see Russell, 1973). This distinction is made in the same spirit as—though it is not identical to—that which Locke made between primary and secondary qualities (see p. 26). Piaget presented a formal statement of these rules in the groupings but whenever a concrete operational judgment is justified this is done by giving an informal statement of this rule or by rules regarding the possibility of reversing the transformation and the identity of the substance. For example, the child who says 'It's the same because although the level is higher the glass is thinner' is evincing an understanding of the covariance principle of Grouping VII. Indeed it is in the nature of the human conceptual system that quantity, weight, area and so on cannot be appreciated without reference to the rules whereby they are taken to perdure throughout certain transformations. (It is of interest in this connection that in *Psychology and Epistemology* (p. 11) Piaget gives the 'operational' delineation of object permanence and the principle of conservation as one of the instances of developmental psychology aiding the clarification of issues in theoretical physics.)

For our present purpose the most important feature of these rulebound judgments is that they possess many more 'degrees of freedom' in their application than perceptual judgments. By their very nature, rules could always have been otherwise and can be misinterpreted in different ways. As regards the possibility that the rules for the application of abstract concepts might have been different, a conceptual system might have evolved along a different route. For example, had our perceptual apparatus been such that we could directly perceive quanta of energy we might have been judging that a lump of coal remained the 'same amount' as a light beam after a transformation of it. Just as fancifully, within another system the water in the third beaker might only be judged to remain the same amount in certain circumstances because shape is included as an extra 'semantic marker' in the concept; so that if the beaker were straight-sided it would be the same amount and if curvilinear the question of sameness of amount would not arise. On the other hand, because perceptual judgments are reliant on what is seen, rather than deduced from multidimensional correlations, they lack such degrees of freedom. As regards the possibility of misinterpretation, rulebound concepts can be misinterpreted perceptually, and indeed are by preoperational children: amount is judged in terms of height or width. Such misinterpretation is not possible for perceptual concepts because in this context there is no level below the perceptual. This means that perceptual misapplication of a rulebound concept cannot be corrected by indicating another perceptual feature without at the same time making reference to the rule. For example if the child says that there is more water in the third beaker because the level is higher it is not enough to point out the corresponding decrease in width unless the child already knows the covariance principle crucial to conservation—the rule at the heart of the abstract concept. Likewise, we cannot show him that there is still the same amount to drink just by returning the liquid to the original container because all he will be seeing is a change from equality to inequality and back again: he still has to cognise the covariance rule.

These considerations also highlight an essential difference between transitivity and conservation. In transitivity, although the *inference* is abstract the A, C *question*, being unidimensional, requires only a perceptual judgment; but in conservation the very question 'Is it still the same amount?' is an abstract question and so it can be argued that *being able to understand the question implies understanding the conservation principle.* We have here a genetic epistemological problem. Its epistemological face is the issue of whether it is possible in principle to distinguish linguistic competence from concrete knowledge in this context. Its genetic face involves a developmental investigation into the relation between linguistic comprehension and cognitive level. The epistemological problem must be answered with reference to the developmental facts, yet the empirical findings have to be interpreted within a certain epistemological framework. Within Piaget's genetic epistemology language is taken to be a reflection of operational level and thus a separation of the linguistic from the cognitive would not be seen as justified, and neither would it be predicted that specifically linguistic difficulties of anything but a trivial nature could be discovered which are crucial to performance of conservation tasks. An answer to the epistemological question will emerge from what follows, but first let us review some of the experimental attempts to tease out linguistic and cognitive factors in conservation.

The first strategy for separating verbal from cognitive competence which will be considered is the avoidance of abstract terms like 'same amount' and 'more' in the instructions. Braine (1959) and Bruner (1966) have been foremost in suggesting that children should succeed on such conservation tasks at a much earlier age. This avoidance is achieved by what is known as the 'anticipation-of-levels' task. In this situation the child is presented with a standard beaker containing liquid together with an empty comparison of different width. He is then asked to indicate on the comparison how far up the level of the liquid poured from the standard will come. Consequently, earlier ages for conservation have been reported (Bruner *et al.* 1966; Halford, 1968). Another version is to ask the child to give a 'fair share' of water to another child in a differently shaped beaker; even 4 and 5-year-olds were able to perform correctly here (Cohen 1967).

A study by Larsen and Flavell (1970) confirmed that if the anticipation instruction contained the phrase 'same amount' the task was significantly more difficult than if they contained 'this water'. However this was only found if the comparison beaker was narrower than the standard, not if it was wider (Cohen had not included a wider comparison). Also they found little evidence of the ability to anticipate levels in their group of 5-year-olds; these children often placed the standard and comparison side by side and simply traced a straight line from one vessel to the other. Moreover, in an examination of the relation between anticipating the relative displacement of the trailing ends of the sticks in length conservation and the actual ability to conserve length they found 'little evidence that this kind of compensation necessarily precedes or accompanies conservation, or vice versa' (p. 272). It seems that we have to conclude that the degree of abstraction of the instructions does affect performance in some conditions but as anticipation does not unequivocally precede conservation this is of little theoretical significance.

Piaget's view of anticipation-of-levels performance (Piaget and Inhelder, 1963) is that it does not, by definition, test the child's knowledge of conservation. Being able to appreciate then an increase in one dimension necessitates a decrease in another and vice versa, is not all that is involved in conservation, he argues. The child must also know that the actual quantity of substance itself is not being changed. Piaget is undoubtedly correct that these kinds of knowledge are quite different; indeed the ability to anticipate levels seems more akin to a skill determined by mental imagery. In general the anticipation-of-levels task is a measure of what the child knows will happen rather than what he knows to be the case. Whatever is discovered about the relation of this skill to conservation, its quite separate epistemological status will be unaltered.

Another way of exploring the relation between verbal understanding and knowledge of conservation is to argue that, if the pre-operational child is failing to conserve due to linguistic incompetence, language training should bring about correct performance. The work of Bruner (1966) is again relevant in this context. Bruner's view of conservation development clearly diverges from Piaget's. He argued that the preoperational child has a basic understanding of the identity of substance throughout transformations but that because he is perceptually dominated, the gross changes in appearance seduce him towards the judgment that quantity has changed. Only by coming to encode the situation symbolically in language can the child succeed, because language encapsulates reality as opposed to appearance, embodying the 'ultimate structure of thought'. Frank (in Bruner, 1966) a co-worker of Bruner, employed a training method the aim of which was to encourage linguistic encoding by literally screening out perceptual cues. This involved asking the children to make judgments, or predictions, about the amount, or level, of liquid when poured into a container of a different shape behind a screen. This was employed to activate a linguistic competence which the child was taken to possess already, allowing him to argue 'same water therefore same amount', uncontaminated by perceptual cues. Many non-conservers did indeed judge that the amount remained the same. When the screen was removed the child was presented, according to Bruner, with a conflict between an 'ikonic' (perceptual) and a symbolic representation of the situation in which the symbolic was supposed to win out and bring about a consequent improvement on a post-test of conservation. This improvement was found in subjects above the age of 4 years.

Peill (1975, pp. 54–55; 103–107) has made some telling criticisms of Bruner's rationale, as did Piaget (1967) in reviewing the Bruner *et al.* volume. They both emphasise the question of whether conservation had really been induced by the screening procedures. If it had, this would be extremely significant whatever the weaknesses of rationale. Piaget's contention is that conservation was never induced as there had been no check for 'pseudo-conservation' where the child knows the correct answer without genuine knowledge of the conservation principle—though, puzzlingly, his arguments seem mainly relevant to anticipation-of-levels procedures. Whether or not this is fair criticism, other workers using pre and post-tests equally as inadequate from Piaget's viewpoint have failed to support Bruner's theory (for example, Strauss and Langer, 1970).

Another well-known verbal training technique is the 'verbal rule instruction' method of Beilin (1965) which, unlike the Bruner method, was not derived from a new theory of conservation. In this, children were presented with the rules that govern conservation in a verbal form and saw them coordinated with manipulation of the experimental materials in length and number conservation. This was found to be the most effective training method as against three nonverbal methods and a control condition. Smith (1968) supported the efficacy of this procedure for weight conservation against another two nonverbal methods. In the same context Lumsden and Kling (1969) gave non-conservers of size training in the multidimensional interpretation of the word 'bigger' which brought about a significant increase in size conservation responses relative to an untrained group. Yet on the other hand, Piaget's Genevan co-workers, Inhelder and Sinclair (1969), failed to discover any facilitating effects of language training on conservation. In reply to this significant piece of negative evidence Beilin (1971) pointed out that his verbal rule instruction method had not been used and concluded that available evidence still supports its efficacy. But he says 'The mechanism that accounts for its effectiveness is the algorithmic function of language that enables language rules to serve in problem solving *even in those instances in which an adequate operative structure is not available to the child.* Screening procedures function in an analogous fashion' (Beilin, 1971, p. 96; my italics) which amounts to an admission that language training need not have been bringing about any fundamental cognitive change.

This introduces the problem of producing criteria for real cognitive change, as opposed to the learning of a formula for correctness without real understanding, on which the interpretation of training studies hinges. Genevans refuse to accept any training studies which do not bring about operativity as they define it and stress the following factors: resistance to counter-suggestions, transfer to other kinds of conservation and to nonverbal testing procedures, giving full verbal justifications for the judgment, and the durability of the change through time. As some of these are more important than others Inhelder and Sinclair (1969) have suggested a hierarchy of criteria. On these criteria no training methods of any kind have ever been successful. Mermelstein and Meyer (1969) assessed four training techniques including Bruner's and Beilin's in a study of number conservation by the stringent Piagetian criteria and concluded that none of them were effective as neither the generalisability nor the durability criteria were met.

However, there is some circularity in the Piagetian position. As Beilin (1971) has pointed out, Genevans insist on strong criteria because the architecture of their theory depends on them. But to insist that training studies are only relevant if they actually bring concrete operations into being by their necessarily brief and artificial methods is unrealistic: the human cognitive system could surely not be so labile as to be capable of fundamental alteration by such experiences. Yet neither would it be advisable to open the floodgates and accept that improvement in conservation performance after training of any kind is evidence that Piaget has underestimated some particular experiential factor. If we did this the picture would be very confusing because almost every training method ever devised, from S–R to Brunerian, has brought about *some* post-test improvement in conservation. It appears that this present muddle has been brought about partly by Piaget's neglecting to set out clearly the kinds of experience which, on his theory, should and should not force accommodation through a conflict between assimilatory schemes. But with regard to our present problem, we should take evidence for the efficacy of verbal training as coming from studies which show *facilitation* of cognitive change in the direction of operativity arising out of a clearly verbal component of training against a wide range of techniques which do not include this component. However there are considerable difficulties encountered in designing such experiments and the bewildering variety of techniques which do produce facilitation, coupled with Inhelder and Sinclair's negative evidence makes the current state of the positive evidence seem rather weak. Furthermore, the durability criterion especially has to be taken seriously, for the facilitation of a judgment which only lasts for a few days can never be regarded as significant.

Our third strategy for examining the role of verbal factors in conservation is the development of nonverbal analogues to the standard procedure; if the preoperational children are failing through linguistic incompetence they should succeed on these. One nonverbal method was included in the Mermelstein and Meyer (1969) study mentioned above. This involved showing the children conjuring tricks in which the amount of liquid really appeared to increase with pouring it into another vessel and a row of counters seemed to be halved in number by deformation. If a child showed surprise at this turn of events it was concluded that he had some expectation of conservation and thus 'passed'. The authors found that only in the nonverbal number (but not liquid) conservation trick did a higher proportion of children pass than on the verbal version, which conflicted with an earlier study of Mermelstein and Shulman (1967) which found that a higher proportion of children did pass the nonverbal liquid task as opposed to the standard verbal version.

In the study by Mehler and Bever (1967) discussed above a nonverbal condition was included in which the children were shown two rows of sweets and asked to take which one they wanted to eat. However, as we have seen, this was not a test of conservation and it could not be assumed that children always chose what they took to be the larger. A study by Maxwell (unpublished data) employed a similar technique but deformed one of the rows as in the standard Piagetian procedure and told the children a story beforehand about a greedy little girl who always took the bigger share, so the question could then be about which of the rows this little girl would choose. The nonverbal task was not significantly easier than the standard conservation of number task.

Perhaps the most well-known attempt at a nonverbal analogue of a conservation task is one of number conservation based on the matching-from-sample paradigm. In this situation the subject is presented with a series of choice stimuli differing from one another and a sample stimulus which is identical to one of the choices in at least one respect. The task is to match the sample stimulus to its counterpart among the choice stimuli, which can be sets of items on display cards in the case of number studies. The numeric skills of monkeys and birds have been assessed in this way and more recently Wohlwill (1960) has adapted the procedure for use with children. The apparatus consists of a vertical board containing three rectangular appertures each covered by a card showing the stimuli (usually sets of dots) behind which are trays which can contain a reward of some kind. A sample card is presented to the child and he is told that one of the three cards has the reward behind it and that he will be able to find it every time if he looks first at the sample card. In order to test for conservation, counters can be used instead of a sample card which duplicate one of the choice cards in number and shape of arrangement. When the child has succeeded on this the counters can be deformed and the child asked to proceed as before, thereby testing his ability to judge invariance through a transformation.

Wohlwill's main reason for employing this test was to compare and rank the various subskills which go to make up the number concept—addition, subtraction, one-to-one correspondence, conservation and so on—not to contrast nonverbal and verbal competence. Therefore, the results were presented in terms of the relative ease of the tasks rather than at which age certain tasks were passed. Similarly, Wallace (1972) also employed this method primarily to study the developmental relationship between addition–subtraction and conservation, and counting and conservation. Nevertheless, we can also learn something about the relationship between nonverbal and verbal competence from examining the data. From Wallace's study we see that just under the third of a group of 5 to $5\frac{1}{2}$ -year-old children and over two-thirds of a group of 6 to $6\frac{1}{2}$ -year-olds passed such a nonverbal conservation test on which no children between 4 and $4\frac{1}{2}$ years were successful. Although Wallace employed a standardised version of the Genevan testing procedure with the same children he does not present data for comparison, therefore we cannot directly contrast the ease of the two tasks. In any case, the evidence here for a nonverbal competence in number conservation is not very impressive: Piaget himself found success at age 6 to be quite common with the standard procedure (Piaget, 1952).

Moreover, there are certain features of the procedure which make it difficult to equate with the verbal test. In general the test does not present sufficient perceptual conflict. For example, in Wohlwill's testing procedure, the counters were actually covered after they had been deformed, obliterating the perceptual conflict which is the essence of the Piagetian procedure: the child must see two qualities clearly differing in one dimension, such as height, after the deformation. Although Wallace did not cover the counters, his procedure encountered a similar conceptual difficulty. In deformation, the counters were not made any more perceptually similar to the displays on the incorrect choice cards so again no conflict was present: there was no reason to change to another choice card.

There is, however, a very important piece of evidence from Mounoud and Bower (1974) of not only a nonverbal but a sensorimotor ability to conserve weights in infants. The sensorimotor weight 'judgments' they employed were the adjustment of the force of hand grasp and the degree of arm muscle tension relative to the expected weight of an object. There was only direct perceptual evidence *after* the object had been lifted, unlike Furth's experiment with deaf children. Once the infants were able to relate these anticipations to the visual index of the object's size they could be tested for weight conservation through changes in an object's shape. Here the infants saw an object that they had previously picked up being doubled in length and halved in width (it was hinged). After the age of roughly 18 months they used the same anticipatory force to grasp the object after elongation. Thus far then the evidence for sensorimotor competence is good but for nonverbal competence on the conceptual plane very weak.

The final strategy for examining the role of verbal instructions involves accepting at the outset that only the standard Piagetian procedure can assess knowledge of conservation but affirming, in view of the abstract, rulebound nature of the conservation vocabulary, that there is an ineluctably linguistic component to conservation competence involving the ability to interpret the instructions correctly. In order to assess the importance of this linguistic component an attempt can be made to determine whether the preoperational child is naturally inclined to interpret them wrongly when not being tested for conservation. Such an attempt was made in a study by Russell (1975a). If it were discovered that the child does interpret the instructions correctly independent of conservation testing then his conservation failure must be due to the perceptual experience of witnessing the transformation and its results. If, on the other hand, he interprets them incorrectly, then faulty comprehension must be at the heart of his failure. If correct interpretation is not found the next step is to determine whether the misinterpretation is due to semantic immaturity or to a basic cognitive incapacity or 'disequilibrium'. To answer this question, purely semantic training was used in the study which would be effective in changing the interpretation if the failure were only semantic.

In order to test the interpretation in 5-year-old children of the abstract term 'same amount of room' as employed in studies of the conservation of two and three-dimensional space, Russell used as the standard a square (*two-dimensional* condition) or cube (*three-dimension* condition) filled with much smaller squares or cubes which were supposed to represent 'animals' in a 'zoo'. In one set of conditions the child had to *select* an empty comparison from a series in response to the instruction to pick the zoo which had the 'same amount of room in it for the animals' as the first zoo, and in other conditions he had to *produce* the standard himself. Half of the children were then given *semantic* training away from the experimental apparatus in which the experimenter told each child a story illustrated by drawings relevant to a multidimensional interpretation and gave him feedback as to his incorrect interpretation. The other half were provided with concrete *manipulative* feedback as to the degree of correctness of their interpretation by transferring the animals into their chosen zoo directly after testing.

The results were that the children from the two-dimensional conditions who had to select the comparison tended to pick a square irrespective of its size, thereby interpreting 'amount' as 'shape'. In the three-dimensional selection condition where the exigencies of the scoring procedure made it impossible to present a very close approximation to the cube in the comparison series there was a high level of interpretation on the correct multidimensional principle. This relates to a finding of Bryant (1972) that when the opportunity for misinterpreting instructions in terms of length changes alone was not present in a test of number invariance, children as young as 3 years responded correctly. On both two and three-dimensional conditions children *produced* comparisons of the same height as the standard irrespective of comparison width or depth, thus interpreting 'amount' as 'height'. Semantic training was only significantly effective in the selection conditions. However, this post-test improvement was not significantly greater than the non-significant degree of improvement after the concrete feedback training.

It appears therefore that the interpretation is incorrect from the outset *before* transformation, and thus that non-conservation is not due to witnessing perceptual changes. As regards the effects of semantic training, it must be admitted that they were sufficiently limited as to suggest a basic cognitive incapacity or disequilibrium on the part of the child rather than the lack of purely semantic knowledge—or at best a semantic habit very deeply ingrained. One way of explaining the cognitive effects of the instruction is to use Piaget's phrase and say that it 'centres the thought' of the child on unidimensional features. Of course, this claim is quite different to Piaget's that the perceptual nature of the child's non-conservation arises out of the disequilibrated nature of his thought, quite independent of linguistic factors. The present account therefore implies that the child's thought is not spontaneously perceptual in character and that therefore, unless he is asked to make a judgment with an instruction containing abstract terms like 'same amount' which he can only interpret unidimensionally, he should be able to cognise conservation. Thus we return to the question of nonverbal competence.

The Mounoud and Bower (1974) study provided evidence of a form of nonverbal competence in weight conservation but on the behavioural rather than the conceptual plane. Also, as Bryant (1974) points out, only one object was involved rather than an equivalence between two which, as we shall see, is necessary for a genuine test of conservation. A recent experiment by Russell (1978) employed a procedure to determine whether 4 to 6-year-old non-conservers could appreciate length invariance in a nonverbal conceptual task and whether they could verbalise the basis of their judgments after they had been made. The method is best understood with reference to figure 3.1 which represents lined squares of cardboard with lengths of

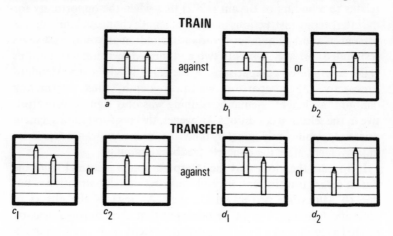

Figure 3.1

pencil glued to their surface. In the training series the children were presented with a pair of cards on each trial, an a card plus b_1 or b_2 card, and were instructed to 'pick the card that you think has a picture on the other side of'. Half of the children were allocated to the 'equal' group and half to the 'unequal' group. For the equal group a coloured picture was always present on the reverse side of the a cards with the b cards blank, and vice versa for the unequal group. Thus one group of children was trained to a criterion to choose pencils of equal length and another to choose pencils of unequal length. On the transfer series the c cards *were always correct*. The rationale was that if the equal group could carry information about length invariance across a transformation (which they did not witness) from a cards to c cards they would find the transfer task easier than the unequal group and thus choose the correct card on the first trial of transfer and take fewer errors and trials to attain criterion on the transfer task. The unequal group should either tend to choose d cards or respond randomly on the transfer. Each child was asked after he had made his choice on the first transfer trial, but before the cards were turned over, why he had chosen as he did, and was retested for conservation directly after the end of the transfer series.

There were also two controls to insure that if children from the equal group succeeded in transferring information from a to c cards this was due to the nonverbal nature of the procedure rather than to any other of its features. It was demonstrated that a standard *verbal* test was neither easier with cue lines present as on the testing cards nor when the child saw an a card replaced by a c card instead of seeing a pencil being moved up.

The equal group made significantly fewer errors on the transfer series. Also on the first trial the equal group tended to pick c cards correctly, implying some understanding of invariance, and the unequal group responded randomly. What was most striking was that with very few exceptions the correct children from the equal group could verbalise the basis of their choice usually saying that the pencils were the 'same size'. Yet on being retested for length conservation by the standard procedure they still evinced *no* understanding of the invariance principle.

It is paradoxical that these non-conservers were able to use the abstract term 'same size' to justify their performance on a nonverbal length invariance task yet failed to conserve when the phrase was used by the experimenter in his instructions. It seems that preoperational children are able to use abstract language correctly in the description of, or reflection on, their judgments but are not able to use this language in *directing* their judgments. Overall these results do support the notion that interpreting the instructions wrongly is the disequilibrating experience in conservation. Moreover this suggests an alternative view of the acquisition of conservation. Instead of the child's cognitive structures undergoing a fundamental change as Piaget proposes, it may be his knowledge of the objective criteria for the truth of concrete judgments which changes. The child becomes aware that the 'knowledge' he possesses in a private form is objective and public, that when other people talk about the 'size', 'amount', 'position' and so on of something remaining the same in a context of change, they are using the multidimensional criteria which he uses himself rather than a unidimensional criterion. On this model the preoperational child cannot appreciate that something other than a perceptually obvious, 'pointatable' change can be a public criterion for the truth of a concrete judgment. Seeing these rulebound criteria as intersubjective is tantamount to the acquisition of a, what Baldwin calls, synnomic form of knowledge.

There is a conceptual argument from Elkind (1967) and a set of empirical findings from Elkind and Schoenfield (1972) which appear to present obstacles to the present line of reasoning. Elkind argued that Piaget confounds two kinds of conservation in his design: the conservation of a single variable quantity ('identity' conservation) and the conservation of the relation of equality between the standard and the variable ('equivalence' conservation). This equivalence conservation is dependent on the ability to make a transitive inference in terms of 'standard = variable before; variable before = variable after; therefore standard = variable after'. The Elkind and Schoenfield results seem to lend empirical support to the conceptual distinction because giving conservation tasks with only *one* quantity enabled even 4-year-olds to conserve. Is, then, failure at the Piagetian kind of conservation due to an inability to make the transitive inference? It is not, because the inference is not necessary for success. In conservation what is presented to the child is two items with two states of one of the items. In transitivity, on the other hand, there are three items each with a constant state. As was argued above, the problem in transitivity is to deduce a perceptual, unidimensional judgment about an invisible relation (A, C) by applying an abstract rule to a series of perceptual, unidimensional relations. But here the

A, C relation is visible and multidimensional; the 'middle term' is multidimensional; and the child is asked to make an abstract judgment. Again, it is one thing to describe performance in terms of a rule and quite another to explain the performance by reference to it. Quite apart from these considerations the non-conserver's perceptual justifications show that he has a basis for his, albeit incorrect, judgment. Would a child whose failure was inferential produce such consistent justifications and would he not lack any basis for the 'standard-variable after' comparison?

Regarding the success of the preoperational children on the single quantity experiments, this can not only be encompassed within the present account but actually complements it. As the results of Russell's interpretation study suggested, preoperational children were misinterpreting the instructions prior to any transformation, hearing which could be regarded as the disequilibrating experience in conservation. In the one quantity situation there can be no pre-transformation instruction, thus no abstract terms and thus the child's thought is not centred on unidimensional features. (This is rather similar to a behaviouristic point commonly made against the conservation experiment that by the perceptual equalisation of the amounts at the outset the child is 'reinforced' for a perceptual answer). When he is asked if it is still the same amount after transformation he is free to judge on the basis that nothing has been added or subtracted because there is no comparison present and thus no opportunity for perceptual interpretation.

However Bryant (1974) reports that the Elkind and Schoenfield results still hold if crosses are left to mark the previous location of the counters, thereby presenting the possibility of a perceptual comparison. If this is so it may either be because preoperational children are less likely to interpret instructions perceptually *after* a transformation, or because they only compare immediately present physical quantities in their perceptual judgments.

Explaining the Elkind and Schoenfield results cannot be divorced from the epistemology of conservation concepts—from the status of our knowledge of physical properties like quantity, size, and so on. These are in no way *properties inherent* in individual substances but what is equivalent to sets of them; this being another aspect of the abstract nature of these concepts. Thus a certain quantity is abstracted from what some substances have in common, so that it becomes the respect in which they are equivalent; and thus Russell and Whitehead in *Principia Mathematica* were led to define number as the class of equivalent classes (and some notion of equivalence must remain, despite Piaget's strictures against their definion). For this reason the children in the Elkind and Schoenfield study cannot be judged to have knowledge of conservation if they still fail what Elkind calls equivalence conservation.

Relating the present explanation of conservation to what has already been said about the rulebound nature of concrete operational thought, one might anticipate Part 4 and say that these rules should be seen as inherent in the human conceptual system—culture in the broadest sense. Thereby the hypothesis arises that they are passed down to the child through interpersonal experience, through education in the broadest sense—a position similar to that of Bruner (1966; 1974). Evidence that the acquisition of conservation is facilitated by exposure to conservers would support this account. Studies in which non-conservers and conservers are paired in a training period and asked to make a judgment about a conservation matter show both that the conserver's answer tends to prevail *irrespective of social dominance* and that the training effects are fairly impressive (Miller and Brownwell 1975; Murray 1972; Silverman and Geiringer 1973; Silverman and Stone 1972). Exposure to the conserving judgments of a model has also proved a very successful facilitatory method (Rosenthal and Zimmerman 1972; Zimmerman and Rosenthal 1972; Zimmerman and Rosenthal 1974a). In their most recent study on this topic Zimmerman and Rosenthal (1974b) showed that modelling caused the trained groups to spontaneously generalise their learning and to manifest conservation in nonverbal behaviour. Suffice it to be said at present that the view which stresses the acquisition of rules from society by coming to share objective criteria for judgments, as against the attainment of equilibrium in mental structures, would support Baldwin's genetic epistemology rather than Piaget's.

Returning to the genetic epistemological problem broached above, as to whether it is possible to draw a distinction between linguistic comprehension and concrete operational knowledge, we have suggested that we can and must concentrate on the factor of linguistic interpretation to explain how the child comes to acquire the knowledge. Indeed concrete operational knowledge is not conceivable without some form of linguistic competence for, as Baldwin stressed, knowledge as opposed to practical success (e.g., predicting water levels, sensorimotor conservation competence) is public property. A similar point was implicit in the conclusion of the transitivity section. The 'nonverbal' kind of knowledge evinced in the length study is unsocialized and private and thus imperfect. Language is the means whereby the essential commonness and public status of knowledge is maintained. This will be taken up again in Part 4.

3.4 LANGUAGE ACQUISITION

That this section is rather different from the previous three is dictated by the nature of the topic. The issues are not experimental in the same sense as data are usually taken from childrens' utterances in their everyday life. Also, the present state of the field must be understood in the light of the impetus which Noam Chomsky's linguistic theory gave to developmental research, rather than as arising from the influence of Piaget. Therefore, we will not be dealing with experimentation directly inspired by Piaget's theory but with the degree to which the theory can be accommodated within the current state of developmental psycholinguistics and indeed influence its development; this being dictated by the fact that Piaget does not offer a theory of language acquisition as such.

Chomsky (see 1965, chapter 1; 1968) first came to the general notice of psychologists through his chastisement of B. F. Skinner in his review (Chomsky, 1959) of Skinner's book *Verbal Behaviour*. Chomsky insisted that the psychology of language cannot be understood by treating it as just another piece of behaviour: we have to begin with a consideration of the structure of language itself. Under the influence of Chomsky's theory psycholinguistics developed from a backwater—a subfield of human engineering—into a field of intensive psychological and epistemological contention. Chomsky very deliberately adopts a rationalist approach (even to the extent of calling one of his books *Cartesian Linguistics*) and argues that examining the structure of a human capacity such as language is tantamount to examining the structure of the mind which processes the capacity. The natural corollary of this is that such a structure will be innate in the human species.

Chomsky employed a mixture of philosophical, linguistic and empirical arguments to suggest that the human child must have innate 'knowledge' of the universal principles under which languages are organised. He argued that it is logically impossible that human language could be acquired by the learning principle of 'inductive generalisation'. His linguistic theory holds that all sentences have a deep and a surface structure related by transformational rules. The deep structure is the abstract, underlying, propositional form of a sentence which determines the semantic interpretation and thus the meaning. Transformational rules are applied to the deep structure to produce the surface structure—the sentence we hear and the superficial grammatical features we assign to it (see Greene, 1972). On the basis of his linguistic theory Chomsky proposed that, as the child is exposed only to surface structures it would be linguistically impossible for him to extract the deep structure of the language, which would enable him to go on generating meaningful utterances himself, unless he already had some prior 'knowledge' of the principles on which 'sound' and 'meaning' were related. He also suggested that it is empirically impossible that a child should acquire the grammar of his language in the relatively short time that he does unless he knows something of the universal principles of its organisation. Thus there are taken to be both 'formal' and 'substantive' linguistic universals, the former representing innate 'knowledge' of principles such as the deep–surface distinction and their relation by transformations (not the actual rules of course, otherwise the child could only acquire one language) and the latter the universal syntactic (such as subject–predicate, noun, verb) and phonological features of all languages. Chomsky's use of 'knowledge' will not detain us here except to say that it is entirely different from the usage employed above, as will be discussed in Part 4.

McNeill (1966, 1970a, 1970b) is the psychologist mainly responsible for mediating Chomskian theory into the study of language acquisition—although he has since adopted a different line (McNeill, 1974a). How might one empirically test such a theory as Chomsky's? McNeill assumed that child speech can be assessed syntactically as soon as two words are conjoined (usually at around 18 months). One can then set about showing that this and further conjoining is organised by prior principles rather than as the result of learning features present in adult usage. McNeill had to demonstrate that the only way in which rulebound features of the earliest two and three-word utterances could be explained was by assuming that these rules arose out of the child's innate syntactical capacities. He had two main pieces of evidence. First, that the position in two-word utterances of a certain set of words was fixed—the so-called 'pivot' class. As well as always coming either first or second these pivot words were supposed never to appear alone or with other pivot words; all other words being assigned to the 'open' class. Second, that in a child ('Adam' from the Brown and Bellugi (1964) study) who had three identifiable grammatical categories, nouns (N), verbs (V) and pivot words (P) and was producing either two or three words at a time, only those combinations were produced which were consonant with 'basic grammatical relations' such as subject–object, main verb–object, and so on. (For two-word utterances there are $(3^2 =)$ 9 possible and 4 permissible combinations; for three-word combinations $(3^3 =)$ 27 possible and 9 permissible combinations.) Thus, Adam produced combinations such as 'Adam write' $(N + V)$ and 'Mommy get ladder' $(N + V + N)$ but not combinations like 'write get' $(V + V)$ or 'Mommy get write' $(N + V + V)$. McNeill argued that this was evidence for innate linguistic knowledge. For a while this kind of analysis seemed extremely persuasive and a form of 'new rationalism' gained strength and confidence sufficient for McNeill to step back 250 years to side with Samuel Bailey against George Berkeley (McNeill, 1969).

In the present context it would be unwise to become involved in the question of how such distributional evidence can and cannot be interpreted, but the possibility of alternative explanations should at least be raised. Is, for example, the following account really too simple-minded? We might propose that the first thing the child does is to acquire some kind of understanding of word meaning in terms of the use to which words are put. Thus he would know pretty well what a Mommy is; what the act of writing is; that getting has something to do with people moving things from elsewhere to him; what a ladder is, and so on. Given such a child, the probability of an utterance like 'write get' occurring would be very low indeed. There might conceivably be a bizarre situation to which it could refer, or it could be the result of an odd kind of telegraphic elision ('write [my name then] get [me another piece of paper]'). But the probability of utterances like 'Adam write' would be immensely greater. It is only when concentration is entirely on form at the expense of meaning and function that the earliest combinations making some kind of sense to the adult (and this is what being 'consonant with basic grammatical relations' really means here) appear remarkable and mysterious. It also makes explaining development difficult if not impossible: McNeill had to diverge from Chomskian theory in his explanation of the later differentiation of the other grammatical categories from the pivot grammar to give a basically functionalist account of how the pivot class acquired its membership (McNeill, 1970a, pp. 1093–99). In any event, the strictly Chomskian view of language acquisition proved, early on, to be untenable. It strenuously neglected semantic and cognitive factors and proposed a device (the 'Language Acquisition Device') to account for acquisition that was ill-defined and so abstract and mechanistic that it seemed to have no discernable connection with psychological processes. Also, further studies showed that there was very scant support for basic empirical assumptions such as the pivot rule (Brown, 1973). But at bottom it was—and is— inconceivable that any developmental linguistic data could only be explained by proposing innate syntactic knowledge.

Thus by the late 1960s a move was already underway towards the acceptance of cognitive factors underpinning the acquisition of language rather than purely linguistic structures—from an excessive formalism to one that was tempered by psychological reality. The work of Bloom (1970) of Schlesinger (1974) and of Greenfield and Smith (1976) is particularly representative of this continuing trend. Bloom argued that the pivot grammar had little explanatory power and suggested instead that such regularities as were found in the child's earliest word combinations could be explained by positing underlying semantic relations which had to be interpreted with reference to the speech context. For example, the fact that 'Mommy sock' had to be interpreted as meaning either something like 'Mommy is putting my sock on' or as 'Here is Mommy's sock' depending on the context, suggests that just recording this as an example of 'Open + Open' is a very superficial characterisation. Bloom did not stray very far from Chomskian concepts, however, and provided a derivation of such two-word surface forms from a kind of deep structure because an underlying grammatical relation could be supplied for each semantic relation.

Schlesinger's approach was more clearly semantic. He proposed that the rulebound nature of the early utterances can be explained by positing semantic relational concepts such as agent and action, possessor and possessed, location of object which depend on the way the child cognises his environment, and thus on developing cognition rather than innate linguistic structures. Some of these semantic relations are taken to be universal. Data from Bowerman (1975) and from Greenfield and Smith (1976) have supported this notion.

Bowerman studied early speech samples from four quite divergent languages—Finnish, Luo, English and Samoan—and found that for two-word utterances five relations were present in all of them (agent–action; action–object; possession; demonstrative; qualification) and four were present in some of them. The Greenfield and Smith study was concerned with one-word utterances and thus had to assimilate contextual features in order to characterise the inherent relations. Schlesinger diverged somewhat from the authors' original interpretation to regard these utterances as epitomising various kinds of underlying situational relation. For example, 'Mommy' when said to demand something, when said to draw attention to the object out of reach and when said to get help in performing an action reflects three quite separate kinds of relation between agent, action and object. So he proposed that, as we are capable of cognitively organising the world in many different ways, one of the things the child has to do in learning language is to discover which of the relations between objects, states, actions and qualities are marked in the syntax of the language he is learning. He has to learn what Schlesinger calls the 'I markers' of the particular language. For example English does not mark any syntactic distinction between the animate and inanimate agents in 'the boy cut the bread' and 'the knife cut the bread', although we certainly cognise the difference. In this way Schlesinger can present an interactional account: a language is constructed on a cognitive framework but can affect cognition through the syntactic filter of its 'I markers'—a consideration which tends towards the 'linguistic relativity hypothesis' of Whorf (1941).

However Brown (1973, p. 142) has argued, in comparing Schlesinger with Bloom, that it is possible to write a grammar on the basis of Schlesinger's theory with a kind of semantic deep structure having a rule-governed relation to the surface form and that many of the differences between the two accounts are terminological. But the third theory of Greenfield and Smith (1976) is quite untranslatable into Chomskian concepts. Like Schlesinger they say that 'the child's actions and perceptions are being structured in terms of semantic functions like Agent, Action, Object, Location etc. and that words are being inserted into such a cognitive–perceptual–action framework from the outset' (p. 30) but go beyond this to propose that communication between child and adult is central to the development of grammar—indeed that the child learns syntax from what adults say about his language. The adult understands what the child is intending when he uses a word in a particular context and then expands this into a sentence. The child learns from this something about how words are ordered in relation to environmental events and states and organised within utterances. Such an account would have to predict that adult expansion of the child's utterances should facilitate syntactic development. Neither naturalistic nor experimental studies have so far discovered any such energising effects (see Brown, 1973, p. 464).

In view of these developments it is not surprising that psycholinguists have turned to Piagetian theory in the hope of finding support for their cognitive proposals; for Piaget's theory is founded on the notion that the logicalities of thought stem from sensorimotor coordinations and that language reflects the degree of logicality which thought possesses. In a similar vein Bruner, among others, has proposed a 'grammar of action' beginning in early infancy—see Bruner (1968) and papers in Bruner and Connolly (1974). There is a particularly neat demonstration of what appears to be an isomorphism between the coordination of action and grammar development in an experimental study by Greenfield, Nelson and Saltzman (1972). They found that when infants were encouraged to nest a series of cups one inside the other three identifiable strategies appeared, developing in the following order between about 12 and 36 months. First, in the 'pairing' method the infant just puts one cup inside or on top of another without going any further; in the 'pot' method one cup was static and he brought other cups to put inside or on top of it; in the 'subassembly' method, once cups had been nested by pairing they were moved as a unit and put inside another cup and so on. The authors suggest that pairing reflects the 'actor–action–acted upon' relation which parallels the simple syntactic form of 'subject–verb–object'. The pot method reflects 'actor–action–acted upon' then another sequence with the 'acted upon' item changing, which parallels two 'subject–verb–object' sequences conjoined by *and*. In the subassembly method we have an 'actor–action–acted upon' relation itself becoming the actor in a similar relation: one 'subject–verb–object' sequence being embedded within another by 'which'. This order of simple sentences then being conjoined and finally being embedded within each other is found in the developmental sequence of their acquisition, the authors conclude from a review of studies carried out by others. They were also able to relate nesting strategies to the developmental finding that animate nouns are subjects and inanimate nouns are objects of the earliest sentences, by interpreting 'cup in hand' as animate. There is also the suggestion that such a sequence may be universal: children from a Mayan community in South Mexico showed a similar sequence of strategies. In a different context, the fact that it is not till some four years later that such seriation tasks can be carried out conceptually affords another example of the behavioural anticipating the conceptual—found also in the Mounoud and Bower (1974) conservation study—and consonant with Piagetian theory.

Yet it has to be admitted that such studies, although inspired by Piagetian principles, do not actually extract a theory of language acquisition from Piaget's theory. Such an isomorphism does not explain how language is acquired but rather supports a general parallelism between thinking in words and in actions. It is possible to apply more distinctively Piagetian notions to the acquisition of language. Morehead and Morehead (1974) have attempted this. In a theoretical paper they describe Piaget's account of the development of the sign out of the index, the imagery of imitation and the symbolism of play (see p. 105) and then relate the stages of sensorimotor development, in a very interesting way to Bloom's (1973) data on the early utterances of her daughter Alison between 10 months and 2 years.

At 10 months (sensorimotor Stage 4) Alison's utterances had an index-like character and were highly dependent on immediate imitation. She could use 'away' after having been repeatedly told to throw certain objects away when mouthing them. (Bloom (1974b) later showed that there are definite individual differences in the tendency to immediate imitation and clear syntactic differences in the spontaneous and imitated speech of imitators.) During what looked like Stage 5 Alison started to use two forms of word: substantive terms like 'chair', 'book' and 'back', and function words like 'stop', 'more' and 'up' as 'orders and expressions of desire'. Bloom reports that the first category had a 'high mortality rate' but that the second quickly became established. This, the Moreheads suggest, is due to the fact that internalised action schemes which allow for the retention of a representation independent of context on which naming is dependent have not become established in Stage 5. The child is still very much action-based; thus the establishment of the function words. At the end of Stage 5 the child plays in an 'adultomorphic' way that is unimaginative and literal: blankets are used for covering, brooms for sweeping and so on. They see this characteristic reflected in the way Alison started to produce the surface features of adult speech. She sometimes talked in a kind of gibberish which imitated the phonetic and intonation patterns of speech but had no meaning. Finally, with Stage 6 and the internalisation of action in imagery there is evidence for the first time of a real separation between sign and signifier: in play the child uses objects in ways different from their intended use; there is deferred imitation; and in her speech Alison overgeneralised, saying 'Mommy' when she saw her mother's glove and calling other males 'Dada'.

The Moreheads refer to one especially interesting characteristic of speech during Stage 6. Viewed from the Piagetian angle speech at this stage will reflect the combination of internalised actions in novel, 'insightful', anticipatory ways even though it cannot be expressed syntactically. Thus, three children studied by Bloom started to produce sequences of single words without grammatical relation but with a fairly complex action component. For example Alison handing her father a peach and a spoon: 'Daddy . . . peach . . . cut'. The intonation contours and the long pause between the words suggest their syntactic separateness. My daughter Charlotte produced a similar sequence at 18 months. She said 'Push [push-chair]. . . . lepcub [leopard cubs] . . . meat . . . Gramma' *some hours* after she had seen from her push chair, and in the company of her grandmother leopard cubs being fed at the zoo. Though one, perhaps crucial, difference is that the child was here a passive spectator of the scene. In this way, according to the Moreheads, the cognitive stage is set for the appearance of syntax. This either seems to derive from physical knowledge (such as existence: 'that ball'; recurrence: 'more milk') or 'logico-mathematic' knowledge (agent–action: 'daddy walk'; possessive: 'mommy sock'). In both cases the words follow a definite order of occurrence.

Of course these are very early stages: the Morehead's parallel-drawing may not stand up to new data and will seem overzealous to many. But it cannot be denied that at a basic level linguistic development must be dependent on sensorimotor capacities. Yet this still does not get us very far in extracting a theory of language acquisition from Piaget. Of course linguistic development is hardly likely to outpace sensorimotor development (for example, the child is not likely to evince an object concept in his speech which he does not show in his behaviour), but positing a sensorimotor substrate, a necessary condition, is a long way from explaining how language gets off the ground in the first place, how it continues to develop after the sensorimotor stage and indeed how its formal features ever came to develop (Brown, 1973, p. 239). Even the foremost Genevan psycholinguist H. Sinclair (1973) does not hold out very much hope of deriving a developmental linguistic theory from Piaget. Nelson (1974) suggests the basic problem is that the relation between verbalised preconcepts and the sensorimotor schemes from which they are derived is indeterminate: Piaget does not forge the necessary link between the sensorimotor and the verbal-conceptual. 'Logical structures appear to develop independently of specific context just as syntactic structures seem to develop independently of lexical content in current theories. But as Sinclair de Zwart has pointed out, one must influence the other, and this seems especially true early in development' (p. 274).

The matter is further complicated by the fact that Piaget appears to assign two (albeit complementary) roles to language in his theory, neither of which are leading ones. One is auxillary: language is the most pervasive of the symbolic functions—with deferred imitation, symbolic play, drawing and dreams being the others—and, as such, forms the necessary but not sufficient condition for the construction of logical operations. Without it the 'operations would remain at the stage of successive action without ever being integrated into simultaneous systems or simultaneously encompassing a set of interdependent transformations . . . would remain personal and would consequently not be regulated by personal exchange and cooperation' (1954, p. 98). The other role is as the reflection of the subject's state of operational equilibrium, and thus as the medium through which this equilibrium can be assessed by the clinical method. One of the very few things that Piaget has in common with Bertrand Russell is the assumption that language is 'transparent' in this way. There seems to be an isomorphism between the operations and verbal concepts being proposed. The consequences of this view for Piaget's account of conservation were tackled in the previous section. Within Piagetian theory language just seems to appear and play its rather subservient part.

The evidence which Piaget most frequently cites (along with the Inhelder and Sinclair verbal training experiment) in support of his view of language, is experimentation with deaf children by such workers as Furth (see p. 156). Apart from the fact that this work *does* in fact show deaf children to be impaired relative to hearing children, there are considerable difficulties of rationale and procedure in the way of drawing definite conclusions from such studies about the role of language in thinking. A dilemma of rationale is whether to use nonverbal or verbal testing procedures. Nonverbal techniques are, of course, fairer to deaf children but there is a severe limitation on the kinds of task which can be performed totally without instructions, let alone without the use of abstract terms; so it is rather like a high-jump competition in which the bar can never be raised above 2 feet. The other alternative is to employ some other form of symbolic representation to instruct the child and present the materials. But there are severe limitations on what can be explained without the use of language. Moreover, to instruct deaf children by the use of sign language or lip-reading procedures is merely to employ them as a group of children with a relatively inefficient language system rather than as children 'without language'. When these difficulties are resolved there is still the question of subjects. It is extremely difficult, if not impossible, to find deaf children totally lacking any form of verbal—symbolic skill. Even if one discovers children who have never been taught lip-reading or signing the chances are that they have been able to find some way into the verbal system by either of these routes for themselves. 'Nonvocal' does not imply 'nonverbal'. Notably, when verbal instructions (in this case signing) were used by Furth (1966) in a study of liquid conservation the deaf children were found to be severely handicapped relative to hearing children—not even being able to understand what was expected of them till the age of about 10 years. Oleron and Herren (1961) found a retardation of 6 years in a similar task. In fact it is strange that Piaget wants to predict lack of retardation in deaf children who lack verbal skills when he regards a sign system as a *necessary condition* for concrete operational thinking! Moreover he proposes that as blind children lack the deaf children's sensorimotor abilities though they have a fully-developed language they *should* be retarded by some years. Evidence from Cromer (1973) indicates that the concrete operational structures do not appear to be delayed in blind children.

Cromer (1974) has also produced a review of the language acquisition literature around the question of evidence for a cognitive account which Piaget would generally support as against the Chomskian view—managing to trace a clear path through the jungle of complex data. Of course Chomsky's theory is not the inverse of Piaget's (he does not hold that language structures thought in a

Whorfian fashion) but he does believe that linguistic structures are innate and implies that the course of language development is largely determined by factors within the linguistic system apart from the course of cognitive development. Cromer presents a considerable range of evidence for the cognitive theory (for example, that before a form is made syntactically explicit the child is able to express it with the primitive means at his disposal) and also some evidence for independent linguistic development (for example, that the timing of the appearance of grammatical forms between languages is due to the degree of specifically linguistic complexity which their expression involves). However it might be said in passing that one crucial piece of evidence Cromer gives for the linguistic independence theory is somewhat debatable. With reference to the work of the Gardeners (1969) who taught the chimpanzee Washoe to communicate in sign language he supports Brown's (1973) contention that although the chimp's sensorimotor intelligence was comparable to the human infant's, her grammatical competence in terms of word order was not and that, therefore, she lacked a specifically grammatical competence. But, reverting to the Morehead's distinction between two kinds of early word combination one reflecting physical knowledge and one reflecting logico-mathematical knowledge (of the relations between things and events), it appears that Washoe lacked the latter kind which implies a *cognitive* incapacity in framing relational concepts. McNeill (1974b) has suggested that Washoe did have a sort of grammar but one based on an 'addressee–non-addressee' rule in terms of who was giving and who was receiving information rather than on relations between actors, recipients and objects in the communication event. Communication is important within chimpanzee society but unlike humans they have little curiosity about objects and their relations (van Lawick-Goodall, 1971) which further suggests a lack of relational sensorimotor understanding on which to construct a grammar. Further developments in this area are eagerly awaited.

Cromer suggests in conclusion a weak form of the cognitive hypothesis on the basis of the Russian psychologist Vygotsky's (1962) theory that thought and language have separate genetic roots, that they develop independently yet they interact at certain stages, that there is a pre-linguistic phase of thought and a pre-intellectual phase in speech and so on.

That so many conflicting claims cannot be resolved by such a formula is not only due to its neglecting to specify the nature of the human language capacity and the nature of the interactions between the systems that are supposed to take place but arises from restricting the issue to language *structures*. No adequate theory of language acquisition can be developed from asking only what is the relative contribution of structures of thought and structures of language. The real dichotomy in developmental theories is not between those which propose a cognitive and those which support a linguistic primacy but between structuralist and functionalist accounts. What Piaget and Chomsky have in common is more fundamental than how they differ: they are both structuralists (see Morehead and Morehead, 1974; Russell, 1975b). Chomsky, for example, is not totally opposed to the notion of cognitive structures underpinning language nor to that of organism—environment interaction. Regarding the relation between cognitive and linguistic structures he says 'It is quite possible that the lack of analogy testifies to our ignorance of other aspects of mental function, rather than to the absolute uniqueness of linguistic structure'; and although he talks of 'a succession of maturational stages leading finally to full generative grammar' he also calls for 'a detailed study of the actual character of the stimulation and the organism—environment interaction that sets the innate cognitive mechanisms into operation' (Chomsky; 1968, pp. 76–8).

A glance at the history of psychological theories of language reveals that the earliest protagonists for structuralist and functionalist accounts were, respectively, Wundt and K. Bühler (see Blumenthal, 1975). Wundt, who like Chomsky was primarily influenced by Humboldt, wrote tree diagrams to illustrate the relational structure of sentence comprehension, introduced a distinction very similar to that between deep and surface structure and a system of transformations between sentence types. Bühler (1934) was primarily a theorist of function. Communication, he argued, must depend not only on the speaker and hearer having the requisite cognitive competence to structure and interpret sentences, but on their sharing the same field of discourse, having in common the same range of objects, events, and ideas to consider, the same set of assumptions and kinds of interest. Thus Wundt's mental structures were replaced by structures of this total field (*Umfeld*) consisting of the practical situation (*Zeigfeld*) in which the utterance occurs and the symbolic field (*Symbolfeld*), the linguistic context. An essential element in language is the function of the utterances within the stream of behaviour, within the context of the exchange of thought. To regard the *Umwelt* as being either in the communicants' heads or in the external world would be a mistake; rather it is a constantly changing schema, continuously constructed and reconstructed by speech, which cannot be located anywhere. Developmentally one can extract the implication that communicative intent, the function of vocalisation, must be prior to the production of language; it is how language development gets under way and why we ever say anything at all.

It is within the conceptual framework established by Wittgenstein and by certain Oxford philosophers after J. L. Austin (see p. 36) that Bruner (1975) has recently adopted a somewhat functionalist view of language acquisition. A large number of Anglo-Saxon philosophers, each in his different way, have recommended focusing on the *use* to which utterances are put *in vivo* as a way of understanding the nature of meaning in language. Bruner argues that when the infant is at the prelinguistic stage he is learning, largely through interaction with a caretaker, that certain acts have determinate usages and that within interpersonal exchanges these acts are related to others in a rulebound manner. By coming to appreciate the function of behavioural elements in the human community he is able to recognise the function of the basic linguistic relations which are isomorphic to these. If we consider, for example, the immense pleasure babies get from throwing things out of their cots for their mothers to retrieve and the many kinds of exchange of objects that goes on between the infant and his caretaker we can regard the child as developing a prelinguistic understanding of agent–action–object–recipient, which could provide 'bench marks' for interpreting the order rules of language involving grammatical objects, indirect objects, verbs, agents and so on. Similarly, when the mother draws the infant's attention to something and demonstrates some function of the object or characteristic of the scene or when she lets the infant take the initiative and follows his line of visual regard (see Collis and Schaffer, 1974) commenting on the object of their joint attention, the infant is being provided with the functional base of the topic–comment or the subject–predicate form.

In the same paper Bruner gives a report of work in progress at Oxford to study these mother–infant interactions in which agent and recipient roles are exchanged, how the rulebound procedures of object exchange are developed and so on. In one situation the infant learned how to participate in a game of passing objects back and forth and inserting 'thank you' ('kew') at the correct point in the sequence—a functional privilege of ocurrence. In another, infant and mother swapped roles of hider and unmasker in a game of peekaboo. In another, the infant developed a behavioural understanding of the subject–predicate relationship and of the embedding of the word 'mouth' as a subject and as a member of a noun phrase in such relationships. In this the infant played various mouth games with her mother: making her pretend to drink, having her nibble her (the baby's) toes and so on. The mother inserted the word 'mouth' within these functional networks. Thus when the infant acquires the word it will not just be as a label for an anatomical item but, because mouths will already have determinate functional roles within her cognitive life, the word will arrive together with its rules for insertion in possible constructions: 'mouth [nibbling]'; 'mouth [dolly's]' usually before the 'predicate' terms become part of her lexicon.

With regard to learning nouns, this notion of functional relations being the framework for future grammatical relations in which the word will be embedded is a very fruitful one. Nelson (1974) has developed a similar theory but with the emphasis on the object's functional roles rather than on the mother–child utilisation of the object, as in Bruner. She also takes her philosophical framework from Cassirer rather than from Oxford philosophy. Cassirer proposed that a concept is a functional entity, not something determined by the properties of its elements. Nelson begins with Cassirer's (1953) argument, one which we encountered in Baldwin, that abstraction theory, whereby the child is supposed to give a common label to objects with common properties, is circular. We have to start with the child developing an understanding of the object's range of functions before he can cognise them and extend his lexicon on the basis of their properties. For example, when he encounters a ball it is not always seen as a round thing lying on the floor, but as an element in a set of dynamic relationships involving people throwing it, its rolling under chairs and so on. The child preverbally 'synthesises over time the various relations into which the ball enters'. There are two constants in all these relations: the ball itself and the 'functional core' of information involving actor, action and movement. From the former the child acquires the foundation of the later abstraction of the ball's properties and extension of his lexicon, from the latter he constructs a cognitive frame for sentences, analogous to Bruner's actor–action–object–recipient functional base.

But in a way this is lapsing back into a cognitive structuralism. Dore (1975, 1976) has recently presented a more strongly functionalist view of language acquisition than Bruner's or Nelson's which locates its philosophical context specifically with Austin (1962) and his notion of the *illocutionary act*. Searle (1969, 1971) has extended Austin's ideas and gives as examples of *speech acts*: 'state, assent, describe, warn, welcome, comment, commend, order, request, criticise, apologise, censure, approve, promise, express approval and express regret. Austin claimed that there were over a thousand such expressions' (Searle, 1971, p. 39). (Bruner also uses the term speech act but with the emphasis, as we saw, more on the 'act' than the Austinian theory it encompasses.) Searle goes on to say 'I think it is essential to any specimen of linguistic communication that it involve a linguistic act. It is not, as has generally been supposed, the symbol or word or sentence or even the token of the symbol or word or sentence which is the unit of linguistic communication, but rather it is the *production* of the token in the performance of the speech act that constitutes the basic unit of linguistic communication'. The speech act is called an act because it is what people do when they speak, and it is what they speak in order to do. This is the intentional core of language without which there would be no speech. Conversely, without the necessary cognitive competence there *could* be no speech.

In his study of the development of speech acts Dore (1975) drew up nine examples of what he called 'primitive speech acts' in a child at the one word stage: labelling, repeating, answering, requesting (action), requesting (answer), calling, greeting, protesting, practicing. One of the significant advantages of such an approach is that it enables us to sidestep the position, which cognitive structuralist theorists like Greenfield and Smith (1976) adopt, of reading profound linguistic significance into the child's earliest utterances on the basis of nonverbal context, as if they were the tip of a structural iceberg large enough to support later grammar. Dore quotes another such theorist Ingram (1971) as viewing 'crying, gesture and intonation as formal features of the child's syntax'. These primitive speech acts are not evidence of preverbal structures, rather they show us the functional route which the child must take towards the acquisition of linguistic structures.

How on this account do grammatical features develop? As well as illocutionary force the speech act will express a rudimentary proposition which, to the extent that the child acquires control over word order and other grammatical features, can be regarded as a sentence. What he learns is how to realise his illocutionary intentions within the grammar of the language. Dore speculates that this might occur by the illocutionary force determining the modality of the sentence which thence determines the grammatical elements. For example the illocutionary force of *demand* determines the modality of *imperative* which leads the agent to be deleted from any proposition.

But in his eagerness to avoid reliance on cognitive structures Dore seems to be throwing the baby out with the bath water. For having abandoned a cognitive substrate he then has to explain basic grammatical structures such as the predicating and the referring expression as being *innate linguistic* universals. He says that 'there appears to be no convincing explanation of what could be the basis for the child's learning about predication' and that 'it does not seem possible that a child . . . could learn WHAT a referring expression is'—surprising claims indeed when Dore's paper shares not only the speech act terminology but also the same journal issue as Bruner's paper! In fact no empirical or conceptual considerations are forcing us to admit innate linguistic structures; clearly there must be some synthesis between the speech act and the cognitive structural approach.

As was said before, the functionalist account implies that communicative intent is prior to actual speech. Dore began by delineating the primitive speech acts at the appearance of the first words, but the linguist Michael Halliday (1975) has proposed that illocutionary function can be ascribed prior to the production of words—when the child is just producing sounds which, in the large majority of cases, bear little or no phonological relation to words in the language. In his book *Learning How to Mean* Halliday reports the study of one child, Nigel. He ascribes six different functions to Nigel's prelinguistic vocalisations at 10 months

1. Instrumental (the 'I want' function)
2. Regulatory (the 'do as I tell you' function)
3. Interactional (the 'me and you' function, such as greeting)
4. Personal (the 'here I come' function, for example expressing feelings)
5. Heuristic (the 'tell me why' function, demand for a name for example)
6. Imaginative (the 'let's pretend' function).

Later there came a seventh: the Informative ('I've got something to tell you') function. In the next stage, when words came to be articulated, the functions of Nigel's utterances could be categorised under two headings: *pragmatic* or *mathetic*. In the former case he was using language to do a job for him, the function which derived from the earlier instrumental and regulatory categories, what Halliday calls the 'goods and services' function. In the latter case he used language as an instrument for learning about his environment. Here he used new words not to ask for more things but in 'contexts of observation, recall and prediction'; for example, 'stick,' said on seeing a stick, then said to report that he saw a stick, then setting out for a walk and saying what he will see on it. As dialogue developed in this child, these two functions merged and the functions of his language could be regarded, says Halliday, as 'abstract' because they became embedded in grammar. Grammar develops, he proposes, 'as a means of incorporating the functional potential into the heart of the linguistic system. It allows for meanings which derive from different functions to be encoded together, as integrated structures, so that every expression becomes, in principle, functionally complex' (p. 48).

Naturally, there is still the process to be explained whereby these functions are integrated within grammatical structures. But Halliday is concerned with, as the title says, learning to mean rather than with the total process of the acquisition of language. The point is not that function is all we have to explain but that learning to mean is a necessary prerequisite of language acquisition. Meaning precedes speaking; it could hardly be otherwise.

The position we have arrived at is this: there are cognitive and functional aspects to language acquisition existing in a state of mutual dependence. The value of Piaget's theory is that it provides an account of the cognitive competence which is necessary for linguistic development. But all the arguments in favour of the functional elements prevent us from holding that this competence by itself brings language about. Speaking can only be understood as something done for a purpose, as are actions. Language cannot be the result of achieving a certain level of cognitive competence plus the requisite vocal and imitative skills. However, even including functions we are still driven back to the question: 'Given a cognitively competent infant capable of vocalising meanings, how does he learn the full grammar of his language?'

Since the Chomskians Bever, Fodor and Weksel (1965) were set loose on the psychologist Martin Braine because he suggested that the pivot—open distinction could have been derived from parental speech by 'contextual generalisation', psycholinguists have been rather wary of saying that the child acquires grammatical knowledge from what people say to him or to each other as they go about their business. Chomsky would, of course, argue that the structure of language shows us that cognitive and functional abilities are not sufficient for the child to extract this knowledge from adult speech. But—and this is what the Braine–Bever *et al.* controversy hinged on—formal grammatical complexity and psychological complexity do not have to be regarded as being the same. Although an accurate description of the human language system has to be of great complexity this does not necessarily mean that the knowledge necessary to use language has to be of the same order of complexity. If such an implication were necessary we would have to ascribe knowledge of the principles of mechanics to everybody who could ride a bicycle (Mischel, 1974). The psycholinguist's task now seems to be to give the details of how the child who is capable of expressing a set of communicative functions, and of cognising an objective, spatio-temporally and causally structured world, which he is able to represent both in images and symbols, acquires knowledge of the structure of his own language from the language to which he is exposed. At least we now have had some good ideas about the instruments at his disposal.

That we have been mainly concerned here with the intentional and cognitive aspects of meaning does not imply that the *conventional* structure of language can be regarded as of secondary importance. As Halliday pointed out (see above quotation) once language acquisition is under way, function becomes abstract—dissolved in the conventional rule-structure of the language that is being spoken. Another way of saying this is: what we can mean is a function of what we are saying. Wittgenstein (1953) expressed this point by the following rhetorical instruction to do the impossible: 'Say "it's cold here" and mean "it's warm here"' (*Philosophical Investigations*, paragraph 510). As we saw above Baldwin emphasised that the commonness of language and its synnomic force can only be explained by synthesising the functional and the structural elements. If acquiring language were only a question of learning the structure, language would not be *for* anything, but without the conventional structure the meaning which could be expressed would lack the commonness of knowledge. Linguistic, like cognitive, structures are external to the child, they are in Popper's sense 'without a knowing subject'; the child has by the functions and structures at his disposal to join in this objective knowledge.

3.5 OVERVIEW

In each of the four topics that have been discussed we have encountered issues which are broadly epistemological. Before I come to consider in Part 4 the relationship between the empirical and the philosophical in genetic epistemology let us look back at some of these.

In Section 3.1 I considered the question of when one is justified in attributing to the infant knowledge of the independent existence of objects. There are a number of reasons why this is not just a matter of semantic nicety. The main reason is that the point at which knowledge is ascribed determines not only the kind of explanation for acquisition but also the possibility of offering any explanation (as opposed to a description) of the development. We considered one theory which ascribed knowledge at 5 months. Because it began by assuming the explicandum it functioned rather as an 'adultomorphic' description of the development from this age onwards. Our concern was also with what will and will not serve as an explanation when we discussed the hypothesis that the infant's Stage 4 'place' error was due to a weak memory. It also relied on an assumption of prior knowledge. Because it was argued that knowledge could be ascribed as soon as mental imagery came into play, the general question of the dependence of knowledge on representation was raised. It was proposed that, although further research might show that the possession of any representational device was not a sufficient condition of object knowledge, it is broadly true that all knowledge is representational and therefore that representation is a necessary condition for knowledge.

A number of interdepending non-empirical issues were raised in the section on transitivity which again revolved around the question of when (this time, conceptual) knowledge can be ascribed to the child. The necessity was indicated of avoiding both the hard-line Piagetian position which defines transitivity in terms of its concrete operational status, and the information-processing approach which is able to characterise a preoperational success based on mental imagery but cannot explain the performance based on knowledge of the principle. Criteria were offered, independent of any prior theory of transitivity, for ascribing to the child knowledge of this logical principle as distinct from achieving success by expeditious processing of the information. The problem was briefly mentioned of characterising consciousness of this rule in such a way that it offers an explanation of the acquisition of the principle. Describing behaviour in terms of a rule and explaining behaviour with reference to knowledge of a rule were differentiated.

In the section on conservation the distinction was drawn between judgments in the conceptual system that are perceptual and those that are abstract. Because, in contrast to transitivity, the ability to comprehend abstract terms like 'amount' in the instructions is a necessary feature of conservation knowledge, the central question of conservation is how linguistic understanding relates to concrete knowledge. An answer to the empirical part of this genetic epistemological question was suggested by the hypothesis that the disequilibrating experience in conservation is faulty interpretation of the instructions prior to transformation of the materials. However, although one can separately manipulate verbal and nonverbal factors within conservation testing and can construct hypotheses about the interrelation of linguistic and non-linguistic factors in this knowledge, understanding of conservation itself is indissociable from knowledge of the linguistic rules governing the judgment. The Baldwinian view of conceptual knowledge as public property was adopted to suggest that a common sign system is the necessary medium for the 'publicity' of conservation.

It was argued that a theory of cognitive competence cannot alone account for the acquisition of language because it omits functional considerations: 'what we do when we speak and what we speak in order to do'. The centrally important distinction between functionalist and structuralist accounts of language was introduced which can be generalised across the entire field of cognitive development. It was noted that the proponents of theories of language acquisition acknowledged their philosophical bases: seventeenth century rationalism, analytical philosophy (especially J. L. Austin) and the genetic epistemologist Cassirer. It was concluded in this section that although there *would* be no language produced if it did not fulfil a function in human life and that there *could* be no language without the requisite cognitive competence, the conventional structure of the system, external to the learner, was of central importance. And this conventionality is the commonness of language without which the commonness of knowledge could not be established.

Part 4

Critique

In this final Part I want to examine some of the major issues in genetic epistemology—the relative contributions of function and structure, social factors, consciousness and so on—and also to discuss the status of genetic epistemology as a field of study. Often this will be attempted within the framework of the following question: how good a run for its money can we give Baldwin's theory? In seeking to make out a case for Baldwin's genetic theory of knowledge relative to that of Piaget the aim is not to turn back the clock and advocate a wholesale acceptance of Baldwin's taxonomy, but to draw out what is useful to modern psychology from this pre-behaviourist theory. The weaknesses of Baldwin's theory—especially its lack of original empirical material—will be glossed over somewhat, but they are more often weaknesses of omission than of practice.

We saw in the Introduction how philosophical type (2) questions such as 'What are the necessary conditions for the acquisition of knowledge?' are those most clearly relevant to genetic epistemology because they concern the process of acquisition rather than the nature and status of something that we possess. Both Aristotle and Kant had this kind of question in mind but it was Kant who provided the philosophical framework within which Baldwin and Piaget established their theories. They were both in their different ways concerned with the processes necessary for objective knowledge and they both rejected empiricist and rationalist solutions in order to regard knowledge as the outcome of an interaction between an active organism and a changing, challenging environment.

Yet although they inherited this interactionism they both went beyond Kant, again in different ways. Baldwin took Kant's idea that reflexive self-consciousness is necessary for objective knowledge and added that neither is possible without a prior consciousness of other people as knowers who agree about the criteria for things being the case—a system of common meanings. Also, Baldwin had nothing in his system which corresponds to Kant's categories. Piaget, on the other hand, accepts the Kantian principle that the mind must contain such a set of general, fixed principles; in Piaget these operational structures become equilibrated to produce objective knowledge so that the structures of concrete and formal thoughts are Piaget's 'categories'. As Hamlyn (1978) points out, there is a clear parallel between Kant's and Piaget's interactionisms: Kant saw objective knowledge as the result of subsuming intuitions (perceptions) according to certain principles in a system of mutual dependence (see p. 29) and Piaget posits cognitive structures to which intuitions are assimilated while the structures have to accommodate to the intuitions. But the important difference is that these principles, for Piaget, are not prior to experience but develop from action, and prior to action there are the functional invariants of the biological system. Piaget most often cites Kant only to take issue with his apriorism, which he seems to regard as the predominant feature of Kant's philosophy.

Indeed, it should not be forgotten that Kant's apriorism, in what Strawson (1966) calls the 'unacceptable face of the Critique,' (see p. 33) can inspire quite a different kind of theory to that of Baldwin and Piaget—a 'crude, innatist psychology'. This is, in fact, what has been attempted by Konrad Lorenz (1941), who has tried to establish the thesis that these prior conditions are biological: instincts and innate conceptual frameworks. Apart from the fact that this seems to be treating Kant as if he were a rationalist, there are two consequences of this way of putting Kant to psychological use at least one of which is unacceptable. Strawson indicated that this innatism produced in Kant the 'disastrous' theory of the noumenon, the unknowable 'thing in itself'. It produces in Lorenz, when allied to evolutionism, the notion that evolution is moving in the direction of closer and closer approximation to the noumenon. Piaget (1971, pp. 313–16) concurs with this. The other consequence Piaget does not accept: if these *a priori* principles are constantly evolving and varying between species they lose 'the very thing which gave them their value, which is their necessity'.

4.1 PIAGET'S STRUCTURALISM

The treatment of epistemology in contemporary Anglo-Saxon philosophy as a subfield of philosophy and thus as a normative discipline entails the position that a *genetic* conception of epistemology must tend towards incoherence. We can no more write off this belief as the expression of intellectual parochialism than we can its converse, so it would be well to begin with a statement by a philosopher of the incoherence which Piaget's genetic epistemology is supposed to represent.

Although D. W. Hamlyn (1971a) makes some very telling points against Piaget's conception of genetic epistemology which I shall consider later there is the problem that much of what he says, although levelled against Piaget alone, is also in opposition to any genetic epistemology with an empirical content. He argues that the basic hypotheses of Piaget's theory are philosophical and that Piaget presents empirical evidence for them: the Kantian reconciliation between philosophical rationalism and empiricism 'by an appeal to the facts'; the notion that causality originates in action being set against the Humean theory, although Piaget's theory is 'supposed to rest on empirical evidence'; the hypothesis that veridical perception comes about through the statistical process of decentration and recentration (see p. 113) resulting from the 'philosophical' position that 'objectivity is constructed on the basis of, and in proportion to, the activities of the subject'. Hamlyn has also presented a similar kind of thesis against Gestalt theory (Hamlyn, 1957); for example, the figure–ground hypothesis, he argued, refers to a necessary feature of all perception and is thus not an empirical hypothesis but a statement of epistemological fact.

In the present paper Hamlyn's conclusion is that 'Piaget's theory is a blend, not only of the empirical and the *conceptual*, which would be both acceptable and inevitable, but the empirical and the philosophical. While *empirical investigations may throw up suggestions for the philosopher and vice versa* and while these suggestions may well be valuable, I am inclined to think that a theory which rests on both empirical and philosophical considerations must have a degree of incoherence' (p. 23, my italics). There are two important matters about which Hamlyn is somewhat unclear. First, there is the necessity for some line of demarcation between the 'conceptual' and the 'philosophical'; we are not told when a proposition has moved beyond being a conceptual framework and has become a philosophical theory. In this connection, because Kant, a philosopher, was the first to propose an interactional account of knowledge this should not imply that the only way in which an interactional theory of cognitive development should be regarded is as a piece of philosophy; and why is it not a conceptual framework? In the same spirit: it may be historically the case that originating causality in action is a 'perennial' answer to the problem of causality by philosophers, but, also historically, these could only be offered as philosophical theses because there was no psychological science established at the time. In any case, a question about the origin of a concept must surely entail empirical considerations: Piaget's theory of causality in the infant is not *supposed* to rest on empirical evidence, it does so rest. Hume's theory, which makes causality dependent on the experience of constant conjunction (see p. 28) *can be treated* as an empirical hypothesis and one which Piaget's observations can be said to have disproved. The fact is, such an hypothesis may be regarded either philosophically or psychologically. As a philosophical theory it states that all we know of causality is constant conjunction, that there is no 'necessary' succession from cause to effect apart from that which we lend to the sequence ourselves. There can be no *evidence* for or against this. What Piaget seems to be doing with both Kant and Hume is treating them as 'throwing up suggestions', in Hamlyn's words, but in the shape of empirical hypotheses; which brings us to the second unclear aspect of Hamlyn's conclusion.

The second problem is the relation which is not supposed to hold between the philosophical and the empirical. On the one hand Hamlyn accepts that 'suggestions' may mediate between philosophy and empirical research in either direction, but when is something a suggestion and when is it a line of implication? With regard to the work on perception, Piaget begins with, what Hamlyn would call, the 'philosophical' thesis that objectivity is constructed on the basis of activity and then takes his experimental data as supporting this. The pertinent questions would then seem to be: is the initial position tenable? do Piaget's results really support such a position?— questions which are short-circuited by the initial assumption that experimental findings are not directly relevant to epistemology. Although Hamlyn is very far from being a positivist, his arguments against Piaget's genetic epistemology seem to rest on, though not an absolute distinction between analytic and synthetic knowledge, at least the derived thesis that there can be no shades between the philosophical and the empirical and that there is only one way of utilising the theses of philosophers, which is philosophically. I shall consider later the question of when a theory should be regarded as generating empirical predictions and when it should not; the point being laboured here is that a genetic epistemology with empirical content cannot be written off as fundamentally incoherent, although we shall have reason to agree with Hamlyn later regarding criticisms that he makes of specifically *Piagetian* genetic epistemology.

Hamlyn does not wish to discount an epistemology whose arguments are presented in a genetic form and he has shown (p. 19) how some of Aristotle can be construed in this way. Indeed he proposes (Hamlyn, 1978) that there can be something which we might call genetic epistemology without incoherence, which would be an investigation into *how knowledge is possible*, into the necessary conditions at any particular developmental stage for the individual's continuing to acquire knowledge and understanding. This would involve constructing the framework within which cognitive development has to take place, with intelligibility as the necessary criterion for a condition being within this framework. We know, for example, that some routes to knowledge could not be taken because these routes are unintelligible to us knowledge-possessors *as* routes to knowledge; and, in this sense, intelligibility cannot be illuminated by empirical research.

But does this have to rule out any genetic epistemology which does consider empirical evidence? As a philosopher Hamlyn is surely free to take Piaget to task for confusing empirical and philosophical questions where he finds him doing this, but the attack is on too broad a front if it is aimed at any field of study which treats the empirical evidence as a relevant consideration in the framing of a philosophical thesis and philosophical theses as determining how we regard our empirical evidence.

Succeeding Hamlyn in the same collection is a paper by Stephen Toulmin who is notable as one of the few philosophers sympathetic to genetic epistemology, and who will be encountered in the final section of this Part. After Toulmin's paper is one by the psychologist Bernard Kaplan in which he chides both Hamlyn and Toulmin for taking too narrow a view of genetic epistemology. The narrowness, Kaplan argues, resides in the fact that it is inaccurate to regard Piaget's genetic epistemology as being essentially about cognitive development in the individual: it is mainly concerned with the growth of scientific knowledge in the human community. The source which Kaplan employs to support this interpretation is Piaget's *Introduction à l'Epistémologie Génétique*. Piaget does indeed say here that 'Under its limited or special form, genetic epistemology is the study of successive states of a science as a function of its development. Thus conceived, genetic epistemology could be defined as the positive science, empirical as well as philosophical, of the becoming of positive science *qua* sciences'. Even Piaget's broader conception of genetic epistemology as the 'study of the mechanism of the growth of knowledge' has as its 'distinctive characteristic' the analysis 'in all domains pertaining to the genesis or elaboration of scientific knowledge, the passage from states of lesser knowledge to states of more extended knowledge' (1957, pp. 13–14; Kaplan's translation). It is a still easier task for Kaplan to produce textual evidence that Piaget is quite aware that, depending on the norms of the particular discipline, there can be separately constituted the philosophical task of determining how states of knowledge should be characterised, and genetic psychological questions about the course of development towards this understanding.

It is certainly true that in recent years Piaget has been more concerned in his genetic epistemology with the progression of scientific knowledge and with fostering interdisciplinary cooperation between Genevans, logicians and scientists than with the course of cognitive growth, but it is incorrect to suggest that genetic epistemology should now be regarded exclusively as the study of the *phylogeny* of knowledge. For example, in *Genetic Epistemology* Piaget says 'The fundamental hypothesis of genetic epistemology is that there is a parallelism between the progress made in the logical and rational organisation of knowledge and the corresponding formative psychological processes' (p. 13) and then goes on to say that as 'there are children all around us' ontogenesis is by far the more accessible study. In that book he considers mainly ontogenesis. When Piaget writes of wishing to 'establish' a genetic epistemology he means as an interdisciplinary field of study; he has himself been practising genetic epistemology from the beginning in tackling traditionally philosophical problems by genetic methods. (Genetic epistemology can be practised without a grant from the Rockefeller Foundation!) To the extent that Piaget is correct that there are common functions and structures in ontogeny and phylogeny he is justified in extending the method to the growth of the sciences. Therefore one does no injustice to Piaget's genetic epistemology by focusing on individual development as Hamlyn did and as we have done here—as was argued in the Introduction.

What is perhaps most significant about the Kaplan quotations from Piaget is their characterisation of genetic epistemology as a science. Piaget characterises even epistemology as a science in his book *Insights and Illusions of Philosophy* (1972c). We find here, as well as more implicitly in all Piaget's writing, the desire, not so much to coordinate philosophy and psychology towards an explanation of the acquisition of knowledge but to collapse the 'epistemological' into the 'genetic'. In general the role he assigns to philosophy is one of providing 'wisdom' rather than 'knowledge'. This wisdom comes about through the opportunity which philosophy affords for the 'coordination of values'—of providing a *Weltanschauung*. Piaget's view of knowledge is almost positivist: as 'possessing safeguards and *methods of verification*' (p. xii, my italics). For Piaget, knowledge is identical to scientific knowledge, thus epistemology is a science or nothing. This is not by any means incorrect (except to a chauvinist on behalf of the Anglo-Saxon construal of philosophy) but it does reflect Piaget's especially continental conception of the discipline (see p. 13). Before examining the consequences of this position for his genetic epistemology it would be of relevance to mention how Piaget's view of philosophy and thus of epistemology came to be determined by his acquaintance with it.

Although *Insights* is something of a popularisation of arguments that Piaget has presented in a more technical form elsewhere it does provide a very instructive account of his view of philosophy. In the first chapter Piaget presents an intellectual autobiography which reveals the forces that influenced his conception of philosophy. With the exception of Kant, the philosophers he read were those who either deliberately sought to develop psychobiological theories by philosophising (Bergson), or who tried to derive a philosophical psychology either out of a Kantian kind of idealism (Maine de Biran) or from the analysis of states of consciousness in the Hegelian tradition (Husserl, Merleau-Ponty, Sartre). These were all philosophers who, by implication or design, were opposed to scientific psychology, indeed who believed that the psychological was a subfield of the philosophical—a thesis which diverges fundamentally from the Anglo-Saxon tradition whose members are more modestly determined to keep philosophy and psychology separate, with 'philosophical psychology', in their vocabulary, referring to a set of classical problems such as the relation between mind and brain, knowledge of other minds, and so on. Within the European, broadly phenomenological, tradition however, there is made an unambiguous territorial claim on psychology which involves a desire to absorb the genetic into the epistemological.

The second factor determining Piaget's view of philosophy is educational rather than epistemic, but must be taken just as seriously. Within France, post-Hegelian philosophy has the persistent tendency to regard itself and to be regarded as the highest form of knowledge, superior to scientific investigation, so that an adolescent entering the philosophy school is expected to be a 'thinker' and study the transcendent before he has had a proper acquaintance with the real through science. The consequence has been that French psychology 'was only able to develop on the fringe of official institutions and in constant struggle with the powers-that-be of academic philosophy' (*op. cit.*, p. 25). Philosophy does not hold the same hegemony within the Anglo-Saxon tradition. The education of philosophers still continues to be more classical than scientific but there is now a good measure of natural scientific and psychological knowledge to be found. The British empirical tradition mitigates against anti-scientism and the aims of what is usually called 'analytical' phil-osophy are austerely circumscribed (or inward-looking and disen-gaged according to its critics). Thus, in attempting to reclaim knowledge for science it can be seen that Piaget had to mirror the misguided territorial zeal of French philosophy, but a zeal not shared by Anglo-Saxon philosophers.

Beyond taking issue with Bertrand Russell regarding his theory of number and his sense-data empiricist epistemology (Piaget, 1950), Piaget largely ignores twentieth-century Anglo-Saxon philosophy. But might Piaget's arguments against continental philosophy apply to any academic philosophy? In his introduction to the book, the British philosopher Wolfe Mays* proposes that Piaget's arguments against phenomenology can be applied *pari passu* to the Oxford school of 'linguistic' philosophy. Apart from the fact that this school treats genetic questions as irrelevant to philosophy, as we have discussed, there is a constant appeal to everyday linguistic usage which Mays claims to be comparable to the phenomenologist's reference to intuitively given 'essences', as in Husserl, or 'irrati-onality', as in Sartre. This is certainly debatable; and we shall be discussing later how the conception of philosophy derived from Wittgenstein and Austin can be of enormous value to genetic epistemology. The Austinian theory of illocutionary acts is already proving its worth (see p. 185).

---

*Mays has sought to introduce Piaget's theory to philosophers, especially within Britain. He has not only written accounts of the theory in philosophi-cal journals (Mays, 1954, 1974) but has worked on experimental projects at Piaget's Centre, for example, on the child's acquisition of the analytic–synthetic distinction (Apostel, Mays, Morf and Piaget, 1957). He is also the foremost translator of Piaget's epistemological writings.

As a consequence of adopting the continental conception of epistemology as the study of scientific knowledge Piaget inherits the tendency to stress structure above function, which is one of the main features of rationalism. This emphasis on epistemology as a study of structures, allied to Piaget's original quest for 'structures-of-the-whole', has, it will now be argued, resulted in a problematical genetic epistemology.

Although the notion of *assimilation* has a clearly functional role in Piaget's account of sensorimotor development we find that in his explanation of conceptual intelligence the functional dualism of assimilation and accommodation seems to have little foothold. Thought is explained as the progression of states of internal equilibrium, and assimilation and accommodation can be spoken of only in a context of such generality and abstraction that they seem to have little explanatory power (see Bruner, 1959). The structuralism in Piaget's theory really begins on the conceptual plane although there are structural elements in sensorimotor intelligence such as order relations, subordination schemes and correspondences. The difference is that these are not taken to be explaining development but are seen as the result of the child's intending that certain states of affairs will obtain, and his having to correspondingly alter his behaviour to this end—functional considerations. Intelligence between the ages of 2 and 7 years, however, is explained essentially by the *absence* of equilibrated structures; intelligence thereafter is structural and all understanding is the result of mental structures having been established. This should been seen in the light of Piaget's treatment of epistemology as a science. Positing structures, characterised in logico-mathematical terms, to explain cognition, coupled with the fact that abstract structures can be derived in every field of intellectual endeavour both as method and as theory, results in the view of mental structures as one facet of the universality of structure. Piaget appears to derive his view of epistemology by the following kind of syllogism: all knowledge is structural, the study of structures is a scientific endeavour, therefore epistemology is a science. He makes his position very clear in a short book *Structuralism* (1971b), that the only essential difference between his structuralism and that of other practitioners (Levi-Strauss; Chomsky *et al.*) is that his structures are genetic. Leaving to the end of this Part the general question of the explanatory, as opposed to descriptive, power of structuralism in psychology, what we must do now is consider the conditions under which a structural account is applicable in cognitive development, and what Piaget omits when he moves straight from the hypothesising adolescent to the frontiers of science.

Piaget (1971) gives three characteristics of a structure as opposed to an aggregate: (1) that it should form a whole the elements of which are subordinated to laws in terms of which the system is defined; (2) that these laws are transformational; (3) that it is a 'closed' and self-regulating system. These, of course, all hold for the groupings of concrete operational thinking and the four-group of formal operational thinking. The feature of the human conceptual system which enables cognition to be characterised as a system of rules, structural or otherwise, is that when concrete operational thinking gets under way, the child's knowledge has to be regarded in terms of abstract rules rather than perceptions or 'centrations of thought' (see Section 3.3). But what Piaget further has to demonstrate is that he is justified in ascribing to this knowledge a structure as he defines it, such that this structure accounts for the special nature of thought after the age of about 7 years. He appears to have begun with the structure—the logico-mathematical system—and then related the developmental findings to these as best he could. The 'fit' is by no means perfect. As we have seen, some of the groupings lack psychological analogues, and the problem is more acute at the formal operational stage. A study by Bynum, Thomas and Weitz (1972) has suggested that the evidence given in Inhelder and Piaget (1958) does not justify his characterisation of adolescent thinking in terms of the 16 binary operations of truth functional logic. They attempted to replicate Piaget's results from the protocol of the only subject (Gou) whom Piaget claimed to have employed all 16, using the Inhelder–Piaget method of analysis. They found evidence for only 8 of the 16 and that 8 of the Inhelder–Piaget analyses were faulty.

In general, Piaget proceeds as a rationalist, providing the logical grid within which certain cognitive skills are located and their relations plotted. Of course, the acquisitions at the concrete operational stage do indeed possess a group structure; but this is because the knowledge revealed by the use of the concrete operational tasks can be characterised as structured by the three criteria above. The justification is thus somewhat circular: the child's acquisition of structured knowledge is explained by the fact that his thought attains an equilibrium defined in structural terms, because the principles with which he now operates can be characterised structurally. Explaining here takes the form of characterising the mind of the possessor of knowledge by the same set of principles employed in characterising what he knows.

At bottom, this is a rationalistic way of arguing. Indeed the parallel with Chomsky, an avowed rationalist, is very evident throughout Piaget's account of conceptual thinking (Russell, 1975b). Chomsky's argument that the child must have prior 'knowledge' of the deep/surface relation and that he must extract the deep structure of the language to which he is exposed, is derived from an analysis of the structure of human language in a similar way. There is also to be found in Piaget, more implicitly, the Chomskian argument that there is a direct relationship between the structural complexity of the cognised system and the psychological complexity involved in cognising the system. However, Chomsky is on much firmer ground than Piaget in assuming that the human language system is known and acquired as a structure. This is best understood in terms of Chomsky's well known distinction between linguistic 'competence' and 'performance'. The competence of the speaker-hearer is his knowledge of the rule-system which enables him to produce and comprehend an infinite number of sentences. The performance is his actual speech in concrete circumstances with all the usual ungrammaticalities, false starts and hesitations and as limited by the human information-processing capacity; competence is an idealisation of which these things cannot be said. Whatever problems there might be with Chomsky's account of our knowledge of linguistic rules as non-conscious and mechanistic, such a distinction can at least be made for human language because this competence has a natural *ceiling* comparable to the closed system of the structure. There is a ceiling to linguistic competence because we can no more go beyond knowing how to speak a language than we can go beyond knowing how to play a game; once we can use the language or play the game the question is one about performance: How well?

The speaker-hearer's knowledge of his language is by definition perfect. The implicit claim in Piaget's theory is that (to take the concrete operations) the child's concrete knowledge regarding conservation, transitivity and so on, is perfect; his performance may vary but there is nevertheless established a structural, non-conscious, equilibrated mental machinary of the same epistemological status as Chomsky's rules. Thus, the human being is seen as possessing, after the end of the concrete operational stage, a logico-mathematical system *determining* his concrete judgments and any incorrect judgments of this kind that he might make should be seen as *performance* slips, because the natural ceiling has been attained. But there is an alternative possibility: that Piaget is dealing only with those concrete judgments with which we operate most often, that no ceiling of competence is ever attained in concrete knowledge and, thus, errors made after the concrete operational stage are not performance slips but evidence of the continuous development of concrete knowledge. To take the example of conservation in support of this, what we know of the adult's performance on less standard conservation tasks suggests that this knowledge, although it may *begin* after about 7 years is still very imperfect in adulthood. Hall and Kingsley (1968) have shown that only on those tests of conservation which Piaget employs with children do adults (postgraduate students) automatically succeed. For many other types of conservation the level of performance is generally low.

In this context, what would we expect of the ability to judge the *absence* of conservation? If judging the conservation of properties reflects the logico-mathematical structure of our thinking it would be reasonable to predict that knowledge of when conservation is *not* taking place would be simply the other side of the same cognitive coin and would thus be closely linked to—even indissociable from— knowledge of conservation; and this especially in view of the importance of negation and inversion in group theory. However, on a test of the ability to judge that the area of space bounded by a string frame changes after elongation, 5 and 6-year-old children were found to perform *better* than adults (Russell, 1976). Preoperational children centre on changes in a single dimension and thus judge change (an illegitimate success); adults see that one dimension is getting longer as the other is getting shorter and think that they are witnessing compensation and thus incorrectly affirm conservation. Of course, the reason why many of the adults were misled is that we have to make judgments about changes in substantial areas much more often than about the area of empty space bounded by a flexible perimeter: the difference is one of familiarity. But if our knowledge of concrete transformations is the reflection of a fundamental structural equilibrium should not judging conservation be relatively immune from the contingencies of familiarity? There is, moreover, no justification for saying that the typical failure of the adult is a performance failure: none of the correct adults in the study could justify his judgment on the relevant principle and many of the incorrect adults experienced some difficulty in grasping why conservation was not taking place when the principle was explained to them. In short, interpreting certain perceptual changes as compensation looks more like a cognitive habit—albeit a deeply ingrained one—than evidence of a mental structure as characterised by Grouping VII.

The difficulties with Piaget's structural account of formal operational thinking are more distinct. We have already mentioned evidence from Bynum *et al.* that the 16 binary propositions fall very short of an accurate characterisation of Piaget's empirical data; and there may also be problems with the formal logic of the model (see Parsons, 1959). Moreover, despite assertions that cognitive growth continues after adolescence, Piaget offers no account of cognitive changes after this period. Indeed, the rather small body of evidence currently available does not allow us to construe these changes as mere improvements in performance with an underlying cognitive competence remaining constant (see Looft 1972; Riegel, 1973).

But these points mostly concern a problematical *application* of the structuralist method rather than the developmental consequences of a structuralist epistemology as such. What is more central to our present purpose is that there follows from such an epistemology a neglect of the everyday cognitive life of the human adult when he is not involved in solving formal problems. We move directly from a set of data about how some bright adolescents construct hypotheses to genetic epistemology in the sense that Kaplan takes it—the phylogeny of scientific knowledge. In a seminar discussion at the Catholic University of America, Washington DC in 1970 (quoted in Looft and Svoboda, 1975, p. 57) Piaget expressed his position thus: 'for our purposes studies of adults are completely worthless . . . if one wishes to continue the study of stages beyond adolesence the only method would be to use history, for example the history of scientific thought.'

The comment is revealing not only for the light it casts on Piaget's methodology but also because of the implicit refusal to acknowledge the importance of the conceptual system within which we all have to function in our everyday life. Piaget seems to regard the establishment of systematic hypothesis-testing as the last real structural acquisition in ontogeny and turns to phylogeny for structural changes which are equally as fundamental. Indeed Piaget stresses that his concern is with the 'epistemic subject'—the artificer of structures rather than the individual. That Piaget avows interest only in the epistemic subject is a further consequence of his structuralism: the subject is seen as the functional centre of the solution of problems of a progressively abstract nature (reflective abstraction) and these epistemic functions are seen as making possible the everyday cognitive performance of the flesh-and-blood subject. Structuralism also determines the methodology and the kind of data he comes to consider. Thus, after the age of about 4 years subjects are given more or less formal problems in order to analyse their verbal reasonings and strategies in the light of prior logico-mathematical frameworks, with the question being 'how closely does this answer or strategy approximate to the structure?' In this way examination-like situations are used as diagnostic or clinical tools rather than as instruments for determining how or how well a subject performs, that is, they are taken as measuring approximations to a structural competence not the kind or level of performance. (One of the other consequences of Piaget's ignoring what might be called 'performance' is that Genevans have not produced studies like that of Bryant and others discussed in Part 3; and when these appear they seem unwilling to admit even their relevance.) By limiting his empirical strategies in this way to the solution of one particular species of abstract problem Piaget is artificially circumscribing his theory to deal with only one aspect of human conceptual life.

What can be said about this conceptual system which Piaget seems to take for granted? Certainly it has a structure, at least in a non-controversial sense in which everything that can be objectively characterised can be said to have a structure. The system is the result of the phylogenetic process of consilience within the species about ways of proceeding, of being forced by our necessarily social life to conventionalise our criteria for what is and is not, can and cannot be the case. The outward and perceptible result of this accretion is our language system, and indeed the existence of a conceptual system is inconceivable without some public symbol system—as concluded in Section 3.4. Consilience is central to language; for example, we do not have to agree between ourselves about whether or not some material is combustible (we just see if it burns) but we do have to agree about the application of the relevant word such as 'fuel'. Moreover, the closer we come to logicality in the system the more limited becomes the range over which we can agree. To illustrate: given the verbal concepts of 'fuel' and 'wood' encased in a system of linguistic relations, when we are forced to reflect on how we have been using this system (in a dispute, for example) there is a sense in which we *have* to rule that from the sequence 'All fuel is combustible', 'Wood is a fuel' the conclusion 'Wood is combustible' is acceptable whereas its negation is not. But the notion of validity in general is not completely determined Into this public system of criteria for truth, responsibility, correctness, causal dependence, usefulness, worth and so on the child comes to be cognitively socialised. And it is this which Piaget's structuralist interpretation of epistemology undersells. Indeed Piaget has in common with empiricists and rationalists the implicit assumption that the child acquires his knowledge, as it were, *by himself* without the aid of other people (see Hamlyn, 1974), because his theory regards mental structures as existing in the heads of an aggregate of individuals, having been internalised from interaction between the self and the concrete world. Other people come in mainly as providers of a ready-make sign-system and to present the child with alternative perspectives to aid in the dissolution of egocentrism.

It is certainly not the case that Piaget leaves social factors out of account (for example, Piaget, 1950, chapter 6; Piaget, 1972, chapter 3) but his thoroughgoing structuralism leads him to view social interaction as itself a form of operational activity: 'internal operational activity and external co-operation are merely . . . two complementary aspects of one and the same whole, since the equilibrium of one depends on that of the other' (Piaget, 1950, p. 166). Every process, including the social, is a manifestation of the universal tendency towards equilibrium within structures. Like Spencer (see p. 41) Piaget regards society on the model of the organism, so it is not possible within Piagetian theory to talk of the cultural transmission of knowledge because this process is itself the working out of an equilibration whose principles transcend and underly social phenomena; 'education' is taken to affect only the ease with which operativity is attained (Piaget, 1972a, p. 41).

In seeking to absorb the epistemological into the genetic by a structuralist theory and method Piaget has, at least implicitly, to deny the relevance of the Anglo-Saxon, conceptual analysis kind of philosophy to genetic epistemology, for it is this discipline which seeks to produce an account of the structure (not in the technical sense) of the human conceptual system—a normative epistemology.

However, if we regard the cognitive socialisation of the child into the system as at the heart of conceptual development, the importance of characterising our conceptual system within a normative discipline is manifest—an argument, in fact, for genetic epistemology. To illustrate the importance of such a view let us take an argument from the Hamlyn paper which was discussed above, in which he shows how Piaget's attempt to explain the development of veridical perception, whilst ignoring the criteria for the correctness of perceptions embedded in the conceptual system, leads to difficulties. Piaget argues that the correction of perceptions is brought about by the multiplicity of fixations produced by movement—a *statistical* process. But, Hamlyn argues, once concepts and judgments are involved it is fundamentally unclear how other concepts and judgments could correct 'distorting' judgments. The way in which human beings correct and modify judgments is manifestly not mechanical and statistical but rather involves the purposive utilisation of experience and the construction of new judgments. The notion of correctness and incorrectness of perceptions belongs, in fact, to the *cognitive* field of criteria, because it entails evaluation of the perception against some standard. Therefore the process which Piaget puts forward as explaining the development of perception is not responsible for the correction of primitive tendencies but is what makes any perception possible. We can speak of decentration as corrective only because we have 'a prior conception of how a thing should look'. And this conception is brought about by the exercise of conventional criteria.

4.2 BALDWIN'S PHILOSOPHICAL PSYCHOLOGY

Rather than trying to absorb the epistemological into the genetic, Baldwin seems to proceed as if there really were no difference between a philosophical and a psychological theory, sometimes treating developmental issues as if they were philosophical. The problem is not that Baldwin lacked an interest in experimentation as such but that more often than not the experiments he did perform bore little relation to his genetic theory of knowledge. In *Mental Development*, for example, he reports work on colour and distance perception, on drawing and handwriting in children and presents a methodological discussion of how to observe imitation, but we find no systematic attempt to explore the empirical implications of his system. Moreover, in *Thought and Things* the reader is rarely able to determine how Baldwin wanted his theses to be regarded, whether they were meant to be testable or to be characterisations of the conceptual system. The embryo state of psychology must largely have been responsible for this ambivalence, which, it is hoped, can be resolved by interpretation.

Although Baldwin's theory lacks the empirical interest of Piaget's it does offer an account of the conceptual system within which the child is developing, and of the dialectic not only between the child and the concrete world but between the child and the human community. We have already noted how the functional polarities of assimilation and accommodation when used by Piaget seem to lose their explanatory power after the sensorimotor stage—when they have to encompass that which is conceptually mediated. But because Baldwin is concerned primarily with the self–social world dialectic his theory is ideally adapted to explaining the child's entry into a world of concepts expressed in language; with his own use of the terms assimilation and accommodation being quite different from Piaget's—accommodation being employed in a more diffuse sense to refer mainly to individual adaptation and assimilation usually being restricted to schematic intelligence.

As we saw, instead of the assimilation–accommodation dualism Baldwin employed a number of different terms, depending on the epistemic nature of the particular development, with which to explain the progressive interaction between the functional interests of the developing individual on the one hand and (at first) the concrete world and (later) the conventional system of human concepts on the other—the various modes of 'control' by all that is not the self. In the beginning is the interest and the datum; the interest taking different forms as it progressively adapts to concrete reality—selective, semblant, experimental, imitative, schematic. Then with the adaptation to social reality and the growth of syndoxic meaning the self–social dialectic takes the form of a schematic assimilation of new meanings by imitative absorption set against what Baldwin calls in a special sense 'disciplinary enforcement' (p. 62). However, it is with the development of predication leading ultimately to logical reasoning that we find the following set of functional—conventional polarities: the functional against structural aspects of language acquistion; proposition against elucidation; the construction of abstract against general terms; intension and extension and accretion against erosion of meaning within this; synthesis against analysis—a system of opposing but complementary relationships. A dialectic is still found in the development, by reflection, of the notion of validity within a system of implication: the movement towards greater synnomic force of the proposition being opposed to the negative tendency whereby limitation excludes elements from classes (p. 69). We saw that these dualisms are not resolved until the attainment of the immediacy of reconciliation (see p. 77).

Baldwin is able to propose such a dialectic because, in contrast to Piaget, he sees the child as developing into a *ready made* (though evolving) system. In a sense the child in Baldwin's theory is less active than in Piaget's for he is not constructing reality through his actions which become interiorised and equilibrated within structural systems. But though he is not actively structuring he is necessarily active, because Baldwin lays a correspondingly greater stress than Piaget on functional interests (for example, from the first head turn to the nipple, through play, imitation, to proposition, abstraction and art) and the necessary cognitive plasticity which must be its concomitant. Although Baldwin says that syndoxic commonness is 'hammered onto the plastic surface of the child's mind' he says at the same time that without a corresponding functional assimilation on the part of the child this reality would remain meaningless (see p. 63). This is an unfortunately misleading metaphor, however, because there seems to be little to choose between hammering a plastic surface and etching the *tabula rasa* of the empiricists. One can only reiterate that wihout the functional interests existing in different forms at each phase of development no sense could be made of Baldwin's theory nor could the child come to make sense of the concrete or social world: it is just the difference between a piece of plastic being stamped with a triangle and a child copying a drawing of one. It should also be noted that by proposing plasticity Baldwin ascribes to the child greater potential adaptability to alternative realities—he is paradoxically less active but more 'free'.

As Baldwin regarded the conceptual system as being presented ready-made to the child instead of constructed anew within each childhood, it is not surprising that the epistemology on which he based his theory takes knowledge as being an essentially public property. The roots of the acts of meaning are to be found in the earliest semblant functions (p. 57) and the child's awareness of himself as distinct from the public world must be well elaborated before he can appreciate any symbolic system; but it is with the establishment of common, syndoxic meaning through language that the child really joins the cognitive community as a junior member. Kant held self-consciousness to be a necessary concommitant of objective knowledge; Baldwin goes further and says that the awareness of others as makers of judgments is also necessary. As he argued in his dialectic of personal growth, consciousness of self and others develops from social roots rather than from cognitive structures becoming established by interaction with the concrete world as in Piaget— with the process of imitating other people being central. Piaget's theory of the development of consciousness is almost the inverse of this: the adualism that Baldwin proposed is not regarded as being overcome by the refractoriness of the concrete world, the ejection of the self into the social world and by syndoxic and synnomic commonness, but is seen as resulting in egocentrism which the progressive equilibration of mental structures dissolves— another consequence of Piaget's assumption that cognitive development is in one sense a solo enterprise. Baldwin would probably have regarded what Piaget calls egocentrism as the reappearance of a form of adualism on higher planes of thought as the child has to accommodate to more and more elaborate systems of control and mediation.

Baldwin regarded syndoxic meaning as only the preliminary to objective knowledge. The child has still to cognise others as judging agents and truth as involving the accord of judgments before he can appreciate that although truth depends on agreement this is not a contingent matter and that certain truths are universal, objective and independent of what other people might happen to judge—synnomic meaning. Logic is the result of reflective awareness of the principle of limitation working within the system to make the treatment of certain arguments as valid or invalid not the outcome of agreement but the inevitable result of having established the particular system. By way of illustration, compare the way in which a game is invented: the originators of chess had complete freedom to agree about which moves would and would not be permissible, what would count as taking a piece and when the game had finished, but once that was established they could claim no freedom to rule on what should count as winning or losing the game.

When critics of Piaget have sought theoretical support for the notion that cognitive development originates with a primitive sociability rather than egocentricity it is to thinkers such as the pragmatist G. H. Mead (see p. 39) and the Russian L. S. Vygotsky that they have turned rather than to Baldwin. In his hugely influential book *Thought and Language* (original publication: 1934) Vygotsky offered an account of the developmental relationship between language and cognition similar in many respects to Baldwin's theory. The similarity is mainly due to the fact that Vygotsky inherited a dialectical framework from Marxist–Leninist philosophy which is more akin to the Baldwinian than to the Piagetian dialectic. As Wozniak (1975) has pointed out, Piaget's interactionism is typically given a subject-to-object cast whereas materialist dialectics view the subject as under the determination of the—especially sociocultural—environment. Also, modes of intelligent thinking are regarded within Marxist–Leninist philosophy as *external* to the subject, hence the emphasis on social interaction and on language as the medium for the transmission of the shared sociocultural experience of man. Vygotsky proposed that mental structures arise as a consequence of the internalisation not of actions but of processes of sharing and exchanging thought between two people—primarily the child and the adult—and that thought is structured by virtue of its derivation from structured social activity. But although the parallel with Baldwin is very evident it would be a mistake, as argued on p. 51, to link Baldwin closely to Marxist theory because of his emphasis on the individual as the source of novel social constructs, especially as outlined in his 'dialectic of social growth'.

Another theorist who should be mentioned as sharing Baldwin's belief in the social origin of cognitive development is Heinz Werner. Although Werner was directly influenced by Baldwin as well as by Hobhouse and Cassirer (see Langer, 1970), and although one finds extensive use of the terms 'schema' and 'dialectic' in his work, he cannot be regarded as a genetic epistemologist because he did not address himself to epistemological issues. Development for Werner essentially involves progression from the global to the discrete by way of differentiation and hierarchical integration in motor, perceptual and conceptual systems. In the book *Symbol Formation* (1963) Werner and Bernard Kaplan proposed an account of the growth of the symbolisation (one very influenced by Cassirer) in which the infant is seen as possessing an interpersonally undifferentiated consciousness wherein there is not only an adualism between the self and objects but also between the infant's self and that of his caretaker.

In this 'primordial sharing situation', as they called it, the infant's experience of the other person and of their joint objects of attention are fused, so in contrast to Vygotsky this sharing situation involves three elements. The authors show three intersecting circles to represent this. The child is only able to differentiate his own consciousness, the 'I' from the 'you' and the 'thing', when he can represent the joint referent by a verbal symbol—a *name*. Vygotsky (1933) and to a lesser degree Werner and Kaplan (p. 94) both see imaginative play as crucial to the dissociation of symbol from object—to which we might again compare Baldwin's emphasis on the role of 'sembling' in the growth of meaning (see p. 58).

It would not be fruitful here to explore in detail the similarities and dissimilarities which these thinkers have to Baldwin but it is relevant that, vis-à-vis Piaget, they are all emphasising that the sharing of experiences is a necessary prior condition of objective knowledge. Although Baldwin's dialectic of personal growth, an imitative process, is divergent from Werner's proposals about primitively fused spheres of consciousness, both are proposing that before the child can *think for himself* he has to *experience with others*.

Finally there can be separated from Baldwin's genetic epistemology a normative philosophical epistemology which, as we saw, owes much to Kant. That is to say, Baldwin's account of knowledge as public property constructed out of agreement can be treated as a purely philosophical theory to be contended with reference only to facts over which there can be no real empirical controversy. Broadly, it is the contention of the genetic epistemologist that such an epistemology, in that it tends to result in an agenetic description of one state of human knowledge has to be supplemented by an account of the developmental forces which have and will determine the dynamic process of knowledge; Baldwin did after all present his epistemology within a developmental theory. The time has now come to sketch some principle whereby the philosophical and the empirical in genetic epistemology in general and Baldwin's theory in particular might be demarcated and related. We have said that some aspects of the theory can be treated as philosophy and some as psychology but no suggestions have been offered as to what should be determining these treatments.

4.3 THE TWO FACES OF GENETIC EPISTEMOLOGY

Genetic epistemology does not aim to melt psychological and philosophical issues into each other. That developmental evidence and epistemological theory should be synthesised does not imply that there is a set of hypotheses about which we have to admit ourselves unable to decide whether we should determine their correctness by observing and testing children or by remaining cogitant in our armchairs. Considering philosophical and psychological questions within one discipline is quite different from holding that there is a point at which such a distinction dissolves and we are quite free to regard hypotheses as testable or as not. Such a view would, of course, be disastrous because it would mean trying to establish an area of study, the status of which would be doomed to ambiguity. I shall go on to discuss how such a subsidence can be resisted within genetic epistemology by maintaining an awareness of the possibilities and consequences of testing hypotheses within it. An argument for a genetic epistemology with empirical content will thus emerge.

Typically, developmental psychologists and philosophers working within the Anglo-Saxon tradition of epistemology have little difficulty in deciding what comes under their sphere of interest. One reason for this is the existence of conventions about how theories and propositions should be treated. Thus the philosopher does not discuss the Cartesian theory of innate ideas with reference (say) to Bower's work on infants, and neither does the psychologist turn to the Schematism section of the *Critique* when designing an experiment on concept attainment. But to say that they are guided by conventions is not to imply that the constraints are in any sense trivial or arbitrary because, as we have suggested, the human conceptual system itself is profoundly a convention.

In the area broadly known as analytical or linguistic philosophy or as conceptual analysis there is the general aim of studying the nature of human knowledge with reference only to those facts that are totally without taint of empirical controversy. Especially amongst philosophers who have been influenced by the later Wittgenstein and by Austin, one finds constant appeals being made to how we would normally characterise something (for example, Would we say that remorse *caused* us to drink? Would we say that the Hundred Years War was an *event*?) appeals to how we would normally react (for example, the wish not to be disturbed cannot be regarded as a necessary feature of the concept of pleasure, as Ryle suggested, because one can so wish when engaged in non-pleasurable activity); overall there are appeals to what we would normally want to say, to our knowledge on the boundaries of sensible judgment. These appeals are absolutely necessary and the philosopher is on the same kind of solid ground here as is the linguist when he employs his own 'intuitions' to decide whether a given sentence is grammatical. The philosopher has to stay within the limits of the conceptual system if he is to examine its nature; and in so doing he does indeed 'leave the world as it is'.

In contrast, there is a sense in which the psychologist does not leave the world as he finds it because he is concerned with enlarging human understanding *of* human understanding. It cannot be denied that some psychology has altered the way man sees himself—notably the influence of psychoanalytic theory on our conception of human motivation. Psychologists rarely challenge the conceptual system directly (as, for example, does Skinner) but their theories and findings do feed back into the system and have determinate effects.

It is tempting to believe that it was only in the past that philosophers and psychologists strayed over into each other's territory, but that now the boundaries have been clearly drawn and well policed. For example a psychologist might suggest that although writers on psychology before the behaviourist revolution, such as Baldwin, lacked the reflexive awareness of their own discipline which would have purged their writings of unfortunate philosophising, psychology is now established as a science and such a danger is passed. But all that has been said up till now suggests that this should not be regarded as a danger and that anyway it can never be passed. Similarly, the philosopher might be inclined to look back at Descartes' proposal that the mind moved the body through the pineal gland with a wry smile as at the antics of a precocious infant. But how can he be confident that philosophy has attained an adulthood (along with a more grown-up name like 'conceptual analysis') in which such mistakes are not made? In actual fact empirical psychological assumptions are also to be found in present-day philosophy. Sometimes one finds them extremely sympathetic, though they nevertheless are assumptions. For example Hamlyn (1974) suggests that 'In humans there have to be some instinctive patterns of behaviour, for example, sucking, but so much more depends on what the mother puts the child in the way of' (p. 152). This entails the assumption that cogntive development is dependent on the caretaker providing the child with a necessary set of experiences. Psychologists influenced by ethological or maturational approaches, and indeed by Piaget, would certainly not accept this; likewise Hamlyn's frequent (and Baldwinian) characterisation of cognitive development as the child's being 'initiated into the conceptual system'. Similarly Melden (1961): 'Here the *training received by the very young child* in responding to those about it plays a decisive role in the ability it acquires . . . to recognise others as agents and in doing so grasp the familiar concepts of action and agent' (p. 195, my italics). Sometimes one finds the assumptions less sympathetic. Thus Peters (1958): 'Yet [Pavlov's] experiments on extinction suggest that even a response at this level is not unintelligent; for the dog came to change it in the light of differences in the situation' (p. 112). This implies that the classically conditioned animal is not responding automatically to the bell (CS) but intentionally; for there is a clear, empirical difference between automatic and purposive salivation. And sometimes the assumptions reveal an ignorance of the facts which would have been excusable in the seventeenth century but must today reflect intellectual arrogance and laziness. In a recent televised discussion between an Oxford philosopher and a zoologist the philosopher contended that one of the fundamental differences between animal and human communication was that in the former signing was carried out irrespective of whether or not another animal was present—'They just defecate and run away'!

Why do psychologists have to found their theories and procedures, willy-nilly, on philosophies and why do philosophers tend to find themselves generating psychological assumptions? For psychology, the very fact of producing a theory about the nature of human thought must involve a more or less implicit characterisation of the conceptual system—a notion of intentionality and learning, of the range over which causal explanation is applicable, the functions of consciousness and so on. For philosophy, the area of the conceptual system over which there is universal agreement is not determinate, and seems indeed to be contracting under the influence of the social sciences. There is a centrifugal force at work in philosophy whereby its practitioners, in an effort to avoid trivially semantic issues, find themselves moving from the centre of the system to its outer limits where agreeement about the conceptual conventions dwindles and their judgments take on the form of empirical hypotheses. There is an opposite and rarer tendency whereby psychologists find the conceptual conventions restricting and seek to change them. The most notorious example of this is Skinner and a more contemporary instance is the way in which workers in artificial intelligence contend that we will have to modify our conception of thought and consciousness if we are to accommodate to expected advances within the field (for example, Sutherland, 1971). Genetic epistemology is located around the area where these two movements meet, at the boundary of the conceptual system.

At the confluence of these scientific and philosophical interests the starting point for a possible genetic epistemology has to be a normative epistemology (structuralist for Piaget; functionalist for Baldwin) founded on agreed features of the conceptual system whose nature we examine by reflection on this system rather than by reference to the actual course of development in the individual or the race. As regards Piaget, the existence of hierarchical structures in biology and knowledge is, at one level, non-controversial; it is the epistemic significance of these structures which is debated. Similarly for Baldwin, the fact that we do have to agree with others about what is to count as a correct judgment is a truism. The development of the epistemology can then be extended up to the point at which universal agreement about the 'facts of the case' breaks down, when testable hypotheses are generated—Baldwin's dialectic of personal growth, Piaget's notion of egocentrism, and so on. Sometimes, as with Hume's theory of causality, the theory can be regarded either as philosophy or psychology, as mentioned above. But, in general, psychological theories arise out of epistemologies by, as it were, *stretching* the epistemological theory until it reaches beyond the universally agreed core of the conceptual system. If empirical support is forthcoming it will have the following consequences for the epistemology from which the hypotheses were developed. Most of these 'facts', on whose agreement each epistemology depends for its coherence, are better seen as features of the conceptual system itself (for example, the distinction between actions and movements; the law of excluded middle) but there are others which carry a penumbra of assumptions and possibilities which are accepted, as it were, for the sake of argument—because it is only since the rise of psychology that they seemed to be worth questioning. Supporting data for the relevant developmental hypotheses can fortify these assumptions and even extend them, and negative data can undermine or contract them.

To illustrate, a discussion of rationalism might proceed on the basis of its being within the realms of possibility that the infant could be born with an innate store of knowledge, in the sense of knowing that certain things are the case. However, developmental psychology post-Piaget has tended to suggest that there is no foothold for the view that infants bring anything else with them into the world other than a set of reflexes, pre-adaptive patterns, an assimilatory interest and accommodatory capacity. If, as Piaget and Baldwin are agreed, adualism is the primal state, any notion of innate *knowledge* is untenable. Thus, what philosophers would have once been happy to brush off as nursery anecdote provides a new area of common knowledge with which classical rationalism conflicts. Rationalism is not thus *disproved*, but it has to retreat to a more secure set of assumptions or extend putative assumptions into other areas, thus involving a radical alteration of its conception of knowledge and innateness whilst trying to avoid doing violence to the conceptual system. Similarly, a pure empiricism ascribes to the individual a passive orientation in the acquisition of knowledge and philosophical discussants of empiricism generally agree to assume that this passivity, of which Locke's 'great mirror' is an apt metaphor, is in principle not only conceivable but practically possible. Again we are faced with the psychological evidence that development in infancy appears to be fundamentally an active process, and indeed both Piaget and Baldwin have to ascribe active participation in a dialectic to the child throughout cognitive development. Given a possible future situation in which there is a body of firm evidence universally accepted that knowledge cannot be acquired unless the individual is actively assimilating, an epistemology which entails passivity would be purposefully ignoring the real world as it is known to be. Again, an empiricism could still be maintained by retreating to a safer set of assumptions, by, for example, concentrating on a positivistic form of empiricism which might propose that our judgments get their meaning by being ultimately reducible to statements about possible experiences.

It would be of no avail for a philosopher to attempt to hang on to the classic form of empiricism because developmental evidence is not affecting the *logical coherence* of the system; by seeking, in fact, to make it independent of the state of human knowledge. To apply a *reductio ad absurdum* to this kind of move, here are some conceivable epistemologies which could be proposed in a 'logically coherent' form: our logical knowledge is founded on God appearing to us in dreams to demonstrate logical principles; our knowledge of our own existence is basically visual and would not be possible unless we could see more things than we feel and feel more things than we can smell. What is striking here is not the violation of basic logical principles but that the theories are far outside the range of, literally, common knowledge. However, to the extent that philosophical epistemologies can always confine themselves exclusively to those aspects of common knowledge which are essential for the pursuance of human life, empirical evidence can never bring about their demise. The same might be said to be true of religions, though in a very different way.

Thus what we know about how cognitive development actually takes place is not merely a set of *details* which the psychologist fills into the philosopher's account of how the acquisition of knowledge is possible in general. The 'facts of the case' provide the platform on which philosophers produce their theories. Conversely, the developmental psychologist's data remains unintelligible to him without an epistemological framework within which to view it. The positive aim of this genetic epistemology is thus to exploit rather than avoid this mutual dependence.

4.4 HYPOTHESES

In this section we will consider some aspects of the empirical face of genetic epistemology by first taking two areas of recent contention as test cases of how the process sketched above might function in practice. One is the nature of the infant's innate sensorimotor endowment and the other the possibility that the human infant is innately primed to share experiences with others, as previously discussed in relation to Vygotsky's and to Werner's work.

As regards the question of sensorimotor development both Baldwin's and Piaget's conception of the infant's innate apparatus is in terms of a set of reflexes or 'habits' together with assimilatory interests and accommodatory capacity—a phylogenetic rigidity and an ontogenetic plasticity. However it is possible to adopt a more nativist view to propose that there is some primitive sensorimotor pre-coordination present at birth which is more than reflexive. Furthermore, one can challenge the Piagetian view that sensorimotor development takes place by progressive coordination between action schemes by adopting a conceptual framework after Herbert Spencer (see p. 41) wherein development is seen not as a progressive coordination out of basic elements but as the differentiation and subsequent integration of elements initially fused within a global whole.

This, as we have seen, is the conceptual framework of Heinz Werner (see Werner, 1948) and it also happens to be that within which Trevarthen (see Trevarthen, 1975; Trevarthen, Hubley and Sheeran, 1974) has taken issue with Piaget's account of infant development. Trevarthen has proposed that phylogenetic endowment is not a matter of discrete responses to stimuli but rather an innate set of motor structures which the infant applies at first in a stereotyped manner and which, in the course of development come to be differentiated and integrated within themselves and controlled by other parts of the motor system. These structures are, he argues, prefunctional. There are, Trevarthen and others have found, innate patterns of looking, which he calls 'pre-looking'. Rather than being random, neonatal eye movements show regular and periodic saccades (or 'jumps') as one finds in the sampling of visual information in adult looking. These are not even dependent on visual sensation as they are found when the neonate is filmed in the dark with infrared video and in blind neonates. Also from birth, spontaneous movements of the head from side to side are found along with displacements of the two eyes in the same direction: the eyes may move together in the direction of a distinctive sound for example. One of the achievements of sensorimotor development before the age of three months or so is to integrate saccadic eye movements and the movements of the head which appear when the neck muscles have matured sufficiently for the head to support itself. Thus, rapid saccades become integrated with slower rotations of the head and shoulders, along with inverse, cancelling-out procedures which can maintain an object in the visual field when the head is turning. Similarly, infants can capture and track objects in the first wakeful period after birth—a programme which becomes controlled by and integrated with other motor capacities developing at different rates till the procedure is smooth and regulated after 4 months.

The story is similar for prehension. Trevarthen claims there to be a form of 'pre-reaching' at birth, analogous to the pre-walking found in neonates (see Bower, 1974) wherein the infant shows a coordinated, though weak and stereotyped, reach and grasp pattern directed towards seemingly attractive objects. Development is dependent on the activation of an 'interlocking system of controls . . . produced by developments within the brain' (Trevarthen, 1975). Especially important is differentiation between proximal control of the arm and distal control of the hands. Much play is made of *déclage*-like sequences of the appearance, then apparent disappearance and reappearance of motor functions, which is taken to be due to the fact that motor systems develop at different rates so that the 'embryo' structures become overlaid by other motor developments. Thus pre-reaching is almost suppressed by the increased speed and strength of arm and shoulder movements. This emphasis on differentiation is strongly analogous to the differentiation of morphological structures in the development of the embryo.

Assuming that the experimental evidence of the role of pre-looking and pre-reaching structures in development can be accepted, what consequences are there for the Baldwin–Piaget account of infancy? First, it should be emphasised that this is best regarded as an account of the development of voluntary action which has no necessary implications for the elaboration of object permanence, space, time and causality. The implications of this kind that Trevarthen presents do not appear to be tenable: the evidence does *not* suggest that 'infants are born with a visual space in which external events are seen' (Trevarthen *et al.*, 1974) as it is quite compatible with adualism; and Trevarthen's suggestion that after 6 months looking becomes regulated by memory and recognition—in the way that head movements interlock with saccades presumably—is open to the same kind of objections as were levelled above in Section 3.1 at memory explanations for the object concept. Trevarthen's main point is that intentional action should not be seen as developing out of automatic reflexes by a process of learning but out of innate coordinations by differentiation and integration. In fact, there is no hint of rationalism in these suggestions and they can easily be accommodated within the Baldwin–Piaget perspective. The presence of innate motor structures laid down in the nervous system no more implies innate concrete knowledge than the fact that there is an innate programme for humans to develop feet rather than flippers implies innate knowledge that there is solid ground on the planet. An account of the maturational aspects of motor development (which is what Trevarthen's evidence amounts to) and an account of how the infant acquires sensorimotor knowledge of the concrete world through action by-pass each other as regards the essentials. For example if Trevarthen is correct that hand-regard is not, as Piaget and many others have supposed, a necessary step towards fully coordinated grasping and that the ocular and manual motor systems are innately coordinated to some degree this still leaves us with having to explain what the infant *does* with this motor skill: we still do not know how he 'constructs' his reality. Differentiation and integration of innate motor systems cannot provide a complete account of the acquisition of object permanence, for example; although *Piaget himself* found the notion of the differentiation and integration of *action schemes* indispensible in his account of sensorimotor development. In short, given the existence of pre-adaptive structures, a basically dialectical (rather than maturational) account of sensorimotor development (assimilation–accommodation or interest-datum) is still tenable, indeed necessary.

What kind of evidence then *would* have tended to undermine the basis of agreement on which the Baldwin–Piaget explanation of infant development is founded? One element of this agreement is the assumption that concrete reality is constructed by a self-world dialectic in development, and those who oppose this account have to agree to admit this as a possibility. They would not have to accept this possibility if it could be demonstrated, for example, that infants directly after birth perform Piaget's Stage 5 object-permanence task. This means that, *as regards pre-verbal development at least* the 'genetic' would have to be dropped and the dialectical account presented as a philosophical epistemology from within the boundaries of the conceptual system; thus involving a characterisation of sensorimotor development shorn of suggestions such as that the infant begins from adualism and constructs the concrete world through action. Such an epistemology would probably take a Kantian form and set out the necessary features of the dialectic between the infant's (at least partially) structured understanding and the world of objects if there is to be further acquisition of knowledge. In this same sense, Kant's account of causality in the Second Analogy is presented from within the boundaries of the conceptual system and appears to be immune from empirical disconfirmation.

Now we come to discuss the possibility of a primitive social competence existing in human infants. At present there is a burgeoning interest in early forms of pre-verbal mother–infant communication (for example, Brazelton, Koslowski and Main, 1974; Stern 1974, Stern, 1977) but let us stay with Trevarthen to discuss work he has carried out in this area.

On the basis of studies of mother–infant communication during the early month in which mothers were asked to 'talk to the baby' Trevarthen reports that infants reveal a primitive competence for regulated, conversation-like exchanges. He notes that mother takes her cue from, and even imitates, baby rather than vice versa. The infants employ a form of, what he calls, 'pre-speech'—manual gestures, vocalisations, lip and tongue movements, facial expressions and gross bodily movements which all seem to have distinct privileges of occurrence in the exchange. Indeed it is not uncommon, long before the onset of true speech, to see an infant gesticulating and declaiming in emphatic gurgles like a tub-thumping politician! As to the specific nature of pre-speech Trevarthen is not always clear, and neither do we receive very full information about its incidence. Perhaps it can be best understood by considering the analysis he gives of 10 seconds of mother–infant interaction in Trevarthen *et al.* (1974): infant becomes active, mother vocalises, infant smiles and waves his arms and then vocalises when the mother shakes her head, mother vocalises, infant smiles, waves arms and then vocalises, mother shakes her head, infant produces a flurry of smiling, waving and vocalising, mother shakes her head after the vocalising and so on. Basically, the infant is responding to social signs with other social signs, soliciting and maintaining the interaction with his generation of social signs; the mother falls in with the infant and both find it immensely pleasurable.

This has a contrapuntal relationship to motor developments. It makes its first appearance (what Trevarthen calls 'primary intersubjectivity') after pre-reaching disappears and then, as true reaching is established around 4 months, the infant in many cases actually loses interest in his mother even to the extent of avoiding eye-contact as he begins to take a more active interest in the concrete world. As the mother becomes sensitive to this change and joins him in his exploration of things and their relationships there is a return to a form of 'secondary intersubjectivity' whereby caretaker and infant share the experience of objects often in the form of ritualised play. This might be compared with Bruner's proposal, which we discussed in Section 3.4, that these rulebound procedures form the base structure on which future language acquisition will become established (see also Bruner and Sherwood (1976) on peekaboo and rule structures).

Closely related to the question of a primitive intersubjectivity is that of imitation. Trevarthen makes reference to the work of Maratos (1973), and reports similar findings himself, of imitation of mouth, hand and head movements and of sounds in the very first weeks of life—long before Piaget reports it. Again this form of imitation tends to disappear and reappear roughly in line with Piaget's timetable. Its first appearance is during the period of primary intersubjectivity in a strangely automatic form: usually the adult has to work hard at eliciting it and then it seems to just 'pop out' unheralded by signs of interest or gradual approximation to the model. Some of the most striking cases of this can be seen from photographs which Maratos has taken of very young infants imitating the tongue protrusions of adult models. Melzov (1977), working with 2-week-old infants, reports that such findings, still stand up after rigorous controls have been made. A more deliberate form of imitation appears towards the age of 6 months: the infant fixes his attention on the adult as if puzzled and succeeds by steps of successive approximation. One exciting implication of such early imitation is that if the infant does have some form of innate template of the human face and of movements, which the evidence suggests, it may be that there is even some awareness of what *his* smiles, waves, vocalisings and so on look or sound like to others.

It hardly needs to be pointed out that a host of caveats have to be attached to this kind of work. First there are a clutch of conceptual problems centred on questions about what we are to take a criteria for the *sharing of experiences* (an extremely diffuse notion in itself), what should be regarded as rule-governed communication as opposed to generalised excitement brought about by interesting visual phenomena, and how we are to attribute communicative intent to the infant. Also, great care has to be taken to demonstrate that the infant acts quite differently to people than to things because we would not want to talk about intersubjectivity between baby and his mobile! For example my son at 4 weeks smiled and gesticulated to curtains with a bold, geometric pattern and to a rubber plant with at least the same intensity as he did to his mother; a slow-motion video playback may well have produced qualitative differences of course. Moreover, researchers in this area are seldom careful to indicate how enormous are individual differences in sociability; so how common are interaction sequences such as these described by Trevarthen? By and large one might say that we hardly have *pre-evidence* for a primitive intersubjectivity.

That said, the existence of early social competence as a prerequisite of cognitive development makes excellent sense, especially in the context of the Baldwin—Vygotsky—Werner developmental axis. So what if good evidence *were* forthcoming? Evidence for primitive intersubjectivity and early imitation would be as supportive to Baldwin's account of conceptual development, reliant as it is on the commonness of judgment, as is the evidence for sensorimotor 'construction' of the concrete world through action crucial to Piaget's structuralist account. Although Baldwin's writing tends to hover confusingly between philosophical characterisation and psychological hypothesis-making, certain clear developmental hypotheses can be derived. Regarding imitation, the following two hypotheses would be supported by such work: that prior to his having any knowledge of the concrete world as separate from himself he has an awareness of other people as being imitable; that imitation is primary and does not depend upon any prior cognitive elaborations (any more than does the circular reaction, which is *self*-imitative). Moreover, Baldwin's developmental account of the child's social consciousness is suggested throughout: the imitation of 'projections' of the other resulting in a feeling of 'subjectivity' which is 'ejected' so that other people can be cognised as conscious agents and thus oneself—the dialectic of personal growth. Again in *Thought and Things* he argues that, although the infant's sense of self against not-self has been germinated by the refractoriness of the concrete datum, with the onset of imitation he develops a sense of autonomy for the first time, of being the 'owner' of experiences which can be shared with others. Play is regarded by Baldwin as almost a derivative or consequence of imitation, though of major importance in itself: that given the imitation-derived autonomy play is what the child does with it. Indeed it is bewildering to see how psychologists tend to follow Piaget's lead and regard play and imitation as polarities when so much early play is rooted in imitation to a greater or lesser degree.

If the acquisition of knowledge proceeds from commonness what is to precede the commonness? On what basis might the child *learn* that experiences are shareable? It is from considerations such as these that a Baldwinian account suggests an infant innately primed to share experiences and exchange signals. Also, given a congenital disturbance of this innate predisposition towards intersubjectivity such a theory would have to predict severe cognitive impairment; and thus provide a framework within which *autism* can be explained. So here we have examples of how a basically epistemological theses (knowledge as common property) is 'stretched' towards empirical assumptions and thus predictions.

But if experimentation were to repeatedly reveal a total lack of such social competence and no primitive imitative capacities, the same retreating process could be undertaken by Baldwinian genetic epistemology as was outlined above for epistemologies which had become stretched towards making empirical assumptions. Here certain aspects of the theory could be maintained on a more philosophical level, resting on universally agreed facts such as the presence of imitation in early childhood and that children communicate their needs before they learn to speak. For example, the proposal that imitation of some kind makes possible the distinction between one's own actions and those of others would still be tenable. Indeed it might even be necessary to retreat to the epistemological conception of intersubjectivity in conceptual judgment as presented by Kant (see p. 30).

The remainder of this section will be taken up with some proposals—influenced by Baldwin's theory—as to how the child acquires the kind of knowledge Piaget regards under the heading of the concrete operations. Some of them were implicit in the conclusions of Sections 3.2, 3.3 and 3.4.

It is proposed initially that the child brings to the process of language acquisition two kinds of knowledge: on the one hand knowledge of the regularities in the concrete and the social world, and on the other some primitive knowledge of other minds and competence in imitation. By virtue of this, the acquisition of competence in the use of the categories and structures of the language system has a dual effect: the child's understanding becomes structured by these conventions and there is an enormous advance towards a public mode of consciousness. The fact that there are states of affairs in the concrete, causal and the psychological, intentional world which are made public property through language can be regarded as by far the main determinant of the continuing dissolution of what Piaget calls egocentrism but is perhaps better regarded as a continuing element of adualism in childhood and adolescence.

At the outset, this public consciousness is relatively unstructured by the conventions of the conceptual system. The child is, however, aware of the shared nature of conceptual knowledge, and thus has some notion of the criteria for true judgments, corresponding roughly to Baldwin's syndoxic commonness. There is a still incohate awareness that adult thought involves a rule-system of objective criteria for the truth of concrete judgments. When the child does acquire knowledge, not so much of what the rules are but of their objective 'transpersonal' nature, we have the kind of understanding which Baldwin seemed to be intending by synnomic judgment. Eventually, he is able to reflect on the system itself and evolve a consciousness of what he has been doing all along—'inference' in Baldwin's terminology. One sees here not only Piaget's three-tier structural theory of preoperational, concrete and formal operational, but also something akin to the phenomenological, agenetic analysis, in terms of three levels of consciousness, which Karl Bühler derived from the study of adult introspections: *Bewusstheit*, consciousness independent of mental imagery (the next advance after the interiorised imagery of the sixth sensorimotor stage presumably); *Regelbewusstheit*, consciousness of rules; and *intentio*, by which Bühler meant the conscious act of putting to work the rule system thus cognised. But what is the 'cash value' in terms of substantial hypotheses of preferring notions such as 'Regelbewusstheit' and 'synnomic judgment' to 'concrete operations?'

In terms of the distinction drawn in Section 3.3 between perceptual and rulebound concepts, one can regard the concrete operations as a set of rules which the child comes to apply in his concrete judgments. From a Baldwinian perspective the only source of these rules must be the more cognitively mature members of the human community. In fact, there might be a crudely 'social determinist' interpretation of Baldwin whereby the child would be seen as *imitating* the judgments of others. But this is quite unacceptable owing to the passivity and denial of functional interests which it suggests. A preferable notion, which is employed by Hamlyn, is that of *initiation* into a conceptual system. Initiation is a matter of participating in a process rather than observing and copying its features: there is the necessary element of interaction. It can additionally be proposed that the child acquires basic concepts better from more cognitively mature children than from adults—as other children will express them in the child's own 'language' and through the exercise of common functional interests, usually in play. Of course Piaget does himself emphasise the importance of social experience (although this element has been waning throughout the development of his theory), but in a fundamentally different way. He sees the influence of others (for example, Piaget, 1935, 1950) as being cognitively energising, in that social intercourse with peers presents the child with alternative, *conflicting* perspectives which should speed the dissolution of egocentrism; knowledge is not acquired from others but out of the inevitable mismatch of cognitive perspectives. As Vygotsky puts it, 'socialisation of thought is seen by Piaget as a mechanical abolition of the characteristics of the child's own thought, their gradual withering away' (1962, p. 85).

We would thus have two accounts of peer-group influence which could be called the 'structural' (not wishing to attribute hypotheses to Piaget himself) and the 'synnomic'. The former takes social experience to be necessary and facilitatory because other children present the child with epistemic opposition, clashes of cognitive perspective, which force an internal balance of operations. The other emphasises the fact that (see p. 156) rulebound, abstract judgments can be *justified* unlike perceptual judgments with reference to rules, and that it is witnessing the justification of the relevant principle which influences the child to abandon his perceptual judgment. To test these accounts, groups of preoperational and mixed groups of preoperational and concrete operational children could be observed in order to study the social determinants of the adoption of the correct judgment and the pragmatic and epistemic features of the interactions. Overall, the structural account would predict a high incidence of disagreement involving preoperational children which should be sufficient to energise cognitive change; the synnomic account would predict little cognitive conflict between children because preoperational children do not hold their judgments as objective truths to be contended, and that the only cognitive change energised must have been consequent on hearing the correct principle articulated and justified by a concrete operational child. Perhaps the strongest evidence for the synnomic account would be the cultural transmission of such knowledge by a child from one group of preoperational children to another and from there by another child to a new group, and so on. Such a strategy has been used by Menzel *et al.* (1972) in order to study the transmission of the 'play tradition' between groups of young chimpanzees.

On the present perspective what the child acquires during the concrete operational stage is a socialised, criteria-bound notion of concrete *truth* which, unlike perceptual judgments of unidimensional properties, can be justified by rules. If the thought of the child after the age of about 7 years is different in kind from that of the younger child it is because he possesses a notion of these rulebound judgments as being (1) objective rather than subjective; (2) concerned with the causal rather than intentional world; (3) necessary rather than contingent and (4) universal rather than particular. Thus, another experimental derivation is that there should be a 'quantum jump' in the child's ability to discriminate between judgments on these bases simultaneous with the arrival of concrete operational competence. The child's ability to distinguish between judgments on either side of the divide might be studied. For example as regards particular against general judgments: 'Here is a red chair' compared with 'Red is a colour'; 'My mother has black hair', compared with, 'Mothers are women'; 'I have a pet dog', compared with, 'A dog has four legs'; and so on. It would here be predicted that these distinctions are only *teachable* to concrete operational children, so a 'clinical' kind of methodology of the kind favoured by Russian workers such as A. R. Luria (see Wozniak, 1972) might be utilised.

On this account it would have to be assumed that the child already possesses the 'raw material' of the concrete knowledge in an *unsocialised* form before the concrete operational period. The studies considered above by Bryant on transitivity, by Mounoud and Bower on weight conservation in infancy, and by Russell on nonverbal abilities in length conservation are particularly supportive of this position.

One way of construing the difference between the loosely Baldwinian approach sketched here and the Piagetian is that the former implies a multiplicity of *possible* routes from sensorimotor to conceptual knowledge; that the actual route taken is the conceptual system into which the child is being cognitively socialised, and indeed that there are different ways of travelling in roughly the same direction and different distances travelled depending on the *cultural* expression of the system. Therefore another line of empirical extension would be towards cross-cultural studies. Taking their cue from Piaget, the majority of such studies (see Berry and Dasen, 1971) are implicitly asking the question 'How far along the road to structured knowledge are the children of this culture compared to Western children?—almost a quantitative question. More often than not the answer to such a question can neither support nor challenge Piaget's theory to any significant degree; although one of the foremost workers in the field who has adopted a more critical approach, Alastair Heron, has noted that such studies have shown 'how dependent on cultural homogeneity is Piaget's "concrete operations" stage, the unity of which has been called into question by the results' (Heron, 1975, p. 284).

Of major relevance are cross-cultural studies which focus on qualitative differences, on differences in the way judgments are regarded and how this determines the course of knowledge acquisition. As Bruner and Greenfield (1966) have pointed out, cultures do not so much vary in terms of the efficiency with which they encourage mental equilibrium (in Piaget's sense) as in the orientation to knowledge itself. Employing Kluckholn's distinction between *collective* and *individual* orientations to knowledge (Kluckholn and Strodtbeck, 1961) they showed how unschooled children from Senegal in West Africa have a collective rather than an individualistic orientation to knowledge, so that when faced with the question '*Why do you say* that this glass has got more water than this one?' in a conservation problem they were unable to produce an answer, although they could answer the question in the form 'Why is such and such true?'. Bruner proposes that the collective way of life necessary for survival in a primitive community of this kind must put the group decision above the individual point of view, with the result that these children cannot conceive of justifying their own perspectives with reference to objective rules. Reich (1966) also found this lack of individualistic judgment in Eskimo children performing a concept-sorting task where, unlike western children, they did not pass through an 'egocentric' stage in which cards are sorted by virtue of the child's own relation with the items pictured. Thus, future research may show there to be considerable cultural variability in the way in which the child attains a socialised notion of concrete truth: if the culture is individualistic, for example, his task is primarily one of 'perspective coordination' by objective criteria; if the culture is primitively collective his task is to become conscious of his own perspective as possessing a form of objective validity within a coordinated system.

Another way of relating the collective/individual distinction to the present discussion would be by making it correspond to Baldwin's syndoxic/synnomic distinction. This would imply that children in our western culture possess a kind of collective orientation to knowledge before the concrete operational stage quite different to that in children of a tribal culture.

One assumption fundamental to the present account is that the rules on which rulebound thinking is based are *in the culture*. This can be illustrated by relating the discussion of experimental work on transitive reasoning in Section 3.2 to some studies of verbal problem-solving in the Kpelle tribe of Liberia reported by Cole and Scribner (1974). In Section 3.2 it was concluded that what preoperational children lack is the conscious knowledge that there is an inference to be made, and that this is why they do not store the premises transitively from the outset. The transitive problem—from the presentation of the materials to the A, C question—is a procedure evolved within our culture, so if another culture does not formalise its inferences one would not expect its members to appreciate what is being asked of them. In fact this is what Cole and Scribner report from studies of syllogistic reasoning in problems usually of the form 'If a or b, then c; not a but b; c?' and 'Some a are b; all b are c; are some a also c?' presented with familiar verbal material. Here the tribesmen did not accept the problems at all on an abstract level. Typically they treated them as particularistic statements of concrete fact about real individuals and so answered with generalisations from their own experience. In particular they report a study by Gay which demonstrated how the tribesmen were making no attempt even to retain the premises or the question. This is because they had developed in a culture within which such a cognitive activity was irrelevant to their life.

4.5 AGAINST COGNITIVE STRUCTURALISM

In this section the aim will be to state more definitively some of the notions implicit in what has gone before; in particular two fundamental objections that can be launched against the cognitive structuralist account of the acquisition of knowledge as represented by Piaget. The first concerns the asocial kind of necessity which the structures are taken to possess and the second concerns the way in which consciousness is regarded by such a theory.

The previous section ended with some comments on cultural variability in ways of acquiring and possessing knowledge, and the suggestion that, Protean though Piaget's theory is, there may well be cross-cultural data to which it cannot accommodate. There is also a more philosophical face to this objection. In his book *Human Understanding* (1972) Stephen Toulmin argues that Piaget not only regards the different cultural realisations of the human conceptual system as irrelevant to the truth of his theory but also, in a Kantian spirit, argues that he has discovered developmental universals which must hold for all possible rationalities, transcending the contingent features of our own system. (In this book Toulmin is concerned with the process of conceptual change in the evolution of scientific theories—an historical form of genetic epistemology.) At bottom Piaget is a conservative Kantian: he believes that the necessary form of our knowledge is not something that can be characterised by saying that certain truths are held to be 'necessary' within the system—there has to be some external prop to necessity. For Kant, necessity was something which transcended the bounds of human rationality, could be justified by *a priori* demonstration, and held for all kinds of rationality that there could ever be. Thus, as Toulmin says: 'His transcendental deduction, proving the unique validity of (say) our everyday concepts of "substance" and "causality" were thus intended to demonstrate that these concepts were indispensible for any rational thought whatever; whether in eighteenth century Königsberg, on the planet Jupiter a million years ago, or in the eternal and infinite reaches of Heaven' (p. 422).

What Piaget is producing, argues Toulmin, is a kind of 'historicised Kantianism'. The truth of the conservation of substance, the transitive inference and so on is something for which the child 'progressively recognises the necessity' (Piaget, 1969). The child does not come to acquire the correct criteria for the truth of certain judgments but is forced to adopt the concepts and logic that he does by the very nature of his interactions with the concrete and (later) the personal world. Thus, the fact that substance conserves is not a feature of a highly evolved, sophisticated conceptual system but one feature of the equilibrium in mental structures *necessary* for any kind of cognitive growth. Equilibrium is a necessity; and the necessary truth of a set of judgments and modes of reasoning is a reflection of this equilibrium. As equilibrium is the necessity of intelligence and of life it can be regarded as independent of, even *prior to*, the actual modes of thought of any particular community—human or otherwise. Kant and Piaget would share the view that different human communities, and communities of other intelligent beings that there may be, must develop towards the same destination: for Kant, the 'pure forms of rationality'; for Piaget, progressively higher levels of equilibrated reflective abstraction. It may be recalled how Piaget concurred with Lorenz that evolution is moving towards a closer and closer approximation to the noumenon (p. 196).

One of the purposes of Toulmin's book is to dispute claims that epistemological and logical necessities are timeless absolutes independent of conceptual variability; he takes issue with Russell's and Frege's Platonic view of logic as well as the Kantian *a priori*. Perhaps it will suffice for our purposes to say that such accounts are unsatisfactory because nothing can serve as a justification for itself. Very roughly, Kant attempted to demonstrate that our conceptual system is based on the absolute principles necessary for any such system. The analogy to this is not that of the inhabitant of a house examining the structure and foundations to see whether they fulfil certain building standards, because in this case there is only one house and therefore no standards of comparison. A more accurate analogy would be that of the inhabitant's leaving the house in a rainstorm and attempting to build a shelter in order that he might stay dry as he observes the outside of his house; he wants at the same time to build another shelter from the rain so he will remain dry during the construction of the first shelter—and so on. This person will get wet just as inevitably as the theorist who tries to view the conceptual system completely from the 'outside' will be drenched in nonsense and irrationality. (A genetic epistemologist might remain within the house and attempt to discover the principles which governed the stages of its construction, given that the functions the house has to fulfil are determining its structure.) This point might be seen as somewhat analogous again to Gödel's theorem regarding the limits of formalisation. Gödel showed that no system of formalisation can prove its own consistency: the axioms of a system of logic, for example, cannot be justified by something beyond them, otherwise they would cease to be axioms.

Of course Piaget does not turn to metaphysics for his version of the universals of rationality but to biology and formal systems. Perhaps the book *Biology and Knowledge* (see p. 115) represents his clearest attempt to found human rationality on something outside itself. Here we find a plethora of structural and functional isomorphisms being proposed between the organic and the cognitive: the conservation principle, hierarchies of structure, order and multiplication structures, anticipation, algebraic lattices and so on—with autoregulation itself being the functional universal *par excellence*. Now, it may be objected that whether or not one approves of Piaget's method, he does actually come up with these isomorphisms and makes out some kind of case for human intelligence being a reflective abstraction from basic biological functions and structures. First of all it should be said in reply that it is only by virtue of the structuralist metatheory that such isomorphisms are revealed, and the fact that they are revealed attests to the power, not of Piaget's theory, but to that of formalisation—especially in mathematics. As Piaget says himself: 'There is no known physical phenomenon which has defied expression in mathematical form . . . Generally speaking mathematics today is taking a decidedly qualitative trend, and its involvement with isomorphisms and morphisms of all kinds has opened such broad structuralist perspectives that there is apparently no field—human, biological, or physical—that cannot now be reduced to a fairly elaborate mathematicisation' (*op. cit.* pp. 339–40).

This is the essence of Piaget's cognitive structuralism: making the ultimate goal the extraction of developmental universals from different levels by means of abstract formalisation. Fundamentally, it must be questioned whether constructing parallels between the conservation of the genome between generations and the child being able to judge the conservation of substance, between the inclusion of species within genus and the child performing a class inclusion task, between the fact that Piaget found it possible to describe adolescent reasoning in terms of the 16 functions of bivalent logic and cortical neuronal connections, tells us anything significant about psychology. Also in ontogeny Piaget extracts isomorphisms between developmental levels in order to explain how cognitive growth is directed. And we have already mentioned in this connection Hamlyn's objection to Piaget's taking perceptual decentration as a motoric prefiguration of the cognitive 'decentration' in the concrete operational stage, on the grounds that is is only because we have a prior conception of how a thing should look that we can regard perceptual decentration as corrective. He also suggests, as is being suggested here, that what similarity might be uncovered, is, for this reason, *nothing more than an analogy*.

Piaget employs a kind of two-way reductionism: the higher is explained in terms of the lower at the same time as the lower is being explained in terms of the higher. As in the usual one-way variety, everything mitigates not only against conscious knowledge being given any special status, but also against thought being explained by reference to the conceptual system within which it is operating. Let us take two examples of the latter. Bower (1966) has demonstrated that infants of only 8 weeks have some form of size constancy, and together with Mounoud (1974) that infants of 16 months evince a form of weight conservation. Now when tested conceptually (with verbal instructions) size constancy has been found to be very weak in 8 and 9-year-old children (Zeigler and Leibowitz, 1957); and weight conservation is not found much before the twelfth year. According to Piaget, the delay is due to the fact that the child has to reacquire on the conceptual plane what he has already attained on the behavioural (see Piaget, 1955, final chapter; and 1971a, chapter 5)—hence the reliance on the notion of reflective abstraction. Evidence of such early competences is extremely supportive to Piaget's theory because it consolidates the (largely implicit) view that there can only be one 'route' from the behavioural to the conceptual (see p. 231); for example, that weight conserves is not regarded as a feature of the conceptual system but as a necessary peice of knowledge acquired first *pre*conceptually by interaction with the concrete world in infancy.

But it is being asserted here in opposition to Piaget that only by virtue of what we take as the criteria for equality of size and weight can we judge the infant to have behavioural knowledge of these matters. We find that a very young infant produces about the same relative number of head-turning responses to a cube three times as far away and that a much older infant uses the same hand and arm-muscle tension to anticipate the weight of a deformed object; but this only appears to be a specific kind of lower-level knowledge because we are regarding it through particular conceptual goggles—because the system takes the form it does. (I would wish to argue that the same is not true of object permanence because this is not rulebound knowledge as defined above. The ramifications of this distinction are not explored here for reasons of conciseness.) With regard to size constancy, what was responsible for the incredulity which greeted the initial publication of Bower's results was the common assumption that a two-dimensional world is more primitive than a three-dimensional world, when, given the bombardment by three-dimensional cues, the inverse assumption is no less reasonable (see

Anscombe, 1974). Imagine how a developmental psychologist from another planet, ignorant of our conceptual system, might treat this evidence: would he have to conclude that here was behaviour which would later be unfolded conceptually as something coextensive with what we call 'constancy' and 'conservation' (compare Baldwin's 'Fallacy of the Implicit'). Thus in order that he should demonstrate the necessity for human knowledge taking the form it does Piaget moves *beneath* the conceptual system rather than *beyond* it, as did Kant, with the consequence that he must argue that there is only one possible route from the sensorimotor to the conceptual. Again the structure of the conceptual system itself is seen as failing to provide the requisite bed-rock of necessity.

Perhaps the most fundamental point of divergence between the Piagetian and the present account is that we are here concerned with the fact that conceptual intelligence relies on the acquisition of criteria for the *truth* of judgments, and that these criteria are, of necessity, socially constituted. A mental structure may be equilibrated or otherwise but it cannot be true or false. This perspective is shared with Romanes (see p. 42), with Baldwin, and with Hamlyn after Wittgenstein.

So although, as we have seen, there is a sense in which Kant laid a foundation of genetic epistemology there is also a sense in which his philosophy justified a structuralism which tends against a truly genetic theory of knowledge. How can we extract what is psychologically nutritious from Kantian theory and avoid the unsympathetic transcendental implications? The British philosopher P. F. Strawson has attempted something of this kind with what he calls a 'descriptive metaphysics', wherein there is a deliberate limitation of the programme to the conceptual system as it exists, a search for the foundations of coherent language and thought. The question is broadly: what are the basic elements of our conceptual system without which it would cease to function?

In his book *Individuals* (1959) Strawson began with the traditional distinction between particulars and universals—between spatio-temporal entities and qualities such as colour, shape and so on. Quite unexceptionally, he then proposed that the basic elements in our conceptual system were particulars; but in going on to characterise these as being not particular sense data but particular material bodies and persons he was opposing the traditional doctrine of the British Empiricists still represented in Bertrand Russell's epistemology. The arguments for these basic particulars rested on the necessity for securing identifying reference in a speaker—hearer situation. He then went on to argue that there was a correspondence between the particular—universal distinction and the subject—predicate distinction in grammar such that the introduction of a subject term presupposes an empirical fact which the introduction of a predicate term does not. In general, Strawson was trying to show (1) why a class of particulars were basic amongst others and (2) why all particulars were the basic elements of predication (see Bernard Williams (1976) for arguments against this). In a later study of Kant's *Critique* (*The Bounds of Sense*, 1966), he attempted to extract a descriptive metaphysics, uncontaminated by proposals such as that of a world of noumena, from the body of the work. Tackling the same problem as before from a Kantian rather than an analytical perspective he asked 'What are the bounds of that which we can make intelligible to ourselves as coherent experience?'—rather than what are the prerequisites for linguistic communication. By and large, he found what was bounded to be very like the necessities he had encountered in *Individuals*.

As the aim of descriptive metaphysics is to characterise the basic structure of the conceptual system, it is of obvious pertinence to the philosophical face of genetic epistemology as here conceived. Indeed Strawson's concentration on the act of predicating something on a common item of reference between a speaker and a hearer contains clear echoes of Baldwin's approach. Baldwin constructed his account of the development of conceptual judgment with predication as the starting point where 'elucidatory' meaning was established between interlocutors (see p. 63). However there is a divergence between the two in that Baldwin proposed that the 'hearer joins the speaker in erecting the subject matter into a schema of problematical meaning' which never abandons its 'experimental' aspect, so he might not have concurred with Strawson that one form of predication has to be basic. However, we might regard Baldwin's dependence on the subject—predicate distinction and development from this towards derivably empirical hypotheses as an example of the stretching of normative epistemological theories towards genetic hypotheses discussed above. In this context, the current work of Bruner is very relevant for it appears to suggest that the infant comes to be initiated into a system of predication well *before* he begins to speak.

It may appear somewhat strange that, thus far, very little mention has been made of Wittgenstein; as the present orientation is broadly Wittgenstinian. There are two main reasons for this: we have been encountering Wittgenstinian arguments as mediated through other philosophers such as Hamlyn and Toulmin; and we have not needed to stray very far from Baldwin for what are now considered as Wittgenstinian notions, such as that of knowledge being a system of public agreement in judgments. Wittgenstein's influence has been profound. Indeed he influenced two movements in philosophy by presenting successively versions of the two radically different accounts of necessity which we have been considering. The early Wittgenstein of the *Tractatus* (see p. 35) took the view that necessity is imposed on us (specifically the necessities of logic and mathematics) rather than constructed by us. Indeed the *Tractatus* expressed a kind of structuralist philosophy insofar as it proposed that analysis would reveal there to be a definite unifying structure underlying our linguistic system which is the substratum of necessary truth. Wittgenstein tried to show that all factual propositions were reducible to logically independent elementary propositions; all possible kinds of necessity could then be revealed and analysed in order to show that all these necessities were reducible to tautologies. Thus, there was seen to be a structure of logicality imposed on us to the extent that all our everyday thinking and speaking has coherence and significance only by virtue of its derivation from a fundamental set of propositions about simple objects linked in an unbreakable network of implication. An austere view of human understanding was thus presented which treated our functioning conceptual system as rather like the result of a sloppy workman using a set of precision tools till they become loose and approximate—until the gauge of hairline accuracy is a versatile hammer. The real, tangled stuff of human communication was what the philosopher had to ignore in order to do philosophy.

The later Wittgenstein, as represented especially in *Philosophical Investigations* (1953), did not make a complete break with his earlier thought but in most respects his view of the conduct and aims of philosophy was profoundly altered. Now it was precisely this everyday, ordinary language which concerned him. There was no longer taken to be one touchstone of necessity which determined the system but rather, by our having to put language to use in the world, a system of necessity was evolved. Of course, if we turn away from ordinary language we can study one kind of necessity—as in the

Tractatus—but this is only one amongst many. This involved the crucial claim that the determinants of rationality are to be found in the nature of human social life and the linguistic system which cements it; a proposal which takes logicality to be, in a sense, anthropocentric: a 'Copernican revolution' in reverse therefore. Emphatically, this does not mean that we have complete freedom to construct whatever rules of thought we wish. There is freedom only in the sense that, given different biology, environment, historical circumstance and so on the system *could* have been different; but there is not freedom in the sense of unlimited choice. We have had to 'impose' the particular system of verbal concepts on ourselves in order that we might communicate and have any social existence at all. Fundamental to this is the agreement in judgments, in criteria for truth, correctness and appropriateness that we have been considering.

At one point in the *Investigations* Wittgenstein brings forward a predictable objection to this view: 'So you are saying that human agreement decides what is true and what is false?' (implying that human agreement is just a contingent matter of convenience and choice whereas truth and falsity must surely be something absolute and above mere convention). Wittgenstein replies 'It is what human beings *say* that is true and false; and they agree in the *language* they use. This is not agreement in opinions but in forms of life' (paragraph 241). This notion of forms of life (*Lebensformen*) being that within which there is communal agreement appears rarely in the book and in typically gnomic contexts, but it is at the heart of Wittgenstein's anthropocentrism. It is also introduced with reference to his famous notion of the 'language game' (paragraph 23). The concept of game is maintained not by one common element running through all games but by the overlapping and criss-crossing relationships of game to game. Wittgenstein argues mainly by analogy, and the one he uses here is that of the fibres of a rope securing a ship to the harbour: here one does not require an iron-strong fibre running the full length to give the rope its strength because the strength is maintained by a multitude of intertwinings of flimsy fibres (paragraphs 65–7). Another analogy he uses is that with the family resemblance between members of a family regarding physical characteristics; again there need not be one characteristic (for example, eye colour) which all the members share. Likewise, there are a multiplicity of language games with *no* (thus rejecting the *Tractatus*) common element between them:

giving orders, reporting an event, describing the appearance of an object, speculating about an event, asking a question, and so on *ad infinitum* (compare Austin's illocutionary acts). And these different language games express, and get their significance from, human activities or forms of life; just as men running around after a leather ball attains a significance because it expresses the 'form of game' which we call football. If one begins to note all the respects in which human life is different from chimpanzee life one will be enumerating forms of human life—largely a question of being able to see the trees for the wood! And if there were to be a structuralist version of the famous rope analogy it would be that the strength of the rope is maintained by a finite set of strong fibres and that the other, shorter fibres are merely frayed portions of these. Wittgenstein of the *Tractatus* believed that he had discovered these 'master fibres'.

One of the many important things that Wittgenstein's later philosophy shows us is that the human conceptual system is an organic, inconceivably complex accrescence from the history and psychology of the human species. The Wittgenstinian has an 'empirical' interest in language as it is used and studies the *differences* between the many forms of life expressed through language games, and their interrelationships. When, in contrast, a structuralist such as Piaget is concerned with the underlying *common* abstract forms; which seem to take on an almost infinite generality, not only in life and thought but in the intellectual endeavour, so that even the archetypal functionalist K. Bühler* can be assimilated into the structuralist family (Piaget, 1971b, pp. 51–2).

Therefore, as was argued above, when we say that the child's thought becomes structured at a certain age this is by virtue of the fact that the aspect of knowledge we are considering (for example,

---

* The historical importance of Karl and Charlotte Bühler's work may well be enormous. Toulmin (1969), in discussing the influences which may have moulded Wittgenstein's later philosophy, cautions 'Don't overlook the Bühlers'. K. Bühler's *Sprachtheorie* (1934) is heavily Wittgenstinian. They were all together in Vienna during 1927 and we know that Wittgenstein met the Bühlers, although did not report himself to be very favourably impressed (Bartley, 1974). This would also account for the strongly Wittgenstinian flavour of Vygotsky's *Thought and Language* (first published 1934), wherein much reference to K. Bühler is made. It is difficult to determine of how much more than historical importance K. Bühler is with *Sprachtheorie* remaining untranslated. Werner's view of language is heavily influenced by *Sprachtheorie* (see Werner and Kaplan, p. 52).

the number systems or Euclidean geometry) has, unlike most other aspects, a structure in the technical sense. And that it has this structure is determined by one of the forms of human life: we have evolved this particular network of rulebound concepts to enable us to communicate about certain abstractions away from concrete states— quantity, position, and so on. Thus the groupings and the four-group provide a description of *one* aspect of the system which the child is developing into.

In outlining a possible alternative account, loosely influenced by Baldwin and Bühler, of the acquisition of what Piaget calls the concrete operations there was much reliance on the term 'consciousness' and on conscious knowledge of truths (see also Sections 3.2 and 3.3). Many psychologists regard consciousness as a conceptual dustbin or at best a primitive notion that can be introduced to prop up a theory temporarily until one can provide an explanation in terms of brain processes, stimuli and responses, cognitive structures or information-processing ('black box') concepts. In fact, one of the missions of cognitive structuralism is to dispose of knowledge as something ineluctably conscious and to supplement it with *nonconscious* structures (that is not 'unconscious' in the Freudian sense of having *been* conscious). Thus Piaget denies the relevance of consciousness because 'operational behaviour' makes it redundant; and although he claims that the child reflects on structures as he gets towards the formal stage his view is clearly that mental machinery determines the acquisition of knowledge: ' . . . the subject here can only be the epistemic subject, that is, the mechanisms common to all subjects at a certain level, those of the average subject. So average in fact that one of the most instructive methods for analysing its actions is to construct, by means of machines or equations, models of "artificial intelligence" for which cybernetic theory can then furnish the necessary and sufficient conditions' (Piaget, 1971b, pp. 68–9). Piaget has also proposed that 'The basic operational structures of logic and mathematics lead us to believe in isomorphism between conscious implication, and physical and physiological causality' (Piaget, 1954, p. 146), which brings him still closer to the reductionism mentioned above. And thus Chomsky: 'If we decide to use the word "know" in a narrow sense restricting it to conscious "knowledge of" . . . what is known will be a rather ill-defined and perhaps a scattered and chaotic subpart of the coherent and important systems and structures that are cognised' (1975, p. 165).

However, if the Baldwin–Wittgenstein epistemology is accepted, any notion of 'cognitive structures that express systems of (unconscious) [again: which never have been conscious] knowledge, belief, expectation, evaluation, judgment and the like' (*op. cit.*, p. 24) must be judged to be fundamentally incoherent.

In suggesting that a necessary, determining agency in the acquisition of knowledge from infancy to adulthood is the development of the child's consciousness nothing very novel is being proposed. After all, Piaget's theory up to the concrete operational stage can be construed in this way, and his early work was certainly concerned with the child's consciousness of the world. Furthermore, this does not imply a denial of the role of brain development in determining at least the rate and timing of cognitive growth. Indeed one of the more notable facts about cognitive development is that there is remarkably small individual variability in the rate of development within a given culture and remarkable concordance between children in the time at which they acquire kinds of knowledge, which could reasonably be seen as due in part to maturational factors. But there has been implicit in all that has gone before the denial that an account of neurological growth is sufficient as a theory of cognitive development. The brain is a machine for processing information (and 'black box' models are best seen as theoretical neurophysiology) and to this extent sets limits on what can be cognised; but these are not limits which determine the nature of knowledge—the social product—nor can neurological change bring about the child's initiation into the knowledge system—although it does form a necessary condition for this initiation. There is likewise no denial (as, for example, Chomsky might deny) that brain research is relevant to our understanding of the process of acquisition, to the extent that it will uncover what is determining the child's processing capacities throughout the stages of development.

Apart from a consideration of consciousness, what else does an information–processing account omit? Firstly, it omits the child's *functional interests*: in infancy this covers broadly what Piaget means by assimilation to schemes, that is, what the infant wants to do and takes pleasure in doing from one time to another. Of course these functional interests develop: from the infant shaking his rattle; the toddler building a tower of bricks; the adolescent taking a radio apart to see how it works. When these are given free rein or when they appear to serve no practical or educational end the adult calls these 'play'. It also fails to consider the structure (in the non-technical sense) of the human conceptual system. The interrelation of these three might be represented as follows below:

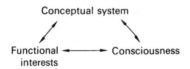

Conceptual system

Functional ←——→ Consciousness
interests

Moving clockwise, the conceptual system as it is presented to the child from the point (or even before) at which he acquires language, determines his consciousness: from the basics such as the subject–predicate distinction up to sophisticated notions such as two events lasting the 'same time'. The level of conscious knowledge in turn determines the kinds of functional interests the child will have: the infant will use a pencil to strike the rungs of his cot, the toddler to scribble, the child to draw, and so on. These examples are manipulative-representational but functional interests are expressed just as clearly in what we do when we speak to each other; so there is here intended the area of mental life encompassed by Austin's speech acts and Wittgenstein's language games. Indeed, another way of conceiving of functional interests is as that which determines the forms of life the child expresses and wishes to pursue at any particular stage in his development, or second in time. Needless to say, there is a phylogenetic component in these interests which diminishes throughout the course of the acquisition of knowledge. Finally, in the third line of clockwise implication, the functional interests do not directly affect the conceptual system itself (at least not in ontogeny) but they do affect the way in which it is manifested to the child in the behaviour of other people.

The process also functions in the reverse (anti-clockwise) direction. The child's level of consciousness will determine to what degree he is capable of construing the conceptual system as it is manifested to him by others. The structure of the conceptual system will determine how the manifestations of the child's functional interests will be treated by more cognitively mature individuals; what the child does is interpreted and influenced in terms of the knowledge system he is being socialised within. Finally, the functional interests will determine the kinds of things that the child will *want* to be conscious of at any particular time.

It would lead us into rather remote territory at the moment to set out fully elaborated arguments for this proposal, but it is only by making reference to consciousness (or its associates such as 'awareness') that the acquisition of knowledge can be made intelligible. If the question goes out 'What does the average child know when he comes into his fourth year?' and the answer comes back in terms of how the child can process information or in terms of abstract mental structures the child lacks, the question remains unanswered, because such answers are not intelligible as answers to that question. Indeed it is as 'making intelligible' that I would wish to characterise the nature of psychological explanation (see Hamlyn, 1970), whether or not this is also true for the natural sciences. And it should be emphasised that increasing intelligibility must be seen as a *necessary* rather than as a *sufficient* condition for psychological explanation.

The necessity for making reference to conscious states in cognitive development is almost less controversial than the question of the *possibility* of ever securing this reference without ending up with an account that is hopelessly subjective or speculative. This rejection of consciousness, not only in behaviourism and cognitive structuralism, but throughout the whole range of scientific psychology, springs from something that could be described as philosophical naiveté on the part of psychologists. Solipsism is the prevailing philosophy of mind within psychology. Psychological solipsism takes the form of rejecting statements about the child's (or experimental subject's) consciousness because there is no possibility of attaining certainty in the ascription of mental predicates to others. One would be guilty of an even greater philosophical naiveté to suppose that Wittgenstein's private language argument (see *Philosophical Investigations*, paragraphs 242–316) has once and for all disposed of this kind of objection but, at the very least, it does show that such as solipsism cannot be taken as the touchstone of scientific psychology. Wittgenstein argued that a purely private language was impossible (for example, one person inventing words to refer to his own sensations) because for any verbal concept to gain a foothold in human language there must be public criteria of application: we do not learn these words from our own case. In the case of sensations such as pain, the pain behaviour (including linguistic behaviour) form these public criteria. The purpose of his argument was not, as has often been supposed, to dispose of mental states in a behaviouristic spirit but to show that the relation between mental states and behaviour is not contingent or arbitrary but that it attains a kind of necessity within the conceptual system; that when we see pain behaviour or hear somebody say 'I am in pain' it is nonsensical to insist that nevertheless we want 'something more' as evidence of the pain; for this is to misconstrue the logic of sensation words as being like that of material object words. Of course, people can tell lies about their mental states, but telling the truth must be at the heart of a form of life (except that of lying!) for it ever to become established as such.

Wittgenstein's argument was concerned with sensation-consciousness rather than that expressed by the epistemic judgment, but, although there are important differences in this connection between statements such as 'I am in pain' and ones like 'That one is the same now, although it is higher up', they both offer public, criteria-bound evidence for necessarily conscious judgments (though only the latter for conscious *knowledge*). Therefore, far from being a justification for behaviourism, Wittgenstein's private language argument tells us: 'Of course behavioural criteria can provide us with knowledge of others' mental states; what more *could* there be?' The difference between the pain example and the case in which we have to evaluate the child's verbal or behavioural judgments is essentially one of degree insofar as they both involve agreement about objective criteria, but that in the former case the agreement is ingrained within the conceptual system and in the latter it is dependent on the findings of psychological research. So we are brought back to the process outlined in Section 4.3 whereby empirical, psychological hypotheses originate at the point at which universal agreement on what is common knowledge breaks down. One of the best ways of studying the child's evolving consciousness is by means of his functional interests, the verbal and behavioural judgments which he expresses in his spontaneous activity; thus breaking into the two-way triangle drawn above. So we certainly require some kind of ethology of child behaviour but one which is centrally concerned with what children *say*, rather than one which treats the child on the model of (at best) the chimpanzee and (at worst) the stickleback.

Strawson also, in a different way, attacked the usual view of consciousness as personal possession. In *Individuals* he proposed that a behaviouristic rejection of consciousness was untenable because it could not be stated without presupposing that which it set out to deny. But his rejection of the Cartesian dualist thesis that states of consciousness have no necessary connection with 'corporeal predicates' (and presumably about what bodies do: behaviour) is of particular interest. 'One can', he wrote, 'ascribe states of consciousness to oneself only if one can ascribe them to others. One can ascribe them to others only if one can identify other subjects of experience. And one cannot identify others if one can identify them *only* as subjects of experience, possessors of states of consciousness' (p. 100) . . . 'If *only* mine, then *not* mine at all' (p. 109). This should make us recognize, according to Strawson, the *primitiveness* of the concept of 'a person': an epistemological thesis which can be again stretched towards genetic hypotheses concerning the importance of primitive intersubjectivity between the human infant and its caretaker.

It is interesting to note that the Wittgenstein and Strawson views of consciousness are strikingly similar to those of a very different kind of philosopher, Friedrich Nietzsche, as Danto (1965) has shown.

4.6 CODA

In this final section I will flesh out some of the suggestions made above, partly as a means of summarising and making them more explicit, partly by way of disclaiming some objectionable consequences which they might seem to imply in their unelaborated form, and partly to illustrate further what is being intended by genetic epistemology. This will be undertaken in five areas. First, the previous section ended on something of an upbeat by affirming the necessity for viewing knowledge acquisition as a function of the development of consciousness; more needs to be said about the limitations of this suggestion and I will spend most time on this. Secondly, I have denied that structures determine knowledge by nonconscious mental operations but that the child's knowledge becomes structured by virtue of the fact that the conceptual system is so structured; the account of these structures and their acquisition requires some elaboration. Thirdly, I have said little about the motivating forces within the acquisition of knowledge beyond vague proposals about the determining influence of functional interests; in general we have to discuss the contribution of the child as a conative agent to the dialectic of cognitive growth. The other two areas involve counterbalancing the pragmatist tendencies which have been uppermost in some of what has gone before. So our fourth issue arises out of the fact that some of the arguments which have been presented cannot be easily distinguished from an extreme conventionalist view of the knowledge which the child is acquiring, which would see the child as acquiring a set of conventions which reflect nothing more than the accretion of agreements made from past expediency. Unmodified, this would entail an unacceptable *consensus* view of knowledge and truth and a conservative kind of epistemology wherein the tendency to agreement as a legitimising activity was the only determining force in the acquisition of knowledge. Also, the pragmatic principle of functionalism has loomed large in the previous discussions and, as with conventionalism, this can lead to unacceptable consequences when its limitations are not made explicit.

4.6.1 *Consciousness*

Knowledge is not something that *happens to* the child. This is the main burden of Section 4.5 and the reason for rejecting the Piagetian proposal that understanding is determined by states of, essentially internal, equilibrium. But in saying that the conscious apprehension of rules of thought and their purposive utilisation is responsible for the acquisition of knowledge one is not claiming that cognitive development is *nothing more* than the growth of awareness, but rather that the conscious element is necessary and determining.

The initial proposal is that there can be no knowledge without some kind of representation in mental activity; which is very close to the Baldwinian principle that 'theoretical' knowledge involves systems of 'mediation', 'controlled' by something determinate in the concrete or personal world. We were first led towards this suggestion at the end of Section 3.1 in discussing when knowledge of object permanence should be ascribed to the infant: knowledge that something continues to exist unperceived is inconceivable without some possibility of representing its continuing existence. On the conceptual plane similar suggestions were made regarding the importance of the language system: only through a sign system can knowledge be made common and objective so that the child makes the world objective to himself by the utilisation of rules ingrained in the linguistic–conceptual system (for example, syntax, inference, conservation principles), which are also modes of representation. Thus knowledge of concrete states, conceptual truths and the making of objective judgments is a function of mental processes which are representable in consciousness. As regards sensorimotor knowledge this means that the agent can represent unperceived events and as regards conceptual knowledge this means that the agent can justify (see Sections 3.2 and 3.3) his judgments by reference to sets of common criteria. It is a necessary condition for the possession of knowledge that it can be made conscious.

Rather ironically, such a proposal would *appear* to locate us squarely behind a 'structuralist' as against a 'functionalist' view of consciousness—at least in the sense that these terms were employed by psychologists just after the turn of the century (see Angell, 1903). It may be recalled that Titchener (1900) in the tradition of Wundt's Leipzig School, attacked the work of Würzburg psychologists such as Külpe and Bühler in Germany and Angell in the USA for their proposal of an imageless thought; all thinking, Titchener maintained, has a sensory content which could be revealed by introspection— and even when introspection failed to reveal this Titchener would only comment on its elusiveness rather than conclude its absence. However, the present proposal regarding the indissociability of knowledge from conscious apprehension is no kin to this philosophically dubious and empirically false notion; indeed we have already endorsed Bühler's *Beswusstheit* (see p. 229). In fact, one does not have to maintain that all *mental processes* are conscious and that it is by virtue of purely conscious processes that judgments are made. For instance, it is surely not the case that between the time of the child being asked 'Is it still the same amount to drink?' and his answering 'Yes' there has to be an intervening train of images or verbal reasonings by means of which the child judges correctly. There *may* be such an intervening phenomenal procession but it is probably rare even in the child and certainly not epistemologically necessary.

On the other hand, consciousness comes in by virtue of the fact that the child 'knows he knows' indeed knows *how* he knows and can thus say—in principle if not always in practice—why he is judging the way he is; and thus we re-encounter Kant's principle of reflexive self-consciousness, and the justification of judgments as truths by objective criteria. There need not have been a conscious mental process prior to the judgment but there is necessarily the ability to make conscious reference to the facts of the case. It is in this way that what I have called 'rulebound' concepts involve consciousness. But what of those which are not rulebound, some of which have been called 'perceptual'? For example, a child may know that he has a pair of red socks, that the lady who looks after him is called his mother, that he goes to school, that there are seven days in a week and so on. He knows these as facts about the world and saying that he knows them is tantamount to saying that he is conscious of them; not that this knowledge can only be characterised phenomenologically but that the child knows these as truths which he will—of course consciously—contend. The preoperational child is well aware that *non-rulebound* knowledge is objective and contendable: when somebody says that his socks are green, that the woman is called his father, that he does not go to school, that there are five days in a week, he does know that this is wrong; he can, moreover, tell lies. So partly in this sense, not in the sense that the acquisition of knowledge is *identical to* the development of consciousness, one can propose that acquiring knowledge is necessarily a function of consciousness—a proposal which is a consequence of making *truths* the objects of knowing.

Of course, it is possible to argue in opposition that this consciousness is just an epiphenomenon of non-conscious mental machinery, a spin-off from some deep, equilibrating process of the mind. The rejection of this (equilibrium) view has been made inevitable by the position adopted here regarding a cluster of interwoven issues in the philosophy of mind—the distinction between reasons and causes for behaviour, the problem of intentionality, the relation between consciousness and brain processes—for an account of the acquisition of knowledge cannot be given without adopting a definite perspective on these issues. To take first the reason–cause distinction; although the arguments will not be rehearsed here, one accepts Peters' (1958) thesis that for the kind of behaviour which we call intelligent there can be no explanation by seeking to reduce what we call the individual's reason for acting to a set of prior causes within or without him. Peters' main justification for this view is that human behaviour must involve the adoption of certain socially-constituted ways of proceeding which necessitate the agent acting 'in the light of' contingencies rather than being determined by them. This is closely allied to the position taken by Hamlyn (1970) that knowledge cannot be the end result of causal processes but must involve the appreciation of relevant criteria and that human learning—*qua* the acquisition of knowledge in the broadest sense—always involves a modification of consciousness. It would be wrong, however, to regard these as philosophical theses in a scientific vacuum: their viability depends on what we know of animal and human behaviour and on what has been and can be achieved in the field of artificial intelligence. Also, assumptions about such issues do more than influence the construction of a 'conceptual framework' but actually determine the kind of empirical hypotheses that will be developed, thus determining, in turn, research procedures and findings, on the basis of which the area of common knowledge within which the philosophical theses can exist is either extended or contracted (see Section 4.4).

I shall take the other two philosophical issues—intentionality and brain states—as starting points from which to elaborate further the present view of consciousness, beginning with intentionality.

The view of Hume and of many susbsequent philosophers was that an intention is an internal event which precedes the performance of an action and is the sufficient condition for it; against which post-Wittgenstinian philosophers such as Anscombe (1957) and Melden (1961) have argued. On the present perspective the main problem with the Humean view is that it presents intention as merely a special kind of causal antecedent—a mental cause—so that there is nothing to prevent the assimilation of intentions to causes. It is the *difference* between intentions and causes which needs to be emphasised.

One genetic consequence of the notion that knowledge does not happen to us is that the child's developing ability to make judgments is seen as involving the *purposive utilisation* of what he already knows, often in order to accommodate to that which he does not know. When taken together with the proposal that all conceptual judgment involves the conscious adoption of socially constituted criteria for truth, this means that although judgments are not made and understanding not acquired as a consequence of trains of phenomenal images or internalised speech they are the result of what can only be characterised as conscious intention. Here again justification is at the heart of the matter. Although only rulebound concepts can be justified when given as answers to questions, any verbalisation or purposive action can be questioned: What did you do/say that? may sometimes be inappropriate but it is never nonsensical.

It is in the sense that they both share intentionality that conceptual thought can be characterised as a kind of interiorised action. However, there is a crucial difference between action and conceptual thought expressed in language: although purposive action need not involve any consciousness of what is being done (Wittgenstein gave the lion stalking its prey as a paradigm case of intentionality) verbal–conceptual judgment necessarily does. The lion does not know that he is stalking prey but it is only in abnormal mental states that we do not know what we are saying or doing; thus we are driven back again to Kant's proposal that reflexive self-consciousness, or as he put it 'The "I think" that must be *capable* of accompanying all my presentations', is a necessary feature of objective knowledge.

So although the mental processes are not always conscious, the *act* of thinking is necessarily conscious in the sense that what we think is a function of what we intend, which is a function of what we want—and hence the interrelationship of consciousness, knowledge and functional interests given diagramatically on page 245. In explaining how the child acquires knowledge we need not search for a set of determining principles which are not amenable to revelation in consciousness and which are independent of the child's conative life.

This is not supposed to imply that we are only conscious of what we wish to be and that thoughts are products of completely free choice, for everybody knows—especially those who often try to concentrate or meditate—that sometimes we not so much choose our thoughts as become assailed by them: unlike knowledge there is a sense in which *individual thoughts* do happen to us. Not only this but solutions to problems, creative syntheses, memories and the like often arrive unheralded by conscious groping, trial and error or previous associations. Does not this fact, manifest to introspection, go against all that has been said up to now about consciousness, and thus the necessarily conscious element in knowledge, *not* being an epiphenomenon of mental mechanisms?

In answer to this it is necessary to return to the distinction between *non*-conscious and *un*conscious mental processes (see p. 243). Structuralists such as Piaget and Chomsky posit non-conscious thought structures which *can* never be conscious owing to their enormous formal complexity, and which *need* never be conscious. Freud, on the other hand, did not regard unconscious mental processes in this way: for him what is unconscious is amenable to revelation in consciousness by virtue of the fact that it was originally conscious. On this basis I believe it is possible to develop some notion of a *cognitive* unconscious epistemologically similar to the Freudian unconscious of affective life. So now the speculations must begin.

A cognitive unconscious develops as a direct result of the growth of conscious faculties, for all the thinking that we carry out unconsciously can, in principle, be carried out consciously. At the outset the child's consciousness consists of sensory data, and what will later be the unconscious and conscious elements of thinking are fused. But as thinking becomes more determined by things and more structured by abstract features of the conceptual system (for example, grammar, logic), as one element of thinking becomes more *public*, in Baldwin's sense, and thus conscious, there is a corresponding, inverse development towards a purely *private*, unmediated kind of thinking which splits away from determination by the data and forms moulding what is essentially public in consciousness. Just as we argued above that consciousness is, in one sense, a public phenomenon, the cognitive unconscious is private insofar as it lacks everything that thought requires to be knowledge—especially it lacks any sensory content, linguistic expression, all that Baldwin meant by systems of 'control' and the reflexive self-consciousness which must accompany this. But although this cognitive unconscious is primitive in character—for knowledge develops away from privacy—it does develop as a mirror image of conscious processes, except that it functions in a seemingly automatic, ballistic and *autonomous* manner. This is not a complete autonomy however but one which comes about through unconscious cognition lacking the reflexive self-consciousness which attends objective knowledge. We are aware that unconscious thought has taken place but are not aware of the process itself because there is no possibility of remembering ourselves thinking through it. So although unconscious mental processes may be revealed in consciousness by reconstructing they are not retrievable in memory as having been carried out by ourselves. This lack of reflexivity would account for the speed with which unconscious thinking occurs.

Apart from speed there is another advantage: problems are solved and creative syntheses made in the unconscious because it has the freedom to make unusual associations and regrouping of data through lacking a context—because there is no determination by epistemic conventions nor by the motives of the moment. However this is again only an autonomy relative to conscious functioning for it is conscious thought which engages the cognitive unconscious by, as it were, setting it problems. The data of the cognitive unconscious (the premises of an argument, perceptual schemata and so on) are there to be processed only because they were initially conscious, and the way in which this data is organised at the outset is determined by the way it was consciously apprehended (see the discussion of transitive reasoning in Section 3.2). Finally, the relation between the cognitive unconscious and the conscious mind is dialectical for not only does consciousness set in train unconscious processes but the *results* of these unconscious processes influence what will be judged.

Of course this is all very unsatisfactory: here are a set of dubious metaphors about compartments of the mind, about mysterious processes and kinds of determination, indeed about the development of something 'we know not what.' But this dubiousness is an inevitable consequence of our lacking concepts to characterise these kinds of thinking (which is in turn a consequence of not needing to communicate about them)—not necessarily because the notions are dubious in themselves. Moreover, it should be stressed that this is meant to be by way of framing the problem and plotting out a sphere of explanation rather than the solution or the explanation itself.

Piaget once explained why he studied cognition rather than emotion by saying that he preferred studying the faculty of reason to the 'tricks of the unconscious.' And it is due to Freud that the affectively charged, associative aspects of unconscious life have been uppermost in our conception of it; the image still lingers of that which is beneath consciousness having—in the well-known metaphor—the character either of a sex-crazed monkey or a maiden aunt! But if there is some place for the notion of a cognitive unconscious which develops as a consequence of conscious development one may study the *principles* by which it functions as well as the trickery it can play in our affective life. Guiding developmental hypotheses here might be that the younger the child the more direct access he has to his mental processes and that with each cognitive advance there is a corresponding development in the autonomous, automatic and ballistic element in thinking. Regarding the lack of conceptual tools for characterising the growth of unconscious thinking, it is the business of genetic epistemology to construct them. Indeed in this construction one notion which may need to be transcended is the distinction between reasons and causes. This is a distinction we have been forced to draw in ascribing responsibility to conscious agents, and thus it has been ingrained in our conceptual system; a system unadapted to dealing with unconscious thought. So we may require a third kind of principle which is not causally determining yet which cannot be characterised as ratiocinative activity as we know it to be. Likewise, it may not be possible to characterise these processes either as intentional or automatic or even as being located at some point between the two extremes; unconscious thinking has a strange status because although it is something that we do it is not done from considerations of which we can ever be completely aware.

Thus we arrive at our third philosophical problem, that of the relation between brain processes and consciousness, for something must be said about the status of these mental processes vis-à-vis neurological processes. Perhaps the best way of avoiding entanglement in a web of philosophical debate at this point is to tackle this question by way of the notion of information processing, and by distinguishing clearly between knowledge and reasoning. I have been labouring the point that knowing something to be the case is not essentially the result of cognitive processes which the individual undergoes, because knowledge has an ineluctably public aspect. Knowledge is apprehended and constructed by individuals but it exists *as* knowledge by virtue of the fact that it is commonly controlled, intersubjective, objective. Knowledge can be considered separately from reasoning: there is a fundamental difference between knowing what is the case, what are the rules for a procedure, on the one hand, and actually carrying out ratiocinative activity like solving a mathematical problem. Although knowledge, in that it is not a possession, is not in itself isomorphic to brain processes or status, there is a sense in which we can regard the active utilisation of knowledge, the process of thinking, as isomorphic, for surely when we think processes go on in our brains.

We are dealing here with information processing which in our present state of knowledge we have to represent in flow diagrams and computer programs rather than in neurological language. What is being affirmed here is that this is information by virtue of the conscious, epistemic functions of the subject; and what is being denied is that an account of the processing can *alone* explain ratiocinative activity. The information processing is 'got underway' by the individual in that what he judges and intends 'determines' the information content and the goals. (Quotes are used here in order to disclaim any simple causal relationship and to recognise the crudity of the terms.) But rather than implying an homunculus working the machinery of the brain this is only by way of denying that the influence is not in the other direction—that the processes which our brains undergo 'determine' the judgments we make; that is, 'knowledge does not happen to us'.

The genetic implication here is that brain development affects the acquisition of knowledge partly as a negative principle: it sets the limits on the information we can handle rather than frames the information itself. It also implies that our logico-mathematical knowledge is not structured by virtue of the fact that the human brain is structured in a certain way, and that it is not a necessary condition for the child's attaining competence (say) in the concrete operations that a definite reorganisation of his brain takes place. It is now these structures which we have to consider.

4.6.2 *Structures*

Piaget holds that the structures of conceptual thinking are rooted in structures of sensorimotor action and that the former develop out of the latter by a reflective abstraction made possible by the equilibration of mental operations. It has been proposed above, however, that to talk of sensorimotor thought being structured is to beg the important questions (p. 237), and that the structure concept itself, being so all-encompassing, seems to do likewise (p. 234). Indeed, it is a reflection of the nature and power of mathematics that the structure concept can be applied so widely (p. 236). Nevertheless, it cannot be denied that human thought—leaving aside pre-verbal behaviour for the moment—is structured. For there is a logico-mathematical grid within which even our everyday commerce with the world is regulated and legitimised. Mathematics, on which all the natural sciences depend, is structured by definition; the number system is surely a structure; and here I am deliberately not using the word in the technical sense of the Bourbaki circle of mathematicians and of Piaget (see Piaget, 1971b, and below).

On the present perspective what has been emphasised relative to the Piagetian account is that these structures exist, as it were, *outside* the individual, that, in a Popperian sense, they are without a knowing subject, a consideration which makes a Platonic view of mathematics still so seductive. But on what criteria should we distinguish between knowledge that is structured and that which is not? First of all, what we have called rulebound concepts are roughly isomorphic to Piaget's structures of concrete operational knowledge. Rulebound concepts—as contrasted with perceptual concepts—involve the correlation of at least two physical dimensions or unidimensional relations (which is the case in all concrete operational problems) and thus they have a kind of abstraction quite beyond that of (say) colour concepts, one which can be characterised by rules enabling the relevant judgments to be justified by such rules.

These rules of thought evolved within the culture through the invention of legitimising procedures to expedite functional demands. For example, the number system may well have arisen out of the exigencies of bartering: the utilisation of units—be they sheep, teeth or trinkets—moulds a system out of practical necessity. At a more basic level, logic—of which the syntax of language is an expression—would have arisen out of the necessity of imposing order on the communicative system to secure common reference (Strawson), in order to construct a system of 'elucidatory truths' (Baldwin)—the logical framework for any thinking. Every logical notion from the law of excluded middle, through inductive and deductive inference to the most complex syllogisms is rooted in a dialectic between interested parties. However, the very enculturalisation of these structures *as* necessary rather than just as functional necessities for some end results in a kind of Platonic status as ideal forms of thinking and calculating. Even grammar may be construed as a system to which we aspire or which we erect as an ideal to be consciously pursued when we speak and write. Also, Popper notwithstanding, only in a limited sense are these structures creations of the human mind, as creation implies some freedom of synthesis and a range of alternatives; the first moves towards (say) a number system conservation of discontinuous quantities, the ordinal/cardinal distinction, addition and subtraction related as reciprocals and so on) were almost forced on early man given the functional interests he possessed (exchanging, sharing, rationing) and the kind of world in which he lived. Moreover, as each rule was erected the degrees of freedom were correspondingly diminished for the next moves towards structure (see p. 156 above) so that the more rules, the greater the determination by the system itself.

Given such a status what can be said about the acquisition of structured knowledge? It does not entail that such structures are handed down to the child fully elaborated like Commandments of Thinking with his having merely to adopt the appropriate receptive orientation. Rather, it might be proposed that the child is 'shown the way into' the system by way of rulebound concepts, which he acquires informally through everyday social interaction, trading on his prior possession of perceptual concepts and a set of functional interests. The perceptual–rulebound progression is the 'bridge' into the system. Moreover, it is not necessary to regard the development of what can be called structures out of rulebound concepts as a quantum jump to a new form of equilibrium or necessity; and, as was argued on p. 206, there are good reasons not to view the concrete operations as a stage which is complete at around the twelfth year. The continuous and potentially infinite process of structuring systems out of lower elements gets underway as the child coordinates his rulebound concepts (such as conservation, class inclusion, transitivity, Euclidian space judgments, time taken as independent of distance travelled) into a system which is *already there*. Given the nature of rulebound concepts certain formal, systematic notions fall into place. For example, an understanding of area and multiplication might come about by the coordination of what the child already knows of the conservation of amounts within boundaries (for example, amount of grass for cows to eat in one of Piaget's experiments) with the ability to additively combine lengths in units. Such a coordination will only be possible when the child is conscious of notions such as conservation, as objective truths, rather than as private, unsocialised regularities (see p. 168).

Thus the Bourbaki mathematicians, in extracting parent structures from the heterogeneous fields of classical mathematics by subjecting the elements of these fields to transformations, were *continuing* the structuring activity which they began in the seventh year of their childhood: they were not discovering how logico-mathematical thinking has to be structured at the outset. Piaget's view of the significance of Bourbaki mathematics is, of course, quite different (Piaget, 1971b). He seeks to justify his cognitive structuralism partly by the fact that the three parent structures which they extracted—the algebraic structures as in classification, the order and the topological structures—are also the three main operational activities prior to the onset of the concrete operational stage. But is it not to be expected *a priori* that the result of extracting structures of such generality will also be very general aspects of childrens' actions on objects, given the fact that mathematics necessarily relates to what people do? Contrary to Piaget it is being proposed here that structures are a product of abstracting activity not a determining agency in the constitution of logico-mathematical thought. Thus, the only way one's thought can be determined by Piagetian structures is by becoming conversant with the work of the Bourbaki mathematicians! Generally, characterising human action and thinking in terms of any formal system whatsoever is not the way to understand how the competences developed, no matter how many kinds of knowledge or planes of behaviour can be encompassed by it.

But we have yet said little about how these rulebound concepts can gain any cognitive foothold given that the child can only cognise immediate perceptual criteria for the truth of concrete judgments. Here it is possible to agree with Piaget about the facts of the case. It can be accepted first of all that, as the infant has a sensorimotor competence in conservation, transitivity, class inclusion and Euclidean space concepts for example (at least in what adults characterise by these terms!) one can view the child from the age of 2 to 7 years as gradually objectivising that which he already acts in accordance with. Piaget is not altogether clear about how what he calls a 'repetition' of the behavioural on the conceptual plane takes place, but he certainly regards the interiorisation of actions as necessary for it, and wants to say that the roots of structure are sensorimotor and that the equilibration of operations is the process essential to the reflective abstraction of knowledge which is already present is a more primitive form. He is more than proposing that behavioural competence exists as a necessary condition, but is saying that the coordinations of action schemes *are* logico-mathematical structures although not yet realised within a language system (Piaget, 1971b). Our problem is how we are to regard the relation between what might be called the *functional competences* of infancy and early childhood and the objective knowledge of middle childhood, having rejected (p. 237) *déclage*-like repetition as the answer.

The infant and young child have a large number of functional competences all of which can be characterised logico-mathematically. He knows that he has to remove his shoes before pulling off his socks (is this a logic of order?); he can pick out the sweets from among a mixture of sweets and marbles (class logic?); he can distinguish a broken from an unbroken circle (topological logic?). In the same vein, should we say that the wood louse which has been conditioned to orientate in a certain manner has been taught the sensorimotor form of the logical inference $P \rightarrow Q, P, \therefore Q$? The fact is that all effective, successful behaviour can be characterised in logico-mathematical terms because it is in the nature of logic and mathematics that they can describe these kinds of phenomena, and as 'forms of life' they have functional roots in action. To illustrate the latter point, I recall being surprised as a student when my tutor in logic suggested that we have a notion of truth because when somebody shouts at us 'Look out!' we want to know if we should believe him. Odd as this may seem it does reflect the fact that logic is rooted in functional interests; and to this we can add that the nature of the logico-mathematical system reflects the functional competences which these interests have produced. Functional interests are necessary for functional competences (the toddler *wants* to retrieve the watch chain; she *can* remove a series of obstacles, in what we might call a transitive manner, to retrieve it); and functional competences are reflected in the structure of logic and mathematics as necessary conditions of their *having any structure at all* not as 'action structures' from which reflective abstraction will produce fully-elaborated formal structures on the conceptual plane. Another way of putting the same kind of point is by saying that as the human child shares certain functional interests with the human race (for example, extracting subclasses from classes, ordering elements) there is a form of recapitulation in cognitive development: the cultural transmission of the structures of the logico-mathematical system is not possible without the functional competences pre-existing in the child which he has developed to expedite these functional interests.

It is possible to account for what Piaget calls the formal operational knowledge of the adolescent in the same spirit. Piaget's theory is that the hypothetico-deductive thought of the adolescent reflects the same kind of operational equilibrium but at a higher level. Yet here we also have a similar confluence of cultural transmission, functional competences and functional interests. As regards hypothesis-testing itself this is a form of life present in (at least some) cultures the functional roots of which are to be found at the stage of the tertiary circular reactions (see p. 100 above) at around 12 to 18 months, in which the infant, having tried out pre-established schemes 'lies in wait for a new experience' to be produced by active experimentation. Of course these trials are not systematic in the way in which Piaget intends by the term 'grouped', but to explain the systematisation, the holding constant of one independent variable to determine the effect of another, we need not postulate any other process than the marrying of this functional competence with the cultural transmission of the form of life. Here also the culture has evolved a system for finding the factor responsible for a particular phenomenon but this system could gain no foothold in the cognitive life of the child without the prior functional interest in finding the procedure for bringing something about and the functional competence of inventive trial-and-error.

But hypothetico-deductive thinking is not the only feature of the cognitive advances at adolescence, for we also see an enormous development in the comprehension and utilisation of concepts of such a degree of abstraction and ruleboundness that their functional roots are hardly discernible. I said before that the structures of concrete operational thinking might have been formed by coordinating more basic rulebound concepts of clear functional relevance such as conservation or addition—subtraction, but where is the functional root in the child's life of a notion such as entropy or logarithm? Moreover, although Archimedes' principle has a clear functional relevance (reflected by its legendary mode of discovery!) as does that of a formula such as πr^2 the notion of a principle *per se*, of a scientific law which transcends contingent regularity, or of a formula as something produced by the system from necessity as well as by man for convenience can be seen as an *imaginative abstraction*. In Inhelder and Piaget's ingenious experiments we see adolescents 'discovering' scientific laws such as the angle of incidence being equal to the angle of reflection; but it would surely be just as wrong to say they accommodate to these laws by virtue of the systematisation of hypothetico-deductive procedures *alone*, as to say that they succeed by recognising a purely functional relevance (for example, seeing the principle at work when playing squash).

The more divorced from functional competences abstract notions become the more justified we are in saying that their appreciation requires an act of imagination rather than a more sophisticated capacity for ratiocination. It is not just individual concepts that are involved here like that of an image being an equal distance behind the mirror as the object is before it, or of all substances having an atomic structure, but the ability to conceive of a quite different kind of reality which science demands.

In discussing consciousness it was suggested that the development of a cognitive unconscious results in the process of thinking gaining a kind of autonomy, well here also there is a developing autonomy in that thinking becomes progressively more independent of its functional origins. In the imaginative abstractions of the sciences the roots of the functional competence may be all but untraceable and the functional interest of solving problems for their own sake hardly justifies the term 'functional' at all.

It would certainly be ridiculous to suggest that Piaget ignores what we have called imaginative abstraction, but the structuralist meta-theory which demands that it be seen as a product of the structuring activity of the mind undersells it and does not make its development, *qua* that of a form of imagination, more intelligible to us. So for both concrete and formal operational thinking it may be more or less possible to characterise it by means of the structures which Piaget employs and these descriptions may or may not make the acquisition more intelligible and furnish suggestions as to the cognitive processes involved, but what it does not do is provide an explanation of the developmental process itself nor an adequate characterisation of the kinds of knowledge to which the child comes to accommodate.

4.6.3 *Motivation*

Our next task is to expand a little on these functional interests which have peppered the discussion so far, by means of some suggestions regarding the role of the child's interests in the acquisition of knowledge, or more generally, the role of motivation in cognitive development. Motivation has had rather a bad press of late and there are a number of reasons for this: the failure of Hullian learning theory, the unpopularity of psychoanalysis within psychology, the inapplicability of S–R theories to cognition and language, philo-sophical arguments against a general theory of motivation (Peters, 1958) and against either mentalistic or behaviouristic conceptions of motivation *qua* affect (Alston, 1969; Kenny, 1963; Melden, 1969), the fact that 'need' theories in social psychology tend either towards clinical generalisation or tautology. Piaget is easily located within this trend by way of his insistence that beyond the equilibration principle we do not require a theory of motivation as a factor energising cognitive growth, that as 'affect' and 'intelligence' are indissociable, the assimilation–accommodation model can comfortably handle both kinds of mental function within the same set of principles (Piaget, 1957). Indeed it is illustrative of the tendency to distrust energising principles in cognitive development that in a recent symposium three major figures in developmental psychology, genetic epistemology and educational psychology were found agreeing that motivational principles beyond Piagetian theory are either not required or not central (papers by Kessen, by Mischel and by Ausubel in Mischel, 1971). What seems to have produced this consensus is the assumption that motivation as a developmental principle can be dispensed with because it inevitably leads to drive reductionism of an S–R or a psychoanalytic variety, to which Piaget's austerely logistical view of cognitive development is infinitely preferable.

But what then is the status of Piaget's equilibrium model such that it can encompass the interests of the developing child as elements of a general process? As Mischel (1971) says, equilibrium is not really—as Piaget calls it—a *process* at all because it does not entail an empirical theory; it is rather an 'analysis or rational reconstruction of how we think in accordance with the norms which govern directed thinking'. Nevertheless Mischel argues that this is a conceptual framework of considerable empirical value because, when coupled with an account of the 'considerations' ('calculations, reasonings, justificatory moves') which weigh with the child at any given stage of development it enables us to understand how the child's thinking develops.

Although Piaget sometimes uses expressions such as the child 'asking himself', as his 'reasonings' and 'doubts' (for example, Piaget, 1957 pp. 62–72) his actual account is not reliant on these conscious ratiocinations, as was argued above. Whilst not strictly being a causal principle equilibrium must have the 'inevitability' of a causal process as well as logical necessity. It is significant that Mischel's construal of Piaget's account in terms of 'considerations which are operative for the child' is very similar to Toulmin's (1970) attempt to account for how *reasons* can have a kind of *causal* efficacy.

What the principle of equilibrium seems to boil down to, however, is that for any cognitive change there has to be conflict or inconsistency existing in the mind of the child or adult. In fact, when applied to sensorimotor development in infancy this is more than a conceptual framework and can be made to yield firm empirical predictions as against (say) a cumulative, S–R learning theory—predictions which have been tested and supported by Bower (1974). But the difficulty arises when we wish to apply the equilibrium–perturbance–disequilibrium model to conceptual thinking. For example, in Piaget's (1967) account of how disequilibrium is energised and resolved in the growth of conservation he says that after a period of oscillating between the two judgments that the amount is greater or that it is smaller he discovers 'the interdependence of the two transformations' with a resultant increase in the probability that 'he will discover that two variations are inverse to each other . . . the child now finds a reversible system' (pp. 154–57). So the child is

capable of recognising inconsistency between incompatible judgments; it is in his cognitive nature that he will *want* to equilibrate these
judgments; and in the nature of his cognitive apparatus that it is
capable of achieving this equilibration.

It is certainly the case that a necessary condition for cognitive
change of this kind is that there should be a recognition of
inconsistency on the part of the subject, but why should this energise
cognitive change unless the subject actually wants to judge 'consistently'? Why does he not remain content to agree to disagree with
those who hold different judgments (see p. 230), as we do, for
example in matters of taste; or why is he not content to have his
judgments changing as they do in phenomenal perceptions (see the
Braine and Shanks (1965a; 1965b) studies of the preoperational
child's inability to distinguish phenomenal and real judgments of size
and shape). On the present perspective, the fact that some kinds of
judgment have to attain consistency, but not others, is in the nature of
the system of concrete knowledge which is being transmitted to the
child; and thus the attainment of consistency between the truth values
of such transformational and multi-relational judgments is a form of
life to which the child has to adapt. As Mischel says, equilibrium is a
principle which reflects the *norms* of our thinking, which in turn, we
might add, reflect forms of life rather than biological necessities of
autoregulation. The motivational aspect of this is what might be
called the 'cultural education' of the child's interests in the direction
of certain kinds of consistency. To say, as Piaget does, that
equilibrium is basically a matter of the 'accord of thought with itself'
(Piaget, 1950) is only to set the problem. Not only does the interest in
consistency have to be explained but the process by which the
disequilibrium is resolved. As regards the latter point it was argued
above that the child has to come to recognise the conflict *as* a conflict
and that the resolution is not something that he can do for himself: he
has to be exposed to the articulation and justification of the relevant
rulebound concept (see p. 231). This is one instance then of how
interests—motivational factors—are embedded in the process of
cognitive change, but we have to do more than say that the social life
of the child educates his interests towards certain standards of
consistency, for how did the interests develop in the first place and
what is their role in the overall scheme of cognitive development?

In sketching the role of interests it is necessary to re-examine the
assimilation–accommodation dichotomy. Baldwin employed the

term accommodation in a much broader sense than Piaget, making it serve for what Piaget would treat as both assimilatory and accommodatory processes, with assimilation sometimes being rather a passive notion, a kind of schematic 'net' or an associative principle. The active principle of assimilating events, objects and so on to schemes was under the determination of the interests—selective, semblant, experimental, schematic. Indeed Piagetian assimilation can be construed as a motivational principle: an assimilatory scheme is like a frame for what the subject wants to do. Thus, what the child has an interest in doing *is* his assimilation and if he wants to do something and fails this is a failure of accommodatory capacity to match up to his interests. In fact, not only *can* assimilation be construed motivationally, it is so interpreted by Piaget, but in order to make motivation redundant as a determining agency. He says that it is ' . . . not necessary for us to have any recourse to separate factors of motivation in order to explain learning, not because they do not intervene. . . . but because they are included from the start in the global concept of assimilation' (Piaget, 1959, p. 46–7; Mischel's translation). But perhaps it is the assimilation principle itself which is redundant. Successful accommodation entails assimilation and unsuccessful accommodation entails failure to assimilate, but the same is not true in reverse because an act of assimilation may not require any new accommodation on the part of the subject. So when considering how *efficacious* behaviour or thought happens to be the assimilation principle is redundant: accommodation encompasses assimilation. Assimilation is the *result* of the fulfillment of interest by accommodation, though sometimes there is a minimum of interest and little accommodation—especially in those people who claim that they have 'fly-paper minds' to which unwanted factual information attaches itself. But if we are concerned with why any behaviour at all or why a particular kind of behaviour, Piaget's notion of assimilation—which construed motivationally is Baldwin's 'interest'—comes into its own. When Piaget writes of assimilation taking place between schemes, however, as in reciprocal assimilation, his usage is different and not dissimilar to Baldwin's associationist usage and to that of Wundt, its originator. Accommodation still remains the plasticity principle however.

What are the consequences of viewing assimilation as a motivational principle akin to interest? It does at least allow us to be bolder in characterising the phylogenetic endowment of the human infant, and it continues, even strengthens, Piaget's biological analogy. Organisms have innate needs for food, warmth, and evacuation; it can be proposed analogously that human beings have innate interests in certain kinds of, at least, visual, tactile and social experiences and towards certain behaviours such as imitation. The baby chimpanzee and the human infant want to do different things and this wanting will inevitably determine how their accommodatory plasticity will be exercised. So cognitive assimilation is not only analogous to biological processes such as that of the assimilation of food because they both involve taking something in, but also because they both involve—however unpopular the notion—drives. It may be recalled that Baldwin's original notion of the circular reaction was hedonistic; and how difficult it is to conceive of the self—other elaboration taking place without the polarities of pleasure and displeasure.

Thus we have an interest—accommodation model and a dialectic similar to that of Baldwin in which cognitive growth is generated by schematic, semblant, experimental, imitative, selective interests, the conceptual heirs of which are the functional aspect of language use, judgmental proposition, abstraction, intension, accretion of meanings and synthesis. The dialectical nature of the system ensures that the motivational aspect evolves with every accommodatory success so there is a mutual determination between what the child wants and what he can do or understand (see figure on p. 245).

Just as in the development of accommodations, that of cognitive motivations can be seen as occurring in a series of discontinuous stages, some of which may be determined by biochemical changes such as those of puberty (as suggested by Bruner, 1959). Perhaps the first great advance takes place at the end of the sensorimotor stage when the self—world dichotomy has been elaborated on the plane of action. For the child may thus have evolved a reflexive awareness of his own interests: to the extent that his ego is differentiated from the world he also has a notion of possessing certain desires and interests, of the refractoriness of the world of things and people, in the development of which the process of imitation may be central, as Baldwin suggests. Seeing his own interests as controllable by the world may be necessary for his conceiving of them as controllable by himself—the genesis of, literal, self-control. Thus, as the awareness of wanting a thing and success in attaining it are differentiated by the child, he also differentiates the wanting and the act—wanting the apple and taking it—so that the action is not an inevitable consequence of the interest. At least at some stage the child must come to regard himself as a wanting agent, who is able to fulfil some of these wants and not others and indulge some and not others. So we have here a third kind of autonomy, this time an autonomy of the child's behaviour over his interests.

If there is to be any ascription of moral responsibility to an agent such an autonomy of behaviour over interests must necessarily have been attained. Baldwin recognised the intimate relationship between motivation and morality in his proposal that moral development is initiated by the earliest selective interests of the infant, as the origin of value and worth, and by the semblant and experimental interests which develop into ideal meanings. Piaget, on the other hand, whose assimilation principle was supposed to remove the need for the determination of behaviour by interests, offers a theory of moral development (see p. 90) which does little justice to the necessarily 'hot-blooded' nature of moral judgment—with Kohlberg (1969) following the same path even further. Of course, to the extent that moral judgments *are* a species of judgment the epistemic aspect of moral development is indispensible; but to the extent that moral judgments have a non-contingent relationship to moral feelings the affective, motivational aspect is also indispensible. It is possible for someone to have attained a high sophistication of moral judgment (Kohlberg's Stage 6 for example) and yet say 'Well this is how I judge the situation morally, but I have never regarded moral considerations as important so I shall do as I wish. Revenge is sweet—though morally primitive of course' (the autonomy of behaviour over interests reciprocally involves the freedom to follow one's interests at the same time as condemning them morally). But if we retain a frankly motivational principle as one side of the dialectic of cognitive development it is not possible for a theory of moral judgment to be produced in an affective vacuum. Conversely, this retains moral developmental issues within genetic epistemology for just as normative characterisations of the conceptual system are necessary for a full explanation of cognitive development, so does the explanation of moral development require ethical theories concerned with moral notions as they are actually used. Moreover, any theory of moral development which produces levels of 'higher' and 'lower' morality has to do more than justify this hierarchy in terms of its ascending cognitive sophistication: there must be some philosophical grounding for the assumption that one kind of judgment is more moral than another (see Peters' and Alston's comments on Kohlberg in Mischel, 1971). At the very least it is well for developmental psychologists of moral behaviour to attain a reflexive awareness of their own moral assumptions and proscriptions.

Although motivation is intrinsic relative to knowledge which is extrinsic and public, the motivation to acquire knowledge is socially determined to a large extent. The apathy which has been noted as characteristic of 'institutionalised' children must surely be at least as much responsible for any consequent intellectual impairment as the diminished quantity and variety of perceptual, manipulatory and verbal experiences which is its usual concomitant. Similarly, the fact that children from socially disadvantaged backgrounds gain less from formal schooling than do their equivalents who are not thus deprived must be largely determined by their literal lack of *interest* in the acquisition of knowledge and competence; certainly, blank indifference to the face of anything outside a severely limited sphere of interest is their most obvious characteristic. Now that the negative influence of fear of punishment and failure is waning within our schools, a motivational vacuum seems to remain; developmental psychology would do an enormous service to society by shedding light on how epistemic motivation is determined by social life and thus how the vacuum might be filled.

4.6.4 *Conventions and functions*

Finally I want to make some brief remarks about not overstating the case that the knowledge which all normal human beings can acquire forms a system of conventions based on agreement between the members of a conceptual system, agreements which have been necessitated by functional considerations of efficacy. For there are important senses in which knowledge is more than conventional and in which functions do not determine the nature of knowledge.

There is a danger of regarding the conventional structure of the conceptual system as having determined our thought to the extent that we are now encased within what some have called a hermeneutical, or interpretive, 'circle'. That is to say, if we wish to understand human nature—including the nature of human knowledge—we can only do so in terms of the system of concepts which we have developed to interpret the behaviour of others. As Taylor (1971) says 'We cannot escape ultimate appeal to a common understanding of the expressions of the "language" involved. That is one way of trying to express what has been called the "hermeneutical circle"'; he sees Hegelianism and empiricism as promising but failing to provide routes out of this circle. Freud's maxim about the limits of man's understanding of himself as being the limits of his anthropomorphism has been used to make a similar kind of point.

It was, in a sense, to escape this 'circle' that Kant and Piaget postulated necessities which were external to the conceptual system—in the one transcendental in the other biological. But despite our having argued against these extra-conceptual necessities (see p. 235) we must take the hermeneutical view of knowledge to be deeply mistaken for important reasons. Only from a completely agenetic perspective can it be sensibly proposed that our thought about ourselves, our explanations of our own behaviour, cannot move outside a fixed system of conventions whilst retaining intelligibility. If we *reflect* on the system we do indeed find a set of established categories (such as reason–cause) and rules of interpretation (purposive–automatic), so the philosopher (see Section 4.3) normally remains within the system for his purposes. But this is precisely one of the reasons why we require a *genetic* epistemology: in order to regard the current conceptual system as a stage in a process, and to view it as determined by principles of development. Adopting this perspective allows us to see our system as the result of a confluence of forces carried forward by the continuing dialectic between the human species and the world.

If the supporter of the hermeneutical view of knowledge then wants to insist that this adoption of a genetic perspective is just what we cannot do except through the 'goggles' of the human conceptual system as it stands, then he would be doing this again through an inability to appreciate developmental principles. It is a fact of human nature, at its most overt in the symbolic play of children between the ages of 2 and 6 years, that we can and do treat (conceptually-mediated) reality as other than it is by deliberately flouting the rules of the system, usually on the basis of our functional interests. In Baldwin's taxonomy this originates as the semblant interests of infancy. Also within this taxonomy, there is a system of *ideal* as well as common meanings, determined by the human interest in what *should* be the case rather than what is the case. The importance of these capacities and interests is genetic: we could not acquire knowledge without the semblant and selective functions, without the activity of delimiting reality from fantasy by producing fantasy (see also Vygotsky, 1933) and of constructing ideals against which reality does not measure. The metaphor of cognitive development which the hermeneutical view of knowledge suggests is that of a model railway train being placed neatly on the lines; but everything we know of the acquisition of knowledge suggests that the relation between the developing individual and the system of knowledge is nothing like this.

Although any explanation of human behaviour must be intelligible to us in a way in which, perhaps, a Skinnerian explanation is not (see Hamlyn, 1970), we should not determine the limits of the intelligibility of psychological theories *a priori* by reflection on the conceptual system as it exists. (Indeed, plotting the boundaries of a basic, communicative intelligibility, as carried out by Strawson, suggests that they are very broad indeed). The intelligibility of psychological theories cannot be decided in an empirical vacuum, for the ability to understand something *as* an explanation of a psychological phenomenon is itself a psychological phenomenon and not completely determined by the conventions of human rationality. Although it is a mistake to think that we are free to tinker with the apparatus of human meanings as we wish (for example see Anscombe (1974) on Richard Gregory's use of the term 'hypothesis'), it is also a mistake to believe that psychologists, whose 'interests' in behaviour are quite different to those of the layman, cannot ever produce new kinds of meaning.

Finally, is it really the case that *interpretation* is at the heart of the human sciences? It is certainly a necessary condition of any explanation of thought or behaviour that it should be interpretable with some reference to our system of meanings, but interpretation for its own sake is far from being the essence of the psychological enterprise. Interpretation as an end in itself can however be regarded as one of the central purposes of the psychological analysis of *abnormal* behaviour such as that in schizophrenia, for even if we know something of biochemical predispositions we have not explained schizophrenia unless we can make it—or rather the schizoid—schizophrenic progression—intelligible to ourselves. It is significant that when R. D. Laing (1959) came to attempt such an analysis he had to move some way beyond the system of our everyday concepts to existential phenomenology; and it is instructive to take existentialism as a test case of the possibilities for erecting 'satellite' conceptual systems. If we consider, for example, the use of the term 'existence' (in Heidegger's claim that only humans exist) we find the potential (for good or ill!) of making an imaginative leap beyond the boundaries of common understanding. However, the existentialist philosophers do not abandon logicality itself which would mean a descent into nonsense (see p. 235), but merely emphasise the diversity of our logics.

Paradoxically, at the other extreme of conventionalism there is emphasised not the *determination* of our thought by the system but our *freedom* to determine the system itself—a view that is equally mistaken. It might be argued that since these conventions are human constructions we are free to develop the system of human knowledge in almost any direction we wish, as it is in the nature of a convention not to be imposed from without. We can see a version of this debate in mathematics between the Platonists who regard the development of mathematical science as the process of discovering what is already there, and the intuitionists who hold that it is we who construct mathematics as we go along. Wittgenstein came close to the intuitionist view in his *Remarks on the Foundations of Mathematics* in which he said that we are 'free' in mathematics at very point—the view to which this other extreme of conventionalism tends. However this does not accord well with the present account: we have already considered in the discussion of structures how we are determined by the structures we have constructed in their extension. Dummett (1958) has expressed how Platonism and intuitionism are not the only alternatives in mathematics: 'If we think that mathematical results are in some sense imposed on us from without, we could have instead the picture of a mathematical reality not already in existence but as it were coming into being as we probe. Our investigations bring into existence what was not there before, but what they bring into existence is not of our own making.' (p. 162). And if this can be said of mathematics it also holds for other areas of knowledge which we can regard as structured in some way. It means—as Dummett goes on to say in fact—that functionalist epistemologies (and logics which explain truth and falsity in terms of the linguistic usage of the terms) do not entail an anthropomorphic autonomy which robs knowledge of its objective status.

Overall, if we look at the functionalisms of Wittgenstein and of Baldwin we do not find the extreme kind of anthropocentrism, which pragmatists such as James seemed to embrace, whereby truth and objectivity are reduced to efficacy and consensus. As Hamlyn (1967) has pointed out, Wittgenstein, whatever his pragmatist tendencies, was firmly in the Kantian tradition. Like Kant, Wittgenstein was seeking necessary conditions for knowledge which were neither logically prior to experience nor derived from it: the forms of life should be seen not only as anthropological phenomena or social norms but as synthetic *a priori* conditions for communication and for anything we can regard as knowledge. Likewise for Baldwin, his functionalism only went so far—so far in fact as the end of the first of the three volumes of *Thought and Things* (called, after all, *Functional Logic*). Syndoxic meaning is purely functional: it is efficacious that we agree with others in our criteria for truth and coherence. But there is a point at which efficacy attains a necessity—synnomic commonness. If Baldwin had stopped at syndoxic commonness there would really have been little to distinguish him from the cruder practitioners of Pragmatism. Synnomic meaning, though derived from agreement, transcends it: its control is independent of what others do or say and it has no function other than to confer objectivity through intersubjectivity. The commonness, the consensus, is necessary for the establishment of objective criteria but once recognised *as* objective our judgments attain an autonomy: my knowledge that substance is conserved through transformations is based on and indissociable from my knowledge that this is a universally *acknowledged* truth, but I do not have this knowledge *because I believe* that others will concur with my judgments and if they did not I would challenge them with justifications. So, for Baldwin, judgments do not have a common meaning merely because they serve a communicative function, and it is in this same sense that we can regard Kant's categories as being intersubjective (see p. 30). So by focusing on the commonness of our judgments Wittgenstein and Baldwin were not attempting to *explain objectivity away* as a social function but were characterising the nature of objectivity itself. Of course, Baldwin was still farther from a purely pragmatic functionalism in his proposals that logic is a reflective not common form of implication knowledge and that there is an ideal system of meaning. Neither of these are functional notions in any simple sense.

In a sense Baldwin was *less* of a pragmatist than Piaget. Piaget founds his system on the process of equilibrium which is, after all, rooted in the notion of organisimic survival; what could be more pragmatic than making knowledge the result of adaptive mechanisms! Baldwin said that this was precisely the kind of theory, fashionable at the time, with which he was out of sympathy. The growth of knowledge, *qua* a system of truths, could not be explained by a theory in which 'the survival value, the pragmatic or instrumental utility, the use and consequence of thought, are taken to be, by a quick and perhaps too violent swing of the pendulum, its entire *raison d'etre* and justification' (1906c, p. viii).

One final charge against functionalism is that, whatever the intentions of its practitioners regarding the importance of certain necessary forms of understanding, it is in the nature of such theories that they cannot encompass any reality which is not a human product, which is something more than the sum of the system's functional parts. As we saw, both Kant and Piaget, in their very different ways, rejected this anthropocentrism and it is not a position that many find congenial as it can lead to forms of skepticism, idealism and subjectivism.

It is possible, of course, to have a short way with this view by adopting a radical anthropocentrism which denies that the conceptual system is anything more than what we require of it. Here Wittgenstein and Baldwin part company. Wittgenstein's anthropocentrism was subtle and complex but anthropocentrism it doubtless was. But Baldwin was, in a sense, more ambitious—or 'overambitious' according to one's view. Wittgenstein did not wish to postulate any meaning beyond the vast network of language games within the conceptual system, whereas Baldwin believed that there was a 'reality' which transcended the different 'realities'. Indeed he primarily intended the term 'genetic epistemology' to refer to what he called 'real logic' which resulted in a *comparison* of the different kinds of reality* (mainly: theoretical, moral, aesthetic), a comparative morphology of meanings, by standing back the farthest possible from this taxonomy to encounter the 'realest real'—the immediate reality of contemplation (see p. 78). This form of transcendent reality Baldwin regarded as a *reconciliation* of the oppositions which the different realities engendered (a *Hegelian* notion). This is not a Kantian necessity but it is one way in which a transcendent notion of human understanding can be achieved within a basically functionalist framework.

Whether or not one regards Baldwin's actual attempt at rec-

---

* (In the metaphor on p. 235 there would be a number of adjoining buildings rather than just one)

onciliation as more mystical than philosophical, one can at least agree
with him that we have access to different realities through a number
of different conceptual subsystems whose interrelations are themselves systematic; within these the finest grain of analysis would be the
language game. Baldwin's functionalism was more systematic than
Wittgenstein's because he was adopting the genetic perspective: the
acquisition of knowledge by the child is nothing if not a systematic
process for it is the point at which the biological and conceptual
systems meet and interact.

References

Aaron, R. I. (1965). *John Locke*. Oxford University Press, London

Adam, C., and Tannery, P. (eds) (1913). *Oeuvres de Descartes* Cerf, Paris

Alston, W. P. (1969). Feelings. *Philosophical Review*, **78**, 3–34

Angell, J. R. (1903). The relations of structural and functional psychology. *Phil. Rev.*, **12**, 1–27.

Anscombe, E. (1957). *Intention*. Blackwell, Oxford

Anscombe, E. (1974). Comment on Professor R. L. Gregory's paper. In Brown, S. C. (ed.) *Philosophy of Psychology*. Macmillan, London

Apostel, L., Mays, W., Morf, A., and Piaget, J. (1957). Les liasons analytiques et synthetéques dans les comportements du sujet. *Etudes d'épistémologie génétique*. vol. 4. Presses Univer. France, Paris

Austin, J. L. (1962). *How to do Things with Words*. Oxford University Press, London

Baldwin, J. M. (1902). *Development and Evolution*. Macmillan, London

Baldwin, J. M. (1906a). *Mental Development in the Child and in the Race*. Macmillan, London

Baldwin, J. M. (1906b). *Social and Ethical Interpretations*. Macmillan, London

Baldwin, J. M. (1906c). *Thought and Things (functional logic)*. vol. 1. Swan and Sonnenschein, London

Baldwin, J. M. (1908). *Thought and Things (experimental logic)*. vol. 2. Swan and Sonnenschein, London

Baldwin, J. M. (1911). *Thought and Things (real logic; interest and art)*. vol. 3. George Allen, London

Bartley, W. W. (1974). *Wittgenstein* Quartet Books, London

Beard, R. (1969). *An Outline of Piaget's Developmental Psychology*. Routledge & Kegan Paul, London

Beilin, H. (1965). Learning and operational convergence in logical thought development. *J. Exp. Child Psychol.*, **2**, 317–39.

Beilin, H. (1971). The training and acquisition of logical operations.

In Rofskopt, M. F., Steffe, L. P., and Taback, S. (eds). *Piagetian Cognitive Development Research and Mathematical Education.* National Council of Mathematics, Washington

Beloff, J. (1962). *The Existence of Mind.* McGibbon and Kee, London

Bennett, J. (1966). *Kant's Analytic.* Cambridge University Press, London

Berry, J. W., and Dasen, P. R. (1971). *Culture and Cognition: Readings in Cross-Cultural Psychology.* Methuen, London

Bever, J. G., Fodor, J. A., and Weksel, W. (1965). Is linguistics empirical? *Psychol. Rev.,* **72**, 493–500

Bloom, L. (1970). *Language Development: Form and Function in Emerging Grammars.* MIT Press, Cambridge, Mass.

Bloom, L. (1973). *One Word at a Time.* Mouton, The Hague

Bloom, L. (1974). Talking, understanding and thinking. In Schiefelbusch, R. L., and Lloyd, L. L. (eds) *Language Perspectives—Acquisition, Retardation and Intervention.* Macmillan, London

Bloom, L., Hood. L., and Lightbown, P. (1974). Imitation in language development: if, when, and why. *Cognitive Psychol.,* **6**, 380–420

Blumenthal, A. L. (1975). Psycholinguistics: some historical issues. In Riegel, K. F., and Rosenwald, G. C. (eds) *Structure and Transformation.* Wiley-Interscience, New York

Bower, T. G. R. (1965). The determinants of perceptual unity in infancy. *Psychonomic Sci.,* **3**, 12–17

Bower, T. G. R. (1966). The visual world of infants. *Sci. Am.,* **215**, 80–92

Bower, T. G. R. (1974). *Development in Infancy.* Freeman, San Francisco

Bowerman, M. (1975). Cross-linguistic similarities at two stages of syntactic development. In Lennenberg, E., and Lennenberg, E. (eds) *Foundations of Language Development: a Multidisciplinary Approach.* Academic Press, New York

Braine, M. D. S. (1959). The ontogeny of certain logical operations: Piaget's formulation examined by nonverbal methods. *Psychol. Monogr.,* **73**, Whole No. 475

Braine, M. D. S., and Shanks, B. L. (1965a). The development of conservation of size. *J. Verbal Learning Verbal Behav.,* **4**, 227–42

Braine, M. D. S., and Shanks, B. L. (1965b). The conservation of shape property and a proposal about the origin of conservation.

Can. J. Psychol., **19**, 197–207

Brazelton, T. B., Koslowski, B., and Main, M. (1974). The origins of reciprocity: the early mother–infant interaction. In Lewis, M., and Rosenblum, L. A. (eds) *The Effect of the Infant on its Caregiver.* Wiley-Interscience, New York

Brown, R. (1973). *A First Language.* Pelican, Harmondsworth

Brown, R., and Bellugi, U. (1964). Three processes in the child's acquisition of language. *Harvard Educational Rev.*, **34**, 133–51.

Bruner, J. S. (1959). Inhelder and Piaget's 'The Growth of Logical Thinking from Childhood to Adolescence': a psychologist's viewpoint. *Br. J. Psychol.*, **50**, 363–70

Bruner, J. S. (1968). *Processes of Cognitive Growth.* Clark University with Barre Publishers, Worcester, Mass.

Bruner, J. S. (1974). Organisation of early skilled action. In Richards, M. P. M. (ed.) *The Integration of the Child into the Social World.* Cambridge University Press, London

Bruner, J. S. (1975). The ontogenesis of speech acts. *J. Child Language*, **2**, 1–19

Bruner, J. S., and Connolly, K. (eds) (1974). *The Growth of Competence.* Academic Press, London

Bruner, J. S., and Greenfield, P. M., (1966). Culture and cognitive growth. In Goslin, D. (ed.) *Handbook of Socialization Theory and Research.* Rand McNally, Chicago

Bruner, J. S., and Sherwood, V. (1976). Peekaboo and the learning of rule structures. In Bruner, J. S., Jolly, A., and Sylva, K. *Play.* Penguin, Harmondsworth

Bruner, J. S. *et al.* (1966). *Studies in Cognitive Growth.* John Wiley, London

Bryant, P. E. (1972). The understanding of invariance by very young children. *Can. J. Psychol.*, **26**, 78–96

Bryant, P. E. (1973). Reply to Youniss and Furth. *Nature*, **244**, 315–6.

Bryant, P. E. (1974). *Perception and Understanding in Young Children.* Methuen, London

Bryant, P. E., and Kopytynska, H. (1976). Spontaneous measurement by young children. *Nature*, **260**, 773–4

Bryant, P. E., and Trabasso, T. (1971). Transitive inferences and memory in young children. *Nature*, **232**, 456–8

Buchler, J. (ed.) (1940). *The Philosophy of Peirce: Selected Writings.* International Library of Psychology, Philosophy and Scientific

Method, London

Bühler, K. (1934). *Sprachtheorie*. Fischer, Jena

Bynum, T. W., Thomas, J. A., and Weitz, L. J., (1972). Truth-functional logic in formal operational thinking. *Devl. Psychol.*, **7**, 129–32

Cassirer, E. (1953). *Structure and Function in Einstein's Theory of Relativity*. Dover Publications, New York

Chomsky, N. (1965). *Aspects of the Theory of Syntax*. MIT Press, Cambridge, Mass.

Chomsky, N. (1968). *Language and Mind*. Harcourt, Brace and World, New York

Chomsky, N. (1975). *Reflections on Language*. Random House (Parthenon Books), New York

Clark, E. (1974). Some aspects of the conceptual basis for first language acquisition. In Schiefelbusch, R. L., and Lloyd, L. L. (eds) *Language Perspectives: Acquisition, Retardation and Intervention*. Macmillan, London

Cohen, G. M. (1967). Conservation of quantity in children: the effect of vocabulary and participation. *Q. J. exp. Psychol.*, **19**, 150–4

Cole, M., and Scribner, S. (1974). *Culture and Thought: a Psychological Introduction*. John Wiley, New York

Collis, G. M., and Schaffer, H. R. (1974). Synchronisation of visual attention in mother–infant pairs. Mimeo

Cromer, R. F. (1973). Conservation by the congenitally blind. *Brit. J. Psychol.*, **64**, 241–50

Cromer, R. F. (1974). The development of language and cognition: the cognition hypothesis. In Foss, B. (ed.) *New Perspective in Child Development*. Penguin, Harmondsworth

Danto, A. C. (1965). *Nietzsche as Philosopher*. Collier-Macmillan, London

de Boysson-Bardies, B., and O'Regan, K. (1973). What children know in spite of what they do. *Nature*, **246**, 531–4

Dore, J. (1975). Holophrases, speech acts and language universals. *J. Child Language*, **2**, 21–40.

Dummett, M. (1958). Truth. *Proc. Aristotelian Soc.*, **59**, 141–62

Elkind, D. (1967). Piaget's conservation problems. *Child Devl*, **38**, 15–27

Elkind, D., and Schoenfield, E. (1972). Identity and equivalence at two age levels. *Devl Psychol.*, **6**, 529–33

Flavell, J. H. (1963). *The Developmental Psychology of Jean Piaget*.

Van Nostrand, New Jersey

Furth, H. G. (1966). *Thinking without Language*. Collier-Macmillan, London

Furth, H. G. (1969). *Piaget and Knowledge*. Prentice-Hall, New York

Gardener, R. A., and Gardener, J. T. (1969). Teaching sign language to a chimpanzee. *Science*, **165**, 664–72

Gratch, G., Appel, K. J., Evans, W. F., LeCompte, G. K., and Wright, N. A. (1974). Piaget's Stage IV object concept error: evidence of forgetting or object conception. *Child Devl*, **45**, 71–7

Greene, J. M. (1972). *Psycholinguistics: Chomsky and Psychology*. Penguin, Harmondsworth

Greenfield, P. M., and Smith, J. (1976). *Communication and the Beginnings of Language*. Academic Press, New York

Greenfield, P. M., Nelson, K., and Saltzman, E. (1972). The development of rule-bound strategies for manipulating seriated cups: a parallel between action and grammar. *Cognitive Psychol.*, **3**, 291–310

Gruber, H. E. (1974). *Darwin on Man: a Psychological Study of Scientific Creativity*, Wildwood House, London

Halford, G. S. (1968). An experimental test concerning Piaget's notions of quantity in children. *J. exp. Child Psychol.*, **6**, 33–43

Hall, V. C., and Kingsley, R. (1968). Conservation and equilibration theory. *J. genet. Psychol.*, **113**, 195–212

Halliday, M. A. K. (1975). *Learning How to Mean*. Edward Arnold, London

Hamlyn, D. W. (1957). *The Psychology of Perception*. Routledge & Kegan Paul, London

Hamlyn, D. W. (1967). Epistemology. In *The Encyclopaedia of Philosophy*. Macmillan, London

Hamlyn, D. W. (1970). Conditioning and behaviour. In Borger, R., and Cioffi, F. *Explanation in the Behavioural Sciences*. Cambridge University Press, London

Hamlyn, D. W. (1971). Epistemology and conceptual development. In Mischel, T. (ed.) *Cognitive Development and Epistemology*. Academic Press, London

Hamlyn, D. W. (1974). Human learning. In Brown, S. C. (ed.) *Philosophy of Psychology*. Macmillan, London

Hamlyn, D. W. (1976). Aristotelian Epagoge. *Phronesis*, **21**, 167–84

Hamlyn, D. W. (1978) *Experience and Growth of Understanding*. Routledge & Kegan Paul, London

Harris, P. L. (1973). Perseverative errors in search by young infants. *Child Devl*, **44**, 28–33

Harris, P. L., (1974). Perseverative search at a visibly empty space in young infants. *J. exp. Child Psychol.*, **18**, 535–42

Harris, P. L., and Bassett, E. (1975). Transitive inferences by 4-year-old children? *Devl Psychol.*, **11**, 875–76

Hearnshaw, L. S. (1966). *The Comparative Psychology of Mental Development*. L. T. Hobhouse Memorial Trust Lecture. No. 36. The Athlone Press, London

Heron, A. (1975). Development, adaptation and change. *Austr. Psychol.*, **10**, 279–89

Hobhouse, L. T. (1901). *Mind in Evolution*. Macmillan, London

Huttenlocher, J. (1968). Constructing spatial images: a strategy in reasoning. *Psychol. Rev.*, **75**, 550–60

Ingram, D. (1971). Transitivity in child language. *Language*, **47**, 888–910

Inhelder, B., and Piaget, J. (1958). *The Growth of Logical Thinking from Childhood to Adolescence*. Routledge & Kegan Paul, London

Inhelder, B., and Sinclair, H. (1969). Learning cognitive structures. In Mussen, J. H., Langer, J., and Covington, M. (eds) *Trends and Issues in Developmental Psychology*. Holt, Reinhart and Winston, New York

Jennings, H. S. (1906). *The Behaviour of Lower Organisms*. Columbia University Press, New York

Kaplan, B. (1971). Genetic psychology, genetic epistemology and theory of knowledge. In Mischel, T. (ed.) *Cognitive Development and Epistemology*. Academic Press, London

Kendler, H. H., and Kendler, T. S. (1962). Vertical and horizontal processes in problem solving. *Psychol. Rev.*, **69**, 1–16

Kenny, A. (1963). *Action, Emotion and Will*. Routledge & Kegan Paul, London

Kenny, A. (1968). *Descartes*. Random House, New York

Kessen, W. (1965). *The Child*. John Wiley, London

Kluckhohn, F. R., and Stodtbeck, F. L. (1961). *Variations in Value Orientation*. Row, Peterson, Evanston

Kohlberg, L. (1969). Stage and sequence: the cognitive-developmental approach to socialization. In Goslin, D. (ed.) *Handbook of Socialization Theory and Research*. Rand McNally, New York

Körner, S. (1955). *Kant*, Penguin, Harmondsworth

Kuenne, M. R. (1946). Experimental investigation of the relation of language to transposition behaviour in young children. *J. exp. Psychol.*, **36**, 471–90

Kuhn, T. S. (1962). *The Structure of Scientific Revolutions*. University of Chicago Press, Chicago

Laing, R. D. (1959). *The Divided Self*. Tavistock, London

Landers, W. F. (1970). Effects of differential experience on infants' performance in a Piagetian Stage IV object-concept task. *Devl Psychol.*, **5**, 48–54

Langer, J. (1970). Werner's theory of development. In Mussen, P. H. (ed.) *Carmichael's Manual of Child Psychology*. vol. 1. Third Edition. John Wiley, London

Larsen, G. Y., and Flavell, J. H. (1970). Verbal factors in compensation performance and the relation between conservation and compensation. *Child Devl*, **41**, 965–77

Looft, W. R. (1972). Egocentrism and social interaction across the life span. *Psychol. Bull.*, **78**, 73–92

Looft, W. R., and Svoboda, C. P. (1975). Structuralism in cognitive developmental psychology: past, contemporary and future developments. In Riegel, K. F., and Rosenwald, G. C. (eds) *Structure and Transformation*. Wiley-Interscience, New York

Lorenz, K. (1941). Kant's Lehre vom Apriorischen im Lichte der gegenwürtigen Biologie. *Blätter für Philosophie*, **15**, 94–125

Lumsden, E. A., and Kling, K. K. (1969). The relevance of an adequate concept of 'bigger' for investigation of size conservation: a methodological critique. *J. exp. Child Psychol.*, **8**, 82–91

McNeill, D. (1966). Developmental psycholinguistics. In Smith, F., and Miller, G. A. (eds) *The Genesis of Language*. MIT Press, Cambridge, Mass.

McNeill, D. (1969). Empiricist and nativist theories of language: George Berkeley and Samuel Bailey in the 20th century. In Koestler, A., and Smythies, J. R. (eds) *Beyond Reductionism*. Hutchinson (Radius Books), London

McNeill, D. (1970a). The development of language. In Mussen, P. H. (ed.) *Carmichael's Manual of Child Psychol*. vol. 1. Third Edition. John Wiley, London

McNeill, D. (1970b). *The Acquisition of Language*. Harper and Row, New York

McNeill, D. (1974a). Semiotic extension. Paper presented at the Loyola Symposium on Cognition, Chicago, April, 1974

McNeill, D. (1974b). Sentence structure in chimpanzee communications. In Bruner, J. S. and Connolly, K. (eds) *The Growth of Competence*. Academic Press, London

Maratos, O. (1973). The origin and development of imitation in the first six months of life. Doctoral dissertation, University of Geneva

Maxwell, M. (1975). A nonverbal test of numbers conservation. Unpublished manuscript, University of Liverpool

Maynard Smith, J. (1966). *The Theory of Evolution*. Penguin, Harmondsworth

Mays, W. (1953). The Epistemology of Professor Piaget. *Proc. Aristotelian Soc.*, **54**, 48–76

Mays, W. (1974). Popper, Durkheim and Piaget on moral norms. *J. Br. Soc. Phenomenol.*, **5**, 233–242

Mehler, J., and Bever, T. G. (1967). Cognitive capacity of very young children. *Science*, **158**, 141–42

Melden, A. I. (1961). *Free Action*. Routledge & Kegan Paul, London

Melden, A. I. (1969). The conceptual dimensions of emotions. In Mischel, T. (ed.) *Human Action: Conceptual and Empirical Issues*. Academic Press, New York

Melzov, quoted in Macfarlane, A. (1977). The Psychology of Childbirth. Fontana/Open Books, London

Menzel, E. W., Davenport, R. K., and Rogers, C. M. (1972). Protocultural aspects of chimpanzee's responsiveness to novel objects. *Folia primatol.*, no. 17, 161–70

Mermelstein, E., and Shulman, L. (1967). Lack of formal schooling and the acquisition of conservation. *Child Devl*, **38**, 39–52

Mermelstein, E., and Meyer, E. (1969). Conservation training techniques and their effects on different populations. *Child Devl*, **40**, 471–90

Miller, D., Cohen, L., and Hill, K. A. (1970). A methodological investigation of Piaget's theory of object concept development in the sensorimotor period. *J. exp. Child Psychol.*, **9**, 59–85

Miller, S. A., and Brownwell, C. A. (1975). Peers, persuasion and Piaget: dyadic interaction between conservers and nonconservers. *Child Devl*, **46**, 992–97

Mischel, T. (1971). Piaget: cognitive conflict and the motivation of thought. In Mischel, T. (ed.) *Cognitive Development and Epistemology*. Academic Press, London

Mischel, T. (1974). Chairman's comments. In Brown, S. C. (ed.) *Philosophy of Psychology*. Macmillan, London

Mounoud, P., and Bower, T. G. R. (1974). Conservation of weight in infants. *Cognition*, **3**, 29–40

Morehead, D. M., and Morehead, A. (1974). From signal to sign: a Piagetian view of thought and language during the first two years of life. In Schiefelbusch, R. L., and Lloyd, L. L. (eds) *Language Perspectives: Acquisition, Retardation and Intervention*. Macmillan, London

Mueller, R. H. (1976). A chapter in the history of the relationship between psychology and sociology in America: James Mark Baldwin. *J. History Behavioural Sci.*, **12**, 240–53

Mundy-Castle, A. C., and Anglin, J. (1969). The development of looking in infancy. Paper presented at the Conference of the Society for Research in Child Development, Santa Monica, California

Murray, F. B. (1972). Acquisition of conservation through social interaction. *Devl Psychol.*, **6**, 1–6

Nelson, K. (1974). Concept, word, and sentence. *Psychol. Rev.*, **81**, 267–85

Oleron, P., and Herren, H. (1961). L'acquisition des conservations et le language: Etude comparative sur les enfants sourds et entendants. *Enfrance*, **14**, 208–319

Parsons, C. (1960). Inhelder and Piaget's 'The Growth of Logical Thinking from Childhood to Adolescence': a logician's viewpoint. *Br. J. Psychol.*, **51**, 75–84

Peill, E. J. (1975). *Invention and Discovery of Reality*. John Wiley, London

Peters, R. S. (1958). *The Concept of Motivation*. Routledge & Kegan Paul, London

Piaget, J. (1924a). *The Language and Thought of the Child*. Routledge & Kegan Paul, London

Piaget, J. (1924b). *Judgment and Reasoning in the Child*. Routledge & Kegan Paul, London

Piaget, J. (1927). *The Child's Conception of Causality*. Routledge & Kegan Paul, London

Piaget, J. (1932). *The Moral Judgment of the Child*. Routledge & Kegan Paul, London

Piaget, J. (1950). *The Psychology of Intelligence*. Routledge & Kegan Paul, London

Piaget, J. (1952a). Autobiography. In Boring, E. G. *et al.* (eds) *History of Psychology in Autobiography*. vol. 4. Clark University Press, Worcester, Mass.

Piaget, J. (1952b). *The Child's Concept of Number*. Routledge & Kegan Paul, London

Piaget, J. (1953). *The Origin of Intelligence in the Child*. Routledge & Kegan Paul, London

Piaget, J. (1954a). Language and thought from a genetic point of view. *Acta psychologica*, **10**, 88–98

Piaget, J. (1954b). The problem of consciousness in child psychology. In *Conference on Problems of Consciousness*, Josiah Macy Foundation, New York

Piaget, J. (1955). *The Child's Construction of Reality*. Routledge & Kegan Paul, London

Piaget, J. (1957a). Programme et methodes de l'épistémologie génétique. In Beth, E. W., Mays, W., and Piaget, J. (eds) *Épistémologie Génétique et recherche psychologique*. Etudes d'épistémologie génétique, 1. Presses Univer. France, Paris

Piaget, J. (1957b). Logique et équilibre dans les comportements du sujet. In Apostel, L., Mandelbrot, D., and Piaget, J. (eds) *Logique et équilibre*. Etudes d'épistémologie génétique, 2. Presses Univer. France, Paris

Piaget, J. (1962). *Play, Dreams and Imitation in Childhood*. Routledge & Kegan Paul, London

Piaget, J. (1967a). Review of Bruner *et al. Contemporary Psychol.*, **12**, 530–33

Piaget, J. (1967b). In Elkind, D. (ed.) *Six Psychological Studies*. Random House, New York

Piaget, J. (1969). *The Mechanisms of Perception*. Routledge & Kegan Paul, London

Piaget, J. (1970a). Piaget's theory. In Mussen, P. H. (ed.) *Carmichael's Manual of Child Psychology*. vol. 1. Third Edition. John Wiley, London

Piaget, J. (1970b). *Genetic Epistemology*. Columbia University Press, New York

Piaget, J. (1971a). *Biology and Knowledge*. Edinburgh University Press, Edinburgh

Piaget, J. (1971b). *Structuralism*. Routledge & Kegan Paul, London

Piaget, J. (1972a). *Psychology and Epistemology*. Penguin, Harmondsworth

Piaget, J. (1972b). *The Principles of Genetic Epistemology*. Routledge & Kegan Paul, London

Piaget, J. (1972c). *Insights and Illusions of Philosophy*. Routledge &

Kegan Paul, London

Piaget, J., and Inhelder, B. (1956). *The Child's Conception of Space*. Routledge & Kegan Paul, London

Piaget, J., and Inhelder, B. (1963). L'image et la pensee: le role de l'image dans la preparation ou dans le fonctionnement des operations. In Fraisse, P., and Piaget, J. (eds) *Traite de psychologie experimentale*. vol. 7. *L'intelligence*. Presses Univer. France, Paris

Piaget, J., and Inhelder, B. (1969). *The Psychology of the Child*. Routledge & Kegan Paul, London

Piaget, J., and Inhelder, B. (1971). *Mental Imagery in the Child*. Routledge & Kegan Paul, London

Piaget, J., Inhelder, B. (1973). *Memory and Intelligence*. Routledge & Kegan Paul, London

Piaget, J., and Inhelder, B. (1974). *The Child's Construction of Quantities*. Routledge & Kegan Paul, London

Piaget, J., Inhelder, B., and Szeminska, A. (1960). *The Child's Conception of Geometry*. Routledge & Kegan Paul, London

Popper, K. R. (1972). *Objective Knowledge: an Evolutionary Approach*. Oxford University Press, London

Popper, K. R. (1976). *Unended Quest*. Collins (Fontana Books), Glasgow

Price, H. H. (1940). *Hume's Theory of the External World*. Oxford University Press, London

Quinton, A. (1963). The a priori and the analytic. *Proc. Aristotelian Soc.*, **64**, 31–54

Reich, L. C. (1966). Reported in Bruner, J. S. *et al. Studies in Cognitive Growth*. John Wiley, London

Riegel, K. F. (1973). Dialectic operations: the final period of cognitive development. *Human Devl.*, **16**, 346–70

Riley, C. A., and Trabasso, T. (1974). Comparatives, logical structures, and encoding in a transitive inference task. *J. exp. Child Psychol.*, **17**, 187–203

Riley, D. A. (1958). The nature of the effective stimulus in animal discrimination learning; transposition reconsidered. *Psychol. Rev.*, **65**, 1–7

Romanes, G. J. (1888). *Mental Evolution in Man*. Kegan, Paul and Trench, London

Rosenthal, T. L., and Zimmerman, B. J. (1972). Modeling by exemplification and instruction training conservation. *Devl Psychol.*, **6**, 392–401

Russell, J. (1973). The relation between verbal and nonverbal concepts in cognitive development. Doctoral dissertation, University of London

Russell, J. (1975a). The interpretation of conservation instructions by five-year-old children. *J. Child Psychol. Psychiat.*, **16**, 233–44

Russell, J. (1975b). Competence, reasons and causes. *Bull. Brit. Psychol. Soc.*, **28**, 299–305

Russell, J. (1976). The nonconservation of area: do children succeed where adults fail? *Devl Psychol.*, **12**, 367–68

Russell, J. (1978). The role of verbal understanding in young children judgments of length invariance. To be published

Schlesinger, I. M. (1971). Learning grammar: from pivot to realization rule. In Huxley, R., and Ingram, E. (eds) *Language Acquisition: Models and Methods*. Academic Press, London

Schlesinger, I. M. (1974). Relational concepts underlying language. In Schiefelbusch, R. L., and Lloyd, L. L. (eds) *Language Perspectives–Acquisition, Retardation and Intervention*. Macmillan, London

Searle, J. R. (1969). *Speech Acts: an Essay in the Philosophy of Language*. Cambridge University Press, London

Searle, J. R. (1971). What is a speech act? In Searle, J. R. (ed.) *The Philosophy of Language*. Oxford University Press, London

Silverman, I. W., and Geiringer, E. (1973). Dyadic interaction and conservation induction: a test of Piaget's equilibrium theory. *Child Devl*, **44**, 815–20

Silverman, I. W., and Stone, J. M. (1972). Modifying cognitive functioning through participation in a problem-solving group. *J. Educ. Psychol.*, **63**, 603–8

Shepp, B. E., and Eimas, P. D. (1964). Intradimensional and extra-dimensional shifts in the rat. *J. comp. physiol. Psychol.*, **7**, 81–92

Sinclair, H. (1973). Language acquisition and cognitive development. In Moore, T. E. *Cognitive Development and the Acquisition of Language*. Academic Press, New York

Smedslund, J. (1966). Performance of measurement and pseudo-measurement tasks by five to seven-year-old children. *Scandinavian J. Psychol.*, **7**, 81–92

Smith, I. (1968). The effects of training procedures upon the acquisition of conservation of weight. *Child Devl*, **39**, 515–26

Stern, D. N. (1974). Mother and infant at play: dyadic interaction involving facial, vocal and gaze behaviours. In Lewis, M., and

Rosenblum, L. A. (eds) *The Effect of the Infant on its Caregiver.* Wiley-Interscience, New York

Stern, D. W. (1977). *Mother—Infant Interaction.* London: Fontana/Open books

Strauss, S., and Langer, J. (1970). Operational thought inducement. *Child Devl.*, **41**, 163–75

Strawson, P. F. (1959). *Individuals.* Oxford University Press, London

Strawson, P. F. (1966). *The Bounds of Sense.* Methuen, London

Sutherland, S. (1970). Is the brain a physical system? In Borger, R., and Cioffi, F. (eds) *Explanation in the Behavioural Sciences.* Cambridge University Press, London

Taylor, C. (1971). Interpretation and the sciences of man. *Rev. Metaphysics*, **25**, 3–52

Titchener, E. B. (1909). *The Experimental Psychology of the Thought Processes.* Macmillan, New York

Toulmin, S. (1969). Ludwig Wittgenstein. *Encounter*, **32**, 58–71

Toulmin, S. (1970). Reasons and causes. In Borger, R., and Cioffi, F. (eds) *Explanation in the Behavioural Sciences.* Cambridge University Press, London

Toulmin, S. (1972). *Human Understanding.* vol. 1. Oxford University Press, London

Trabasso, T., Riley, C. A., and Wilson, E. (1976). Spatial strategies in reasoning: a developmental study. In Falmagne, R. (ed.) *Psychological Studies of Logic and its Development.* Erlbaum Association, New York

Trevarthen, C. (1975). Basic patterns of psychogenetic change in infancy. Proceedings of the OECD Conference on "Dips in Learning", St. Paul de Vence, March, 1975

Trevarthen, C., Hubley, P., and Sheeran, L. (1974). Les activités innées de nourrisson. *La Recherche*, **6**, 447–58

van Lawick-Goodall, J. (1971). *In the Shadow of Man.* Houghton Mifflin, Boston

Von Senden, M. (1932). *Raum-und Gestaltauffassung bei operierten Blindsgeborenen vor und nach der Operation.* Barth, Leipzig

Vygotsky, L. S. (1962). *Thought and Language.* MIT Press, Cambridge, Mass. (original publication 1934)

Vygotsky, L. S. (1966). Play and its role in the mental development of the child. *Sov. Psychol.*, **12**, 62–76 (transcribed from a lecture given in 1933)

Waddington, C. H. (1957). *The Strategy of the Genes.* Allen and

Unwin, London

Wallace, J. G. (1972). *Stages and Transition in Conceptual Development*. NFER, London

Werner, H. (1948). *Comparative Psychology of Mental Development*. Follett, Chicago

Werner, H., and Kaplan, B. (1963). *Symbol Formation*. John Wiley, London

Whorf, B. L. (1941). The relation of habitual thought and behaviour to language. In Spier, L. (ed.) *Language, Culture and Personality*. University of Utah Press, Salt Lake City

Williams, B. (1976). *Problems of the Self*. Cambridge University Press, London

Wittgenstein, L. (1953). *Philosophical Investigations*. Blackwell, Oxford

Wohlwill, J. F. (1960). A study of the development of the number concept by scalogram analysis. *J. genet.* Psychol., **97**, 345–77

Wozniak, R. H. (1972). Verbal regulation of motor behaviour: Soviet research and non-Soviet replication. *Human Devl*, **15**, 13–57

Wozniak, R. H. (1975). Dialectism and structuralism: the philosophical foundation of Soviet psychology and Piagetian cognitive developmental theory. In Riegel, K. F., and Rosenwald, G. C. (eds) *Structure and Transformation*. Wiley-Interscience, New York

Youniss, J., and Furth, H. G. (1965). The influence of transitivity on learning. *Child Devl*, **36**, 533–38

Youniss, J., and Furth, H. G. (1966). Prediction of causal events as a function of transitivity. *Child Devl*, **37**, 73–81

Youniss, J., and Furth, H. G. (1973). Piaget and reasoning. *Nature*, **244**, 314–15

Zeigler, H. P., and Leibowitz, H. (1957). Apparent visual size as a function of distance for children and adults. *Am. J. Psychol.*, **70**, 106–9

Zimmerman, B. J., and Rosenthal, T. L. (1972). Concept attainment, transfer, and retention through observation and rule provision. *J. exp. Child Psychol.*, **14**, 139–50

Zimmerman, B. J., and Rosenthal, H. (1974a). Observational learning of rule-governed behaviour. *Psychol. Bull.*, **81**, 29–42

Zimmerman, B. J., and Rosenthal, H. (1974b). Conserving and retaining equalities and inequalities through observation and correction. *Devl Psychol.*, **10**, 260–8

Index